The Classical Tradition

The British Museum Yearbook 1

The Classical Tradition

Published for The Trustees of the British Museum
by British Museum Publications Limited

© 1976, The Trustees of The British Museum
ISBN 0 7141 0045 5

Published by British Museum Publications Ltd.,
6 Bedford Square, London WCIB 3RA.

Designed by Bernard Crossland
Set in Monotype Baskerville with Walbaum display
Printed in Great Britain at
the Alden Press, Oxford

Foreword

In 1926 it was announced by Sir Frederic Kenyon that 'the Trustees of the British Museum have decided to issue, at quarterly intervals, a periodical publication which will contain descriptions, with illustrations, of the latest acquisitions made by the Departments at Bloomsbury'. Publication of *The British Museum Quarterly* continued uninterruptedly till the summer of 1973, when the Library Departments of the British Museum became the Reference Division of the British Library. The Library Departments had from the outset contributed extensively to *The British Museum Quarterly* and, with their severance from the Museum, it became evident that the basis of the *Quarterly* had to be thought out afresh.

In the forty-seven years of its existence the original terms of reference of the *Quarterly* were slowly modified. It came to include not only the short notes on recent acquisitions which it was originally designed to promulgate, but more substantial articles resulting from retrospective research on the collections. Its successor, *The British Museum Yearbook*, will preserve this dual character. On the one hand, it will publish major articles on aspects of the Museum collections written by outside contributors as well as by members of the Museum staff. These articles, though scholarly, will be directed to the regular museum visitor, not to the specialist. They will be grouped round a common theme. At the same time, the *Yearbook* will continue the practice initiated in the *Quarterly* of publishing short notes on the principal recent acquisitions.

JOHN POPE-HENNESSY
Director

Contents

Notes on selected acquisitions in 1974

Magenta Ware

REYNOLD HIGGINS

Deputy Keeper, Greek and Roman Antiquities

INTRODUCTION

Greek potters were sometimes inspired, by way of a change, to make certain small household containers in the form of statuettes in divine, human and animal shape. The most usual subjects for this treatment were scent-bottles, of which the finest examples were made in the sixth century BC. But another attractive class of plastic vases (as they are called) was made some five centuries later, in the western part of the Greek world, to serve not as scent-bottles but as lamp-fillers and flasks. These objects have never been taken seriously, and were probably never intended to be taken seriously; but as they are not without charm and are unusually well made, they might be thought worthy of a little attention. This periodical is a suitable home for such an investigation, since the British Museum is fortunate enough to possess a good number of well-preserved examples.

The name 'Magenta Class' was coined by the late Professor Sir John Beazley on account of the bright purplish-pink pigment of which traces still remain on the better-preserved examples.[1] He had evidently intended to make a study of them, but in 1961 he very generously handed over his notes to me. I thus learned of the existence of many unpublished vases of this class in the Louvre, and of others in Geneva, Tarquinia, Florence and New York. It is on this foundation that the present survey is based.

TECHNIQUE

Like contemporary terracotta statuettes, Magenta Ware vases were made in a double mould, itself of terracotta. After moulding, much detail, and the necessary vase-attachments, were made separately of clay and fixed with slip. A considerable amount of retouching was also done to remove blemishes and improve definition.

The clay is fine in quality, and as a rule cream-coloured or pale lemon-yellow, with a small quantity of mica, covered with an orange-brown 'glaze', a paler variety of the regular Roman *red gloss*.

Occasionally the clay is light grey, with a poor black 'glaze', an effect obtained from the same materials by firing in a reducing atmosphere instead of the regular oxidizing atmosphere.

After firing, pieces of this ware were decorated, over the orange or black 'glaze', with the standard pigments of the Hellenistic terracotta repertoire. The purplish pink colour which inspired the name 'Magenta' is rose madder, a natural dye made from the root of the plant *rubia tinctorum*. Red and yellow were made from ochres. Blue is the celebrated 'Egyptian blue', made by heating a mixture of sand, soda, and copper. It was at first imported into the West from Egypt, but in the first century BC, as we learn from Vitruvius and the elder Pliny, it was made at Puteoli (the modern Pozzuoli), near Naples, by a certain Vestorius.[2] Black (soot) and white (chalk) were also used. Unfortunately the colours are all very fugitive, so that it is seldom that more than a trace of the original decoration survives, and many Magenta figures have lost all their colouring.

Hallmarks of this class are the very light weight of the figures, because of the thinness of the walls; the fine texture of the clay; the waxy appearance of the surface; and the unusually high quality of the workmanship.

DISTRIBUTION

Of the 125 pieces here considered, 108 have some sort of provenance. If, in addition to the well-attested find-spots, we include those dealers' provenances which seem reasonable, we get the following picture.

Campania	8	Spain (with Morocco)	8
Etruria	7	Delos and Rheneia	11
Italy (Central or South)[3]	25	North Greece	4
Tarentum	4	South Greece	3
Reggio	4	Greek Islands and Asia Minor	5
Sicily (with Lipari)	26	Cyrenaica	3

1 *British Museum, G 153.*

2 *British Museum, Q 330.*

3 *Musée du Louvre, Paris, Cp. 3668.*

4 *Musée du Louvre, Paris, Cp. 3668.*

5 *Agora Museum, Athens, no. 617.*

6 *Musée du Louvre, Paris, Cp. 3647.*

Magenta Ware. Forerunners and parallels

7 *Cat. no. 1 Petit Palais, Paris, Dutuit Collection no. 401.*

8 *Cat. no. 5 Metropolitan Museum, New York,*
06.1021.266.

9 *Cat. no. 4 Museo Gregoriano Etrusco, Rome,*
no. 13251.

10 *Cat. no. 7 Musée du Louvre, Paris, Cp. 3621.*

11   12

Cat. no. 10 British Museum, 1873. 10–20.2.

13 *Cat. no. 20 Formerly Staatliche Museen, Berlin, no. 30.031.*

Magenta Ware. Lamp-fillers

This gives a figure of 82 for the West (Central and South Italy, Sicily, and Spain). Delos contributes a surprising total of 11. It should not be forgotten that in that island, besides Greeks and Orientals, there were native Campanian, South Italian Greek and Sicilian Greek settlers, so that the Delian contribution could be regarded as either Eastern or Western. The same could be said of Cyrenaica, with its total of three.

Greece itself (with Illyria and Asia Minor) contributes a mere 12, of which four come from the far north, a stone's throw from South Italy.

PLACE OF MANUFACTURE

Beazley and others have assigned Magenta Ware to Campania, an attribution which has seldom been challenged. The distribution points without doubt to the West. The large number of handled flasks recently reported from Sicily might suggest a Sicilian origin for that group; but it would be difficult to separate it from the other groups and, on balance, Campania still seems more likely. This attribution is supported by a number of probabilities which, taken by themselves, prove little, but, in conjunction, are more cogent. For one thing, the Hellenistic pottery found in Spain and Morocco, in association with Magenta vases, is generally accepted as Campanian. The fine pale-coloured clay of Magenta Ware, though very different from the coarse material of run-of-the-mill Campanian terracottas, is yet paralleled tolerably well in Campanian pottery of the fourth and third centuries BC, and in the second century forerunners of the lamp-fillers, generally accepted as Campanian (**1,3,4,6**). The find-spot of no. 80, Knossos, would suggest Campania rather than Sicily (see **47**). And the usual Magenta fabric corresponds in clay (though not in 'glaze') to Lamboglia's 'Campanian B', while the less common grey body and black 'glaze' correspond closely with his 'Campanian C'.[4]

No. 69 is signed by the maker, who has the Greek name Dorotheos, so that we should look to one of the Greek cities of Campania, or at least to a city where Greek was still being spoken at this late date by some of the inhabitants. Cumae is a tempting possibility, but no more.

DATING

The style of Magenta Ware is Late Hellenistic, a designation which covers the second and first centuries BC. Can we get any closer? It should be possible, since such a tightly-knit class is unlikely to cover a very long period.

In the first place, the almost universal use of a variety of the Roman *red gloss* in place of the Greek *black glaze* would suggest that the series did not start before the later second century BC.

As bad luck would have it, few of these pieces come from dated deposits, but the rare exceptions provide a consistent picture.

Lamp-fillers are represented in the houses on Delos and the Delian tombs on the island of Rheneia and so can be dated before the great destruction of 69 BC and (in the case of the houses) not too long before that date. They do not occur in contexts of the middle and late first century BC which have yielded Magenta Ware flasks.

An upper limit in the later second century BC is suggested by the discovery of a bull's head lamp of this or a related fabric (5) in a deposit in Athens of the second century BC.[5] And the occurrence of an identical double barred handle on Cnidian lamps of the late second and early first centuries BC (2) gives a similar chronological picture. The connection between Cnidus in the extreme East of the Mediterranean and Campania in the West is rather hard to explain, unless this type of handle was transmitted through the medium of bronze or silver vessels which have not survived.

Of the flasks, the strainer variety has not yet been recorded in any dateable deposit; but the handled flasks are comparatively well dated, and the two varieties are so closely related that what holds good for one will apply to the other.

The typical flask is considerably larger than the average lamp-filler, but a transitional stage is observed in the tombs at Rheneia, where two small flasks occur in the form of the Wolf and Twins (no. 67) and a pig (no. 90): both are lamp-filler types adapted as flasks.

The typical flask starts a little later. The dolphin and the Isis head, nos. 91 and 69, come from a tomb on Lipari which the excavators date around the middle of the first century BC. The actor's head, no. 71, is dated in the second half of that century, and the lion from Knossos, no. 80, comes from a deposit of the late first century BC. There is no evidence from the first century AD. Indeed, the absence of this class in Pompeii is a strong argument for its extinction well before AD 79.

So we may tentatively date the Magenta lamp-fillers between 120 and 70 BC and the flasks (derived from them) between 80 BC and the end of the first century BC.

GROUP A. LAMP-FILLERS

This is the largest and the earliest group, with the widest distribution. Averaging 11 cm. in height and 9 cm. in width, the lamp-fillers were made in a double mould. After moulding, the back was equipped with an inlet and a handle. About five

14 *Cat. no. 11 Ashmolean Museum, Oxford, 1927.45.*   **15** *Cat. no. 14 Musée du Louvre, Paris, Cp. 3628.*

16 *Cat. no. 16 British Museum, 1873.8–20.603.*   **17** *Cat. no. 22 Musée du Louvre, Paris, S 4057.*

18 *Cat. no. 23 Musée d'Art et d'Histoire, Geneva, no. 5850.*   **19** *Cat. no. 24 Musée d'Art et d'Histoire, Geneva, no. 5851.*

Magenta Ware. Lamp-fillers

20 *Cat. no. 25 Musée du Louvre, Paris, Cp. 3639.*

21 *Cat. no. 27 British Museum, 1873.8–20.591.*

22 *Cat. no. 33 British Museum, 1866.4–15.129.*

23 *Cat. no. 35 British Museum, 1887.2–12.2.*

24 *Cat. no. 41 Musée du Louvre, Paris, Cp. 3656.*

Magenta Ware. Lamp-fillers

small holes were made in the wall of the vase and were backed by a curved strip of clay to make a sort of trough, the whole serving as a strainer to trap the sediment.

Below the trough is a semicircular handle of two parallel strips of clay bound together by a transverse strip or (less commonly) by a reef-knot. Such a handle was really a metal form translated into clay, but the transverse strip would in fact serve as a convenient thumb-rest. Similar handles are found not only in Cnidian lamps (**2**), but also on pottery vessels of about the same date.[6] A pour-hole was also pierced in a suitable position at the side.

In the early second century BC arose the forerunners of the Magenta lamp-fillers: hollow statuettes of pale-coloured clay decorated with a poor black 'glaze', having a strainer filler at the back and a lion-head pour-hole at the side. The date of this class is given by a figure of an actor from Sigean in France,[7] like **6**.[8]

Another typical pre-Magenta lamp-filler is the reclining Maenad (**1**).[9] For a third example we might choose the odd group which consists of a seated hooded figure of dubious sex (**3, 4**), a similar, but smaller, figure, and a pig.[10] The black cloak of the larger hooded figure is decorated down the front with two red lines flanking a white line. The cloak is the *cucullus*, a peasant garment of Gaulish origin.

The subjects are very varied and correspond closely with the standard Late Hellenistic terracotta repertoire: mythology, the comic stage, genre scenes, fantasy, and animals.

To start with mythology, in nos. 1–3 a young Pan, holding his throwing-stick in his right hand, reclines against a recumbent kid in a satisfying triangular composition. No. 4 shows the she-wolf suckling the twins Romulus and Remus. For a prototype, we think at first of the famous Wolf of the Capitol, but her twins are a Renaissance addition by Cellini. We know, however, that a statue of the Wolf and Twins was erected by the brothers Ogulnius in Rome in 296 BC, and a coin-type (like our lamp-filler) issued in 269 BC is believed to have been derived from this statue.[11] But the immediate ancestor of this type may well have been a relief on a third century BC Campanian lamp-filler in the British Museum (G 125).

A more unusual subject is no. 5: a pygmy is carrying the body of a crane which he has killed. According to legend, pygmies, who were located variously in India, Africa or Scythia, were in a state of constant war with the cranes.

Satyrs were more popular. In no. 6 one is shown squatting on a rock and holding in his arms a goatskin flask. In nos. 7–9 one reclines wreathed with ivy, naked but for his boots, on a rocky surface. He holds a flask of wine in his right hand and a pair of pipes in his left.

New Comedy is the subject of the finest surviving Magenta lamp-filler, no. 10 (Plate I, p. 287): an actor in the role of a slave who has run away from his master and taken refuge on an altar. The subject is a common one in art, especially in terra-cottas and bronzes, and must have been popular on the comic stage. The colours surviving on this piece give a much better idea than most of the bright and lively appearance of these objects when new. His mask is painted a vivid pink with a red mouth; his hair and sandals are red; the hand which binds his hair and falls on his shoulders is blue; and there is pink on his girdle and on the altar.

A forerunner of the type, covered in a black glaze, and with a lion-head spout (like **6**) was found at Sigean, near Perpignan, in a context of the late third or early second century BC.[12]

In nos. 11–13 a comic actor reclines on his left side, leaning against a wine amphora. In his left hand he holds a garland, so we may presume him to be at a party. His right arm is folded over his head in a gesture associated with tiredness or (in his case) drunkenness.

Nos. 14–15 show an actor in another role. His mask has staring eyes and a snarling mouth. He also reclines and holds a garland, but his elbow rests on a pillow and his right hand is raised to his mouth. The unusual type of mask may belong to the New Comedy, or perhaps to Campanian farce.

Nos. 16–19 depict a common scene at a party. A guest reclines on a couch, embracing a half-naked hetaira; both are garlanded. The popularity of the subject is indicated by the survival of four examples of the type in Magenta Ware and of many variations in Late Hellenistic terracottas.

The form of the Gallic warrior of nos. 20–21 can only be recovered by a combination of the two incomplete figures (**60**). He kneels on his left knee, grasping in his left hand the typical Gallic shield called the *thureos*, and in his right a dagger, pointing upwards. He wears a long cloak, and like many of his race, is clean-shaven except for a long moustache. By the time when these figures were made, the Gauls were no longer seen primarily as enemies, being better known as auxiliaries in the Roman army.

A badly-damaged piece (no. 22) shows a crouching man with a jug. The subject of no. 23 is very popular in terracotta. A boy squats, leaning to his left against a pet goose, which he is embracing with his left arm. The triangular composition recalls the Pan, no. 1. No. 24 shows a very similar boy riding on a dog of the variety known as Maltese. Sentimental studies of children riding animals and birds are very common in the minor arts of the Hellenistic period.

The great majority of these lamp-fillers (and of the flasks too) draw on solitary animals, wild and domestic, for their subjects. Many of the domestic animals are decorated with garlands; evidently an indication that they were destined to be sacrificial victims.

Cat. no. 42 British Museum, 1873.8–20.590.

27 Cat. no. 43 Musée du Louvre, Paris, Cp. 3667.

28 Cat. no. 44 Nicholson Museum, Sydney, no. 98.72.

29 Cat. no. 45 British Museum, 1955.2–16.2.

30 Cat. no. 46 Archaeological Museum, Heraklion, Giamalakis Collection, no. 501.

Magenta Ware. Lamp-fillers

31 *Cat. no. 48 British Museum, 1867.5–8.1212.*

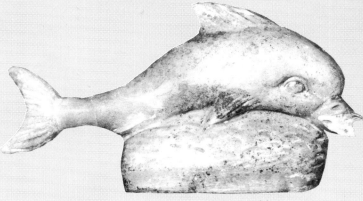

32 *Cat. no. 57 Archaeological Museum, Madrid, no. 20279.*

33 *Cat. no. 51 Ashmolean Museum, Oxford, no. 1927.44.*

34 *Cat. no. 60 Metropolitan Museum, New York, no. 06.1021.265.*

35 *Cat. no. 61 Hermitage Museum, Leningrad, B 3087.*

36 *Cat. no. 62 Hermitage Museum, Leningrad, B 3088.*

Magenta Ware. Lamp-fillers

The lion comes first, represented by two noble examples (nos. 25–26). Then a recumbent bull in several varieties, a sacrificial garland round his head, or his body, or both (nos. 27–34). A garlanded ram in a similar pose (nos. 35–41) has an equally sacrificial look. So has a fine goat (no. 42), and an inferior version (no. 43). Nos. 44 and 44 *bis* are hard to identify, but probably represent a kid.

A dog is represented in three examples, one of which is aberrant (nos. 45–47). There is also a hare (nos. 48–50); and a pig (nos. 51–53), sacred to the infernal goddesses Demeter and Persephone. Nos. 54–58 are dolphins, shown leaping over the waves; a popular subject, especially in the far West, as much, no doubt, for their decorative qualities as for their legendary associations. No. 59 is the only known example of a fish.

Birds are less popular as lamp-fillers; but three cocks (nos. 60–62) and one duck (no. 63) are recorded.

Animal's heads are also occasionally found. A boar's head is known in two examples (nos. 64–65) and a ram's head in one (no. 66).

GROUP B. HANDLED FLASKS

The second type of the Magenta Class is a flask, generally somewhat larger than the lamp-fillers, with a spout like the upper part of a Hellenistic tear-bottle and a ribbon-handle springing from the top of it. As with the lamp-fillers, but with less reason, the front is usually modelled in rather more detail than the back. The purpose of these flasks (as of the strainer-flasks below) is not known; but their association with the lamp-fillers would suggest that they contained lamp-oil, for which they would have been eminently suitable.

The first to be considered (nos. 67 and 68) are two versions of the Wolf and Twins, a subject which has already appeared among the lamp-fillers (no. 4). A head of the Egyptian goddess Isis exists in one example (no. 69). She has a sweet face in the style of the fourth century BC and wears a gold necklace. It is signed by the maker, Dorotheos. Next, heads of actors from the New Comedy founded by the Athenian Menander in the late fourth century BC. They wear the characteristic masks of a slave, with its trumpet-mouth, a young man and a courtesan (nos. 70–72).

A figure of an old woman dressed in a long cloak is represented by three examples (two very fragmentary) from South Italy and Sicily (nos. 73–75). She has a grotesque face with a large nose and thick lips. Her left hand is raised to her chin while her right hand rests on her stomach. If, as seems likely, she is wearing a mask, she must be a character from a South Italian farce. Then two squatting negroes of grey clay with a black 'glaze' (nos. 76–77). One, rather surprisingly, wears round his neck the *bulla*, an amulet of Etruscan origin, which was worn principally by free-born boys, but also by any children and domestic animals as lucky charms. What it is doing round the neck of one who must surely have been a slave is something of a mystery.

The animal world was especially popular. First, a fabulous creature, the griffin (no. 78). Then two pieces perhaps associated with the worship of the god Mithras, a lion grasping with its forefeet a bull's head; one from near Viterbo, the other from a deposit at Knossos of the late first century BC (nos. 79–80).[13] It is tempting to see the latter as the property of one of the veterans from Capua sent by Augustus in 36 BC to settle his new colony Julia Nobilis Cnosus.

Next a leopard, sacred to Dionysus, and therefore shown garlanded, as on a famous mosaic from Delos.[14] He may be represented recumbent (no. 81), or squatting on his haunches (nos. 82–86). No. 83 leaves the species in no doubt, as it is decorated with pink spots. Recumbent pigs are popular (nos. 87–89) and a small standing version, probably slightly earlier, is known from Rheneia (no. 90). A graceful dolphin is recorded from a tomb at Lipari of the mid-first century BC (no. 91).

Birds are more favoured as flasks than as lamp-fillers. Cocks (nos. 92–94) and ducks in considerable quantities (nos. 95–101), are shown garlanded for sacrifice. Finally, two very fragmentary bull's heads complete the series (nos. 102–103).

GROUP C. STRAINER-FLASKS

The third type of Magenta Ware is also a flask, and also probably for lamp-oil. It has a filling-hole in the form of a circular strainer, beside which are lugs pierced horizontally with holes for suspension.

This type is rare, and surviving examples are almost restricted to the Campana Collection in the Louvre, a fact which suggests that it was not as a rule exported outside its centre of manufacture in Campania.

Subjects are similar to those of the handled flasks, and are treated in the same way, but the scope is more restricted. A recumbent leopard, his head turned backwards (nos. 104–105) recalls the handled flasks nos. 81–86. There is one hare (no. 106), while pigs (nos. 107–109) are rather more common.

Finally, as with the handled flasks, we find a cock (no. 110) and also a sacrificial goose with a garland round its neck (nos. 111–112).

37 *Cat. no. 64 British Museum, WT 282.*

38 *Cat. no. 66 Staatliche Museen, Berlin, TC 690.*

39 *Cat. no. 67 Museo Nazionale, Messina, no. 3652.*

40 *Cat. no. 69 Museo Archeologico Eoliano, Lipari.*

41 *Cat. no. 72 British Museum, 1907.12–17.1.*

42 *Cat. no. 73 Museo Nazionale, Syracuse.*

Magenta Ware. Lamp-fillers and handled flasks

43 44

Cat. no. 76 British Museum, 1873.8–20.287.

45 *Cat. no. 77 British Museum, 1873.8–20.288.*

47 *Cat. no. 80 Archaeological Museum, Heraklion;*
excavation no. UM 71.551.

46 *Cat. no. 78*
Staatliche Museen, Berlin.

48 *Cat. no. 79*
Staatliche Museen,
Berlin, V.I. 4292.

Magenta Ware. Handled flasks

OTHER POSSIBLE VARIETIES

Certain lamp fillers in the form of a sandalled foot, and some lamps, particularly those in the shape of a bull's head,[15] may perhaps be Magenta Ware, but their affiliations are not certain, and they have been omitted.

CATALOGUE

This list makes no claim to completeness, but includes all the Magenta Ware pieces known to me, or communicated to me by friends.

The numbers attached to the pieces from Morgantina are those of the catalogue to be published shortly by Professor Malcolm Bell.

In the absence of any statement to the contrary, the pieces listed below may be assumed to be of fine cream-coloured clay, with an orange-brown 'glaze'.

A Lamp-fillers

1 Pan, leaning to his left, against a kid. Ht. 8.5 cm. L. 10 cm. Provenance unknown. Petit Palais, Paris, Dutuit Collection, no. 401.
  Pink on drapery. Pour-hole in animal's mouth. The word ΦΑΩΝ inscribed under base, after firing. (**7**)
   Corpus Vasorum Antiquorum (hereafter, *CVA*), *Petit Palais, Collection Dutuit*, pl. 45: 7 and 9.

2 Pan, as 1. From Delos. Delos Museum.
  Unpublished.

3 Pan, as 1. From Tarentum. Museo Nazionale, Taranto.
  Unpublished.

4 Wolf and Twins. Ht. 8.5 cm. W. 10.8 cm. Provenance unknown, presumably Etruria. Vatican Museum, Museo Gregoriano Etrusco, no. 13251.
  Pour-hole in wolf's left ear. (**9**)
   W. HELBIG, *Führer durch die öffentlichen Sammlungen klassischer Altertümer in Rom*, 1963, 598.

5 Pygmy carrying crane. Ht. 8.1 cm. Provenance unknown. Metropolitan Museum, New York, 06.1021.266. (**8**)
   Sambon-Canessa Sale Cat., 11.5.1903, lot 233. A. SAMBON, *Collection Canessa*, 1904, 74. no. 254.

6 Squatting satyr. Ht. 13 cm. From Budva. National Museum, Belgrade.
   M. VELICKOVIC, *Catalogue des terres cuites grecques et romaines*, Belgrade, 1937, 98, pl. 13, no. 29.

7 Satyr reclining. Ht. 8.8 cm. W. 13 cm. From Italy. Louvre, Paris, Campana Coll., Cp. 3621. (**10**)
  Unpublished.

8 Satyr reclining, as 7 (fragt). Ht. 8.5 cm. W. 9.5 cm. From Italy. Louvre, Paris, Campana Coll., Cp. 3633.
Unpublished.

9 Satyr reclining, as 7. Ht. 8 cm. W. 11.4 cm. From Ampurias. Gerona Museum. Traces of red.
GARCIA Y BELLIDA, *Hispania Graeca*, 1948 (hereafter *Hispania Graeca*), pl. 158, no. 22.

10 Actor seated on altar. Ht. 12 cm. W. 6 cm. Provenance unknown. British Museum, 1873.10-20.2. (**11, 12, and Plate I**)
Pink on mask, girdle and altar. Red on mouth, hair and sandals. Blue on fillet. Black outlining eyes. Pour-hole in his left hip.
British Museum Catalogue of Terracottas, 1903 (hereafter *BM Cat.*), D 322. F. WINTER, *Die Typen der figürlichen Terrakotten*, 1903 (hereafter WINTER), ii, 419:1.

11 Actor reclining. Ht. 9.8 cm. W. 11.5 cm. From Cumae (?). Ashmolean Museum, Oxford, 1927.45. (**14**)
Traces of pink on drapery.
Sotheby Sale Cat., 16.12.1926, lot 64.

12 Actor reclining, as 11. Ht. 10 cm. W. 11.5 cm. From Tarquinia. Tarquinia Museum, RC 6240.
Unpublished.

13 Actor reclining, as 11 (fragt). Provenance unknown. Allard Pierson Museum, Amsterdam, no. 3249.
Unpublished.

14 Actor reclining. Ht. 9 cm. W. 10 cm. From Italy. Louvre, Paris, Campana Coll., Cp. 3628. (**15**)
Pink on lips. Pour-hole by his left elbow.
Unpublished.

15 Actor reclining, as 14. Ht. 9.5 cm. From Cumae. Museo Nazionale, Naples, no. 84927.
A. LEVI, *Le terrecotte figurate del Mus. Naz. di Napoli*, 1926 (hereafter LEVI, *Tc Napoli*), no. 511.

16 Man and woman on couch. Ht. 8.5 cm. W. 10.5 cm. 'From Tarquinia'. British Museum, 1873.8-20.603. (**16**)
Red on lips. Pink on drapery (traces). Black on hair, eyes and eyebrows.
BM Cat., D 213. WINTER, ii, 233.9.

49 *Cat. no. 81 Museo Nazionale, Syracuse, no. 40057.*

50 *Cat. no. 82 British Museum, TB 797.*

51 *Cat. no. 85 Musée du Louvre, Paris, Cp. 3664.*

52 *Cat. no. 91 Museo Archeologico Eoliano, Lipari.*

53 *Cat. no. 87 Cabinet des Médailles, Paris, Janzé Collection, no. 871.*

Magenta Ware. Handled flasks

54 *Cat. no. 92 British Museum, 1911.4–11.1.*

55 *Cat. no. 95 Musée du Louvre, Paris, Cp. 3675.*

56 *Cat. no. 107 Musée du Louvre, Paris, Cp. 3653.*

57 *Cat. no. 110 Musée du Louvre, Paris, Cp. 3696.*

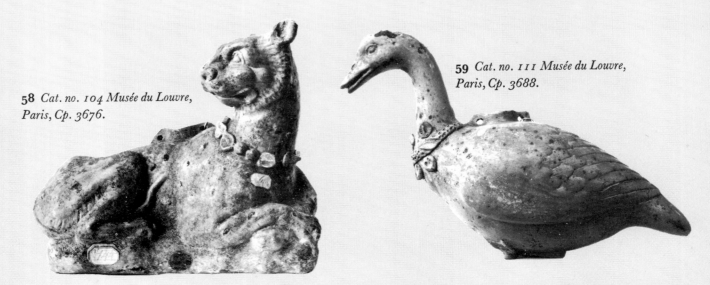

58 *Cat. no. 104 Musée du Louvre, Paris, Cp. 3676.*

59 *Cat. no. 111 Musée du Louvre, Paris, Cp. 3688.*

Magenta Ware. Handled flasks and strainer flasks

17 Man and woman on couch, as 16. Ht. 9.1 cm. W. 11.6 cm. From Italy. Musée d'Art et d'Histoire, Geneva, no. 5849.
Unpublished.

18 Man and woman on couch, as 16. Ht. 8 cm. W. 10 cm. From Sicily.[16] Badisches Landesmuseum, Karlsruhe, B 462.
CVA Karlsruhe ii, 47, pl. 86:9. WINTER, ii, 233:9.

19 Man and woman on couch, as 16. Ht. 8 cm. W. 9 cm. From Sicily.[16] Badisches Landesmuseum, Karlsruhe, B 463.
CVA Karlsruhe ii, 47, pl. 86:10. WINTER, ii, 233:9.

20 Gallic warrior kneeling (head missing). Ht. 8 cm. Provenance unknown. Formerly Staatliche Museen, Berlin, no. 30.031 (lost in the war). (**13, 60**)
Unpublished.

21 Gallic warrior, as 20 (fragt). From Rheneia. Mykonos Museum.
Unpublished. (**60**)

60 *Cat. no. 20 Formerly Staatliche Museen, Berlin, no. 30.031; and Cat. no. 21 Mykonos Museum.*

22 Crouching man, with jug.
Ht. 7 cm. W. 11 cm. Provenance unknown.
Louvre, Paris, S 4057. (**17**)
Most of back missing.
Unpublished.

23 Boy with goose. Ht. 9.6 cm. W. 10.3 cm. From Italy. Musée d'Art et d'Histoire, Geneva, no. 5850. (**18**)
Traces of pink.
Unpublished.

24 Boy riding Maltese dog. Ht. 10.4 cm. W. 7.6 cm. From Italy. Musée d'Art et d'Histoire, Geneva, no. 5851. (**19**)
Traces of pink.
Unpublished.

25 Lion. Ht. 7.5 cm. W. 12.5 cm. From Italy. Louvre, Paris, Campana Coll., Cp. 3639. (**20**)
Red on mouth.
Unpublished.

26 Lion, variant of 25, with head raised. Ht. 8.8 cm. W. 11 cm. From Budva. National Museum, Belgrade.

    M. Velickovic, *Catalogue des terres cuites grecques et romaines*, Belgrade 1957, 90, pl. 14, no. 31.

27 Bull. Ht. 8.5 cm. W. 11.7 cm. 'From Tarquinia'. British Museum, 1873.8-20.591. (**21**)

    BM Cat., D 214.

28 Bull, as 27. Ht. 10.7 cm. W. 11 cm. From Pozzuoli. Metropolitan Museum, New York, 07.286.1311.

    Unpublished.

29 Bull, as 27. Ht. 9.5 cm. W. 12 cm. From Italy. Louvre, Paris, Campana Coll., Cp. 3665.

    Unpublished.

30 Bull, as 27. Ht. 9 cm. W. 11.7 cm. Provenance unknown. (Fogelberg Coll.) Antikensammlungen, Munich, WAF 906.

    Red band on front of base. Darker 'gloss' on eyes and band round body possibly indicates former presence of added white.

    Unpublished.

31 Bull, much as 27, but base has astragal pattern in relief. Ht. 8.5 cm. W. 10 cm. From Ampurias (Emporion). Ampurias Museum.

    M. Almagro, *Las Necropolis de Ampurias*, i, 1953, pl. 17, no. 5.

32 Bull, variant of 27. Ht. 9.5 cm. W. 10.2 cm. Provenance unknown. Formerly de Clercq Coll.

    A. de Ridder, *Collection de Clercq*, iv, no. 108.

33 Bull, differing from 27 in treatment of head and tail. Ht. 8.5 cm. W. 10.5 cm. From Cyrenaica. British Museum, 1866.4-15.129. (**22**)

    BM Cat., C 821.

34 Bull, as 33. Ht. 9.5 cm. W. 12 cm. From Capua. Staatliche Museen, Berlin, V.I. 3762.

    Sambon-Canessa Sale Cat. (Bourgignon Coll.), March 1901, lot 77.

35 Ram. Ht. 9.5 cm. W. 10.5 cm. 'From Syria'. British Museum, 1887.2-12.2. (**23**)

    BM Cat., C 547.

36 Ram, as 35. Ht. 9 cm. W. 10.5 cm. From Italy. Louvre, Paris, Campana Coll., Cp. 3650.

    Unpublished.

37 Ram, as 35. Ht. 9.5 cm. W. 10.7 cm. From Etruria. Museo Nazionale, Florence, no. 4671.
Unpublished.

38 Ram, as 35. Ht. 8.7 cm. W. 11.2 cm. From Etruria. Museo Nazionale, Florence, no. 4672.
Pale grey clay with traces of dull black 'glaze'.
Unpublished.

39 Ram, as 35. Ht. 12 cm. Probably from Sicily. Museo Nazionale, Syracuse, no. 1838.
Unpublished.

40 Ram as 35. Ht. 9.2 cm. W. 11 cm. Provenance unknown. University Museum, Würzburg.
E. LANGLOTZ, *Griechische Vasen in Würzburg*, 1932, no. 890.

41 Ram, as 35, but head only half turned. Ht. 9.5 cm. W. 10.5 cm. From Italy. Louvre, Paris, Campana Coll., Cp. 3656. (**24**)
Matt black on eyes.
Unpublished.

42 Goat. Ht. 10 cm. W. 10.5 cm. 'From Rhodes'. British Museum, 1873.8-20.590. (**25, 26**)
Pink inside ears. Blue on ivy leaves.
BM Cat., C 468.

43 Goat, a coarser version of 42. Ht. 10 cm. W. 12 cm. From Italy. Louvre, Paris, Campana Coll., Cp. 3667. (**27**)
Horns missing.
Unpublished.

44 Kid. Ht. 10.1 cm. W. 10.8 cm. Provenance unknown. Nicholson Museum, Sydney, no. 98.72. (**28**)

44 *bis* Kid. From Melilla, Morocco. Mellila Museum.
I Congresso Arqueologico del Marruecos Espanol, Tetuan 1954, 263, pl. 12, no. 49.

45 Dog lying down. Ht. 4.5 cm. W. 6.5 cm. Provenance unknown. British Museum, 1955.2-16.2. (**29**)
Pale grey clay with traces of dull black 'glaze'. Handle missing.
Unpublished.

46 Dog lying down, as 45, but with cake in mouth. Ht. 7.3 cm. W. 13.5 cm.
Provenance unknown. Archaeological Museum, Heraklion, Crete, Giamalakis
Collection, no. 501. (**30**)
Exceptionally, handle beside strainer.
Unpublished.

47 Dog lying down. Ht. 7 cm. W. 9 cm. From Chalcis. National Museum, Athens.
Archaiologkike Ephemeris, 1907, 82, fig. 17.

48 Hare. Ht. 6 cm. W. 11 cm. From Italy (?). British Museum, 1867.5-8.1212
(Blacas Coll.). (**31**)
Pink inside ears. White on band round neck and as spots on body.
BM Cat., D 212.

49 Hare, as 48. Ht. 6 cm. W. 10 cm. Provenance unknown; presumably South
Italy. Museo Nazionale, Naples, CS 284.
Levi, *Tc Napoli*, no. 790.

50 Hare, as 48. Ht. 7.5 cm. W. 12.3 cm. From Italy. Louvre, Paris, Campana Coll.,
Cp. 3682.
Unpublished.

51 Pig. Ht. 8.7 cm. W. 12.3 cm. From Cumae. Ashmolean Museum, Oxford,
1927.44. (**33**)
Red on eyes.
Sotheby Sale Cat., 16.12.1926, lot 64.

52 Pig, as 51. From Archena.
Hispania Graeca, 178, pl. 127.

53 Pig, as 51. Ht. 9 cm. W. 12 cm. From Cyrenaica. Louvre, Paris, N 4427.
Unpublished.

54 Dolphin. Ht. 9 cm. From Cumae. Museo Nazionale, Naples, no. 8429.
Levi, *Tc Napoli*, no. 510.

55 Dolphin, as 54. From Ampurias. Archaeological Museum, Barcelona.
Hispania Graeca, pl. 111.

56 Dolphin, as 54. From Archena.
Hispania Graeca, pl. 127.

57 Dolphin, as 54. Ht. 9 cm. W. 15.5 cm. From Melilla, Morocco. Archaeological
Museum, Madrid, no. 20279. (**32**)
A. Laumonier, *Cat. de terres cuites du Musée Archeologique de Madrid*, 1921, no. 1016.

58 Dolphin, as 54. From Rheneia. Mykonos Museum.
Unpublished.

59 Fish. From Rheneia. Mykonos Museum.
Unpublished.

60 Cock. Ht. 9.2 cm. W. 14.3 cm. From Italy. Metropolitan Museum, New York, 06.1021.265. (**34**)
A. SAMBON, *Collection Canessa*, 1904, no. 148.

61 Cock, variant of 60, on square base. Ht. 11.3 cm. W. 12 cm. From Italy. Hermitage Museum, Leningrad, B 3087 (Campana Coll.). (**35**)
Unpublished.

62 Cock, as 61, but on oval base. Ht. 12.7 cm. W. 12 cm. From Italy. Hermitage Museum, Leningrad, B 3088 (Campana Coll.). (**36**)
Unpublished.

63 Duck. Formerly market. Provenance unknown.
Hesperia Art, xl/xli, no. A14. (**61**)

61 *Cat. no. 63 Formerly art market; present whereabouts unknown.*

64 Boar's head. Ht. 10.5 cm. W. 10 cm. 'From Capua'. British Museum, WT 282 (Temple Bequest). (**37**)
Inlet-hole in left ear.
BM Cat., D 211.

65 Boar's head, as 64. From Archena.
Hispania Graeca, pl. 127.

66 Ram's head. Ht. 10 cm. W. 15 cm. From South Italy. Staatliche Museen, Berlin, TC 690. (**38**)
Pink on lips, eyes, nose, ears. Strainer-inlet in left ear.
Archäologischer Anzeiger, 1928, 341, fig. 62.

B Handled flasks

67 Wolf and twins, very like 4. Head and top of spout missing. Ht. 16 cm. W. 16 cm. From Messina. Museo Nazionale, Messina, no. 3652. (**39**)
Notizie degli Scavi di Antichità (hereafter *NS*), 1943, 80, fig. 17.

68 Wolf and twins, as 67. From Rheneia. Mykonos Museum.
Unpublished.

69 Head of Isis (damaged). Ht. (presumed), 21.5 cm. W. 13.4 cm. From Lipari, tomb 10 (*c.* 50 BC). Museo Archeologico Eoliano, Lipari.
Inscribed on back (before firing) [Δ]ΩΡΟΘΕΟΓ. (**40**)
L. BERNABÒ-BREA and M. CAVALIER, *Meligunis-Lipara*, ii, pl. 215:1 and 2.

70 Head of actor (slave). Ht. 10 cm. Probably from the Troad. Archaeological Museum, Cannakale (Calvert Coll.).
Winter, ii, 427:1.

71 Head of actor (youth). Badly damaged. Ht. 15 cm. From Morgantina (948). About 130 BC.
To be published shortly. See M. BIEBER, *History of the Greek and Roman Theater*, 1961 (hereafter, BIEBER), 98, fig. 344 for the type.

72 Head of actor (courtesan). Back missing. Ht. 20 cm.W . 14 cm. 'From Rhodes'. British Museum, 1907.12-17.1. (**41**)
Pale grey clay, with traces of dull black 'glaze'. A inscribed under base after firing.
Unpublished. See BIEBER, 98, figs. 361–3 for the type.

73 Grotesque old woman. Lower part missing. Ht. 17 cm. W. 8 cm. From Syracuse. Museo Nazionale, Syracuse. (**42**)
Unpublished.

74 Head of old woman, as 73. Ht. 8.5 cm. W. 7.7 cm. From Reggio. Museo Nazionale, Reggio di Calabria, no. 11552.
NS 1968, 229, fig. 9, no. 22.

75 Head of old woman, as 73. Ht. 6.2 cm. From Morgantina (945).
Traces of pink on face and hood.
To be published shortly.

76 Negro squatting. Ht. 24 cm. W. 10 cm. 'From Ruvo'. British Museum, 1873.8-20.287. (**43, 44**)
Grey clay, with black 'glaze'. Red on lips.
British Museum Catalogue of Vases, iv, 1896 (hereafter, *BM Cat Vases*), G 167.

77 Negro squatting, as 76 but wearing a bulla round neck. Ht. 20 cm. W. 9 cm.
Provenance unknown. British Museum, 1873.8-20.288.
Grey clay, with black 'glaze'. (**45**)
BM Cat. Vases, G 168.

78 Griffin. Ht. 22 cm. W. 20 cm. 'From Crete'. Staatliche Museen, Berlin. (**46**)
Traces of red on head and rear portion; blue on background.
A. FURTWÄNGLER, *La Collection Sabouroff*, i, 1883–7, pl. 72. id., *Beschreibung der Vasensammlung*,
Berlin 1885, no. 2931.

79 Lion grasping a bull's head in its forefeet. Ht. 16 cm. W. 21 cm. From near
Viterbo. Staatliche Museen, Berlin, V.I. 4292. (**48**)
Traces of white and pink.
Unpublished.

80 Lion, variation of 79 (fragmentary). Ht. 14.4 cm. W. 24 cm. From Knossos
(Unexplored Mansion). Late first century BC. Archaeological Museum,
Heraklion. Excavation no. UM. 71.551. (**47**)
Unpublished.

81 Leopard. Ht. 15 cm. W. 14 cm. From Taormina. Museo Nazionale, Syracuse,
no. 40057. (**49**)
Traces of red.
Unpublished.

82 Leopard. Ht. 14.5 cm. W. 12 cm. From Leukas. British Museum, TB 797. (**50**)
Red on muzzle and ears.
BM Cat., C 68.

83 Leopard, as 82. Ht. 15 cm. W. 12.5 cm. From Syracuse. Museo Nazionale,
Syracuse, no. 36783.
Pink on spots.
Unpublished.

84 Leopard (fragt), as 82. Left foreleg and surroundings only. W. 7 cm. From
Syracuse. Museo Nazionale, Syracuse.
NS 1971, 596, fig. 20.

85 Leopard, variant of 82. Ht. 18 cm. W. 12 cm. From Italy. Louvre, Paris,
Campana Coll., Cp. 3664. (**51**)
Unpublished.

86 Leopard (head only), from piece as 85. Ht. 6 cm. From Morgantina (951).
To be published shortly.

87 Pig. Ht. 15 cm. W. 23 cm. Provenance unknown. Cabinet des Médailles, Paris,
Janzé Coll., no. 871. (**53**)
Traces of black and white.
Unpublished.

88 Pig, as 87. Ht. 15 cm. W. 22 cm. From Cumae. Museo Nazionale, Naples, no.
84928.
LEVI, *Tc Napoli*, no. 512.

89 Pig, as 87. Ht. 15.7 cm. W. 21.8 cm. From Halae (?). Archaeological Museum,
Thebes.
Unpublished.

90 Pig, standing variant of 87. From Rheneia.
Mykonos Museum.
Unpublished. (**62**)

91 Dolphin. Ht. 18.9 cm. W. 17.2 cm.
From Lipari, tomb 10, (*c.* 50 BC). Museo
Archeologico Eoliano, Lipari. (**52**)
L. BERNABÒ-BREA and M. CAVALIER, *Meligunis-Lipara*,
ii, pl. 214:5.

62 *Cat. no. 90 Mykonos Museum.*

92 Cock. Ht. 17 cm. W. 23 cm. 'From Acarnania'. British Museum, 1911.4-11.1.
(**54**)
Unpublished.

93 Cock, as 92. From Tarentum. Museo Nazionale, Taranto.
Unpublished.

94 Cock (fragt), as 92. Ht. 12.9 cm. From Morgantina (949).
Traces of pink on comb.
To be published shortly.

95 Duck. Ht. 18 cm. W. 21 cm. From Italy. Louvre, Paris, Campana Coll., Cp.
3675. (**55**)
Unpublished.

96 Duck, as 95. Ht. 18 cm. W. 20 cm. From Cyrenaica. Louvre, Paris, MN 1042.
Unpublished.

97 Duck, as 95. Ht. 15 cm. W. 17 cm. Provenance unknown. Louvre, Paris, N III 251.
Unpublished.

98 Duck, as 95. Ht. 16 cm. W. 22.5 cm. Back restored. From Centorbi. Museo Nazionale, Syracuse.
Unpublished.

99 Duck (fragt), as 95. Ht. 12 cm. Head and neck only. From Syracuse, 'Tomb of Archimedes'. Museo Nazionale, Syracuse.
Unpublished. But see *Archivio Storico Siracusano*, xiii–xiv, 1967–8, 29.

100 Duck (fragt), as 95. Ht. 9.7 cm. W. 10.6 cm. Neck and back only. From Reggio. Museo Nazionale, Reggio di Calabria, no. 11553.
NS 1968, 229, fig. 9, no. 23.

101 Duck (fragt), as 95. Ht. 7.2 cm. W. 8.3 cm. Back with spout only. From Reggio. Museo Nazionale, Reggio di Calabria, no. 11554.
NS 1968, 229, fig. 9, no. 24.

102 Bull's head (fragt). L. 11 cm. W. 7 cm. From Syracuse. Museo Nazionale, Syracuse, no. 69396.
NS 1971, 596, 21, A4.

103 Bull's head (fragt). Ht. 9.5 cm. W. 13.8 cm. From Reggio. Museo Nazionale, Reggio di Calabria, no. 11538.
NS 1968, 227, fig. 7.

C Strainer flasks

104 Leopard. Ht. 16.5 cm. W. 19 cm. From Italy. Louvre, Paris, Campana Coll., Cp. 3676. (**58**)
Black spots on body.
Unpublished.

105 Leopard (fragt), as 104. Ht. 15.2 cm. From Morgantina (950).
White spots on garland and left shoulder. White on teeth.
To be published shortly.

106 Hare. From Tarentum, via S. Giovane. Museo Nazionale, Taranto.
Unpublished.

107 Pig. Ht. 12 cm. W. 25.5 cm. From Italy. Louvre, Paris, Campana Coll., Cp. 3653. (**56**)
Red on base. Two pink stripes round belly. Exceptionally, the suspension-holes are set wide apart on its back.
Unpublished.

108 Pig, as 107. From Tarentum. Museo Nazionale, Taranto.
Unpublished.

109 Pig, as 107. Ht. 11 cm. W. 20 cm. From Chalcis. National Museum, Athens.
Archaiologike Ephemeris, 1907, 81, fig. 15.

110 Cock. Ht. 28 cm. W. 23 cm. From Italy. Louvre, Paris, Campana Coll., Cp. 3696 (**57**)
'Glaze' redder than usual.
Unpublished.

111 Goose. Ht. 17 cm. W. 24 cm. From Italy. Louvre, Paris, Campana Coll., Cp. 3688. (**59**)
Pink on beak and fillet round neck.
Unpublished.

112 Goose, as 111. Probably from Centorbi. Museo Nazionale, Syracuse, no. 36015.
G. LIBERTINI, *Centuripae*, Catania 1926, pl. xxxviii, bottom right.

D Fragments: variety uncertain

113–117 Heads of a lion, leopard, bull, dog and pig. From Delos. Delos Museum.
Unpublished.

118–119 Head of a horse (?) and animal's hoof resting on a base. These, and probably other fragments, from Morgantina.
To be published shortly.

120–124 Five (at least) indeterminate fragments from Syracuse. Museo Nazionale, Syracuse.
See *NS* 1971, 596, fig. 20, and *Archivio Storico Siracusano* xiii–xiv, 1967–8, 29.

Acknowledgements

I owe a special debt of gratitude to Dottoressa Paola Pelagatti for giving me much information and many photographs of Magenta pieces in Sicily and South Italy, a number of them unpublished; and to Professor Malcolm Bell for giving me full information about material from Morgantina which he is engaged in publishing.

I should also like to thank the following for help with information and photographs: Mme I. Aghion, Mlle Z. T. Ailliez, Dr S. Alexiou, Dr A. Andriomenou, Mr D. M. Bailey, Dr D. von Bothmer, Dr L. Bernabò-Brea, Mlle M. F. Briguet, Mlle A. Cacan, Professor A. Cambitoglou, Dr E. Cicerchia, Dr C. Dunant, Professor N. Duval, Dr K. S. Gorbunova, Dr F. W. Hamdorf, Dr I. Kriseleit, Dr G. Maetzke, Professor M. Moretti, Professor A. D. Trendall, and Dr K. Vierneisel.

Photographic credits. American School of Classical Studies, Athens: 5; British School at Athens: 46; Staatliche Museen, Berlin: 13, 38, 48; Musée d'Art et d'Histoire, Geneva: 18, 19; Archaeological Museum, Heraklion, Crete: 30; Hermitage Museum, Leningrad: 36, 36; Museo Arqueologico Nacional, Madrid: 32; Museo Nazionale, Messina: 39; Metropolitan Museum of Art, New York, Rogers Fund, 1906: 8, 34; Ashmolean Museum, Oxford: 14, 33; Bibliothèque Nationale, Paris: 53; Musée du Louvre, Paris, and Chuzeville: 3, 4, 6, 10, 15, 17, 20, 24, 27, 51, 55, 56, 57, 58, 59; Musée du Petit Palais, Paris, photo Bulloz: 7; Museo del Vaticano, Rome: 9; Soprintendenza alle Antichità della Sicilia Orientale: 42, 49, 52; Nicholson Museum, Sydney: 28. 60–62 were drawn by Miss M. O. Miller.

NOTES

1 See G. M. A. Richter, *The Metropolitan Museum of Art. Handbook of the Greek collection*, 1953, 132.

2 Vitruvius, Bk vii, ch. 11. Pliny, *Natural History*, Bk xxxiii, ch. 162. See also H. Frost, *The Mortar Wreck in Mellieha Bay*, 1969, 13.

3 This figure is composed largely of the Campana Collection, which was mostly acquired from Etruria, Latium and Campania.

4 N. Lamboglia, 'Per una classificazione preliminare della ceramica Campana', in *Atti del I Congresso Internazionale di Studi Ligure, 1950*, Bordighera, 1952, 140.

5 *The Athenian Agora*, iv, no. 617.

6 *Hesperia* iii, 1934, 373, fig. 28, D 20.

7 *Gallia* xi, 1953, 95, fig. 5.

8 Louvre, Campana Collection, Cp. 3647. Ht. 13 cm. W. 6.5 cm.

9 British Museum, from Sardinia. 1857. 6-8.3. Ht. 7.5 cm. W. 17.5 cm. (G 153).

10 Louvre, Campana Collection, Cp. 3668. Ht. 11 cm. W. 6.5 cm.

11 R. Thompson, *Early Roman Coinage*, iii, 1961, 116 ff.

12 See n. 7, above.

13 See *Scavi di Ostia*, iv, 200, pl. 96 (top); E. A. Campbell, *Mithraic Iconography and Ideology*, 1968, 288; C. Bonner, *Studies in Magical Amulets*, 1950, 36.

14 J. Charbonneaux et al., *Hellenistic Art*, 1973, 185, pl. 192.

15 For bull's head lamps, see *Délos* xxvi,

nos. 4771–4; *The Athenian Agora*, iv, no. 617 (here, 5).

16 The find-spot in *CVA* is given as 'aus Polizzi'; but Kekulé, in *Terracotten aus Sizilien*, 87, thinks that Polizzi was a man rather than the Sicilian town of that name. There seems, however, no doubt that nos. 17 and 18 do come from Sicily.

Architecture on ancient coins

Contemporary impressions of buildings on Greek coins struck under the Roman empire

M. JESSOP PRICE

Assistant Keeper, Coins and Medals

In the eighteenth and nineteenth centuries the use of coins as a primary source of evidence for life in ancient times was commonplace; but with the growing specialization of scholarship, archaeologists find little room for coins in the teaching syllabus of university courses, and 'numismatics' has become a separate 'subject'. In no field is the absurdity of this more apparent than in the study of ancient architecture. Coins illustrate more than 800 different buildings from the cities of the Greek world alone, and yet they are hardly ever mentioned either in the textbooks on coins, since their study is not the province of the 'numismatist', or in the textbooks on classical architecture.[1] Students are thus unaware that we have to hand fine illustrations of many of the important buildings of the ancient world, engraved by artists who knew them as standing structures and not as foundation stones reconstructed by archaeologists.

It is often objected that such miniature views cannot do more than give a vague outline of the building, and that artists were by no means careful in their depiction of details. There is indeed some truth in this; but among the thousands of coins which use a building as a type, there are hundreds on which the artists who engraved them lavished particular care. It was necessary that the meaning of the type be intelligible to those who handled the coins, and thus there had to be no ambiguity as to which building in the city was intended. It is not rare to find that the artist emphasized a particular architectural detail to give realism to his impression of the building. Different artists picked on different details, so that in a coin series in which the same building recurs again and again, a comparison of these details can lead to an accurate reconstruction of the original. In reducing the three-dimensional building to the two-dimensional coin flan the artist was bound to use certain conventions of shorthand, and it is through a lack of understanding of these that most scepticism arises. Once the conventions are understood, the full value of the coins as documents in the history of architecture can be appreciated.

One of the few buildings on coins to have received detailed scholarly attention in recent times is the temple of Artemis at Ephesus (**63**).[2] The coins can be compared with material from the excavations of the site and with literary descriptions of antiquity, so that we can appreciate not only how the artists approached their subject, but also how far the details of coins can be trusted. The columns, eight in number on the actual building, are on the coins often reduced to give merely the impression of a columned façade. The central intercolumniation is often widened, and the cult image brought to the fore, to identify the building more easily. At other cities, but not in the case of Ephesus, the architrave is sometimes arched to provide more room for the depiction of the cult figure. These three 'conventions', together with simple forms of perspective, were all that the artists required. They are perfectly straightforward, and even if the common appearance of the arched architrave, the so-called 'Syrian arch', may be misleading, such conventions do not detract from a study of the building itself. At Ephesus hundreds of coins survive depicting the temple of Artemis, and the best without doubt is that recently acquired by the British Museum (**63**). The sculptured drums at the base of the columns on the façade can be compared with the actual drums found in the excavations which were one of the remarkable features of the building. Yet, in defiance of the many coins, an archaeologist has during 1974 published a reconstruction of the temple placing the sculptured drums at the top of the columns, immediately below the capitals.[3] His reason for this is that he has thus tried to solve the problem posed by the discovery in the excavations of sculptured plinths, which he has chosen to place at the base of each column; but the coins are explicit: they never show sculpture at the top of the columns; they very often show a drum of sculpture at the base of the columns; and there is no clear example of a drum placed on a rectangle at the base of the columns. It is most probable therefore that the plinths belonged elsewhere, and not on the façade of the building. The coins also show remarkable details in the pediment of the building for which excavations can rarely provide evidence. Here three doors or windows are clearly visible, the central one flanked by figures with raised arms. Knowing the coins, Dr H. Plommer[4] was able to interpret a block of building stone which he found in a nearby church as being the jamb of one of these pedimental windows.

63 *The Temple of Artemis, Ephesus.*
Maximus, AD 235–238. (1970. 9–9. 83).

At Baalbek (Heliopolis) three buildings occur on the coins[5] which can also be compared with their originals uncovered by archaeologists. The temple of Juppiter Heliopolitanus (**64**) is shown in three-quarters view from above. We can appreciate the high podium on which it was placed and the imposing staircase on the façade; and the artist has gone to considerable trouble to show the forest of columns that surrounded the building, some of which have been restored. More important from the archaeological point of view, perhaps, is the gate to the sanctuary (**65**). The arched entrance-way in the centre of the columned portico was discovered by the excavators. The flanking towers are typical of oriental architecture from which they passed to Syrian churches and thence to European cathedrals. The gate at Baalbek can

64 *The Temple of Juppiter, Baalbek-Heliopolis.*
Septimius Severus, posthumous.
AD 211/2. (BMC 3).

65 *The portico to the Sanctuary of Juppiter,*
Baalbek-Heliopolis. Philip I,
AD 244–249 (BMC 16).

be compared with that at neighbouring Capetolias (**66**), where the central tower over the main gateway is even more prominent. Modern reconstructions of the gate at Baalbek have tended to minimize this, until recently[6] it has become merely a coping stone at the top of the pediment. The artist was careful to show the arch of the gate, and there can be little doubt that the proportions of this central tower are also fairly accurate. Archaeologists must admit that it is as prominent as the two flanking towers. As the cult object in the centre of the gate, the artist has placed an ear of corn, as a reminder that we are in the presence not of the Greco-Roman Zeus-Juppiter, but of the great oriental fertility god, Juppiter-Hadad, who presided over the 'city of the sun'. It is in such details that we can appreciate how thin the veneer of civilization can be.

The third building to be shown on the coins of Baalbek is clearly outside the main sanctuary (**67**). A long flight of steps leads 'up' a hill of rocks and trees, and the sanctuary shown in bird's eye view is identified by a winged caduceus to be that of Mercury. It is only in recent years that traces of this temple have been uncovered,[7]

66 *The portico to the Sanctuary of Zeus, Capetolias. Marcus Aurelius, AD 164/5. (1970. 9–5. 1).*

67 *The hill-top Sanctuary of Mercury, Baalbek-Heliopolis. Philip I, AD 244–249.* (BMC 18).

together with part of the great staircase; but the coins show that the temple was a smaller version of that of Juppiter in the plains below, and the façade dominating the sanctuary was probably no less impressive. Today, practically nothing remains.

The interest of the coins centres as much if not more, on those buildings which have not been uncovered by modern excavations, many of which through the ravages of time may never be brought to light. Some may be known to have existed as the centres of great cults; but for most the coins are the only surviving evidence. The cult of Europa-Astarte at Sidon was one of the focal points of the religious life of the Phoenicians, and through its connections with the spread of civilization to Crete and Europe must have had widespread fame. Yet we must rely on the coins of the Roman period for a view of her sanctuary (68). The artist has chosen a simple view of perspective in order to depict more than just the temple building. He has shown above, statues and buildings which in reality stood behind. The entry to the sacred area was formed by two great pillars decorated with floral scrolls which immediately recall the bronze pillars of Boaz and Jachin set up by Hiram of Tyre in front of Solomon's temple at Jerusalem.[8] The sculptures in the gateway probably stood in the courtyard, and beyond we can see the temple of Astarte, with her cult image showing her as Europa on the bull, in which form she found so prominent a place in Greek and Roman mythology. The building itself is rendered rather sketchily; but like so many oriental shrines it seems to have been divided into three parts, the main central 'nave' flanked by side wings. Above these are a further line of columns which should be interpreted as a colonnade at the far end of the sanctuary. Although the bird's eye view gives a clearer impression, the artist of this coin has combined into a single design the main elements of this great sanctuary, and has given enough detail to allow a fair reconstruction, although nothing of the ancient buildings has arrived.

A different kind of monument, but no less interesting, is the gate of the city of Augusta Trajana in Thrace (**69**). In contrast to some of the decorative city gates and victory arches that are found on coins, and in contrast to the religious buildings which we have seen so far, this characterizes the city as a military post, a bastion of the Roman empire. The massive masonry wall is pierced by a narrow entrance, and three crenellated towers provide the necessary protection. Along the whole extent of Rome's frontiers such gates existed, and to these remains the coins add a vivid reminder of the constant threat of invasion, as well as a broad picture of how these military installations looked in ancient times.

68 *The Sanctuary of Europa-Astarte, Sidon. Elagabalus, AD 218–222. (1967. 11–10.11).*

69 *City gate, Augusta Trajana. Caracalla, c. AD 198–210.* (BMC *11*).

The city of Nicaea in Bithynia was in fact overrun[9] by an invasion of the Goths in AD 258, and the coins of the following years which depict a simple hexagon of city walls (**70**) refer to the rebuilding of the city, and in particular to the care given to the defences. These same walls today surround the town of Iznik, and an inscription on one of the gates commemorates the completion of this building project under the emperor Claudius Gothicus (AD 268–270). Here at least we know that the coins can be equated with the erection of the walls and, although we can never generalize since the reasons for the choice of type are legion, it is possible that some other monuments that we find on coins are so used at the time of their building or of their restoration. At Aspendus (**71**) a temple of Zeus of little architectural merit is accompanied by the interesting inscription M. ΑΝΤΩΝΕΙΝΟC ΝΑΟΝ ΕΚΤΙCΕΝ, 'M. Antoninus

70 *The city walls, Nicaea. Quietus, AD 260–262.* (BMC *160*).

71 *The Temple of Zeus, Aspendus. Valerian II, AD 258. (1973. 5–2. 1).*

72 *Aqueduct, Anazarbus. Severus Alexander, AD 222–235. (1974. 1–2. 50).*

dedicated the temple', a clear reference to the fact that the coin commemorated this event, which can thus be dated to the time of Valerian II AD 258.

The unusual appearance of an aqueduct at Anazarbus in Cilicia (**72**) may also allow us to suppose that the coin celebrates the completion (AD 222–235) of an important project bringing an improved supply of water to the city. The arches continue on beyond the flan of the coin, a detail which differentiates it from the normal depiction of bridges on coins (cf. **86**); and the identification of the structure as an aqueduct is confirmed both by the firm ground shown below the arches, and also by the presence below of a swimming figure, the river god whose waters supplied the city. Over the central arch a small tower probably indicates the position of a sluice gate or settling tank. The extensive remains of the city contain a fine example of a Roman aqueduct[10] near which was found an inscription dedicating it to the Roman emperor Domitian in AD 90. One detail links this structure with the coin—the niches or relieving arches still visible between the main standing arches, and noted by the engraver of the coin as small 'windows'. Since the city was extensively damaged by an earthquake under Domitian's successor, Nerva, it is very probable that the original structure was severely damaged or even not completed. Only a single specimen of this coin survives; yet it almost certainly allows us to date the building, or at least extensive repairs to the aqueduct. Although remains still stand, the coin shows us details of the superstructure and decoration which could never have been otherwise restored.

It is naturally unwise to suppose that the depiction of a building on a coin should necessarily be equated with a building project. The temple of Artemis at Ephesus was already nearly 500 years old when it was decided to issue the coin (**63**). Similarly, many buildings are of considerable antiquity even when the coins were struck. The

Acropolis at Athens (**80**), the buildings of which are of the fifth century BC, is found on coins in the third century AD, and the theatre of Dionysus (**73**) was as much a centre of tourism in Roman times as it is today. The building is at once recognizable with its semicircular *cavea* of seating behind the *orchestra*, and to eliminate any possible confusion with other theatres in the city, the artist has shown the walls of the Acropolis above, crowned with the columns of the Parthenon and other buildings. Even the sacred cave of the Nymphs (today a shrine of the Virgin) is shown cut into the rock of the Acropolis. Although the theatre underwent modification in Roman times, the coin type does not emphasize any of these, but gives a general impression of one of the well-loved monuments of the city. It is therefore unlikely that any of the modifications should be linked with the issue of the coins.

73 *The Theatre of Dionysus, Athens.* c. *AD 200.* (BMC *808*).

74 *The Sanctuary of Aphrodite, Paphos.* *Septimius Severus, AD 193–211.* (BMC) *55.*

One of the interesting features of the buildings that appear on Greek coins of the Roman period is that they very often reflect cults and building forms of pre-Greek days.[11] We have already seen the open courtyard, so typical of an oriental sanctuary, at Sidon (**68**); and the semicircular court in front of the temple of Aphrodite at her 'birthplace', Paphos, (**74**) is found on models of sanctuaries 2000 years earlier. Indeed, the temple itself would seem to have derived directly from Mycenaean architecture, having a central tower decorated with sacred horns. Seen in this context the temple of Jehovah at Jerusalem (**75**), used as a symbol of Jewish freedom during the revolt against Rome, can be seen to be in the typical oriental tradition in spite of its Greco-Roman columns. Below the main structure is clearly depicted the barrier which set apart the sacred area to which non-Jews were not admitted. We may compare the temple of the Phrygian god Men at Antioch in Pisidia (**76**) where the barrier is given even greater prominence. At Sidon, Paphos, Jerusalem, and Antioch, the court in front of the building is as much part of the sacred area as the temple itself, and is thus

75 *The Temple of Jehovah, Jerusalem.*
Bar Kokhba, AD 132–135. (BMC *18*).

76 *The Temple of Men, Antioch.*
Gordian III, AD 238–244. (1974. *1–2. 37*).

equally emphasized by the artists. The order of the architecture, as at Antioch, may change; but it is the traditions which dictate to a great extent the overall forms.

In Egypt also the influence of local traditions on the architecture depicted on coins struck under the Romans is very marked, in spite of more than 300 years of 'Greek' culture. Typical is the massive pylon[12] to a temple of Isis on a coin of Alexandria (**77**) showing the same towered gateway that we have seen in Syria. The original defensive purpose of the pylon is emphasized by the windows shown in the upper part of the towers in contrast to the plain masonry at ground level. We can be certain that this represents an actual monument—whether in the city of Alexandria or outside— standing in the second century AD; yet it owes nothing to the Greek or Roman world except the convention of showing the deity on the façade to facilitate its identification. Even this has origins in the eastern world, since underlying such a convention is the ancient practice of bringing out the deity in epiphany for the adoration of the people.

It should now be clear that the artists of these coin types were far more adventurous than is usually believed. Details are carefully noted, and unexpected views are attempted so that far from being stereotyped designs, these miniature buildings have

77 *Pylon to a Temple of Isis, Alexandria.*
Trajan, AD 98–117. (BMC *542*).

much to offer the student of ancient architecture. Despite the restricting size and shape of the coin flan, the artists were remarkably bold in their outlook. At Bizya in Thrace (**78**) the aerial view of the whole town shows us a number of buildings within the walls which the engraver wished to emphasize.[13] The main gate with its portcullis is carefully decorated: there are panels of relief sculpture on either side of the entrance, niches with portrait busts above, and the whole is crowned with a statue group of Victory in a chariot with two warriors. Within the city, colonnaded stoas show the position of the main market place. To the right of this stands a temple, and leading from there (not clear on this specimen) are three columns supporting statues presumably of the imperial family. They appear to stand along a road that goes from the temple and the market place to a large secular building with pitched roofs which is probably connected with the military nature of the city, one of the strategic points on the West coast of the Black Sea.

78 *City view, Bizya. Philip I, AD 244–249. (1970. 9–9.8).*

79 *City view, Amaseia. Severus Alexander, AD 228. (BMC 38).*

A different type of city view is offered by coins of Amaseia in Pontus (**79**). Here the town stands on the side of a mountain in an impressive gorge. The towers of the fortifications are scattered wherever they can be placed on the rocks, and are not continuous stretches of masonry walling. The coins thus show us a view that is remarkably similar to that of today, except that a temple and flaming altar are placed at the top of the design. In fact the mountain divides into two summits, and the artist has shown quite clearly the ridge that separates these. The temple and altar thus do not stand on the mountain, but have been placed above it, incorporated into the design in a form of perspective. Without doubt they represent the great sanctuary of Zeus Stratios which stood within the territory of Amaseia on another mountain ridge. The artist has included two buildings for emphasis within the city: the rectangular cutting in the rock is easily identified as one of the tombs of the Pontic kings, for which the city was famous in ancient as well as in modern times.[14] To the right, a temple occupies the position where now stands a Turkish fortress; and it seems probable that here was built the temple of the imperial cult which assured for the city a primacy over its neighbours.

The city badges of earlier Greek coins have been thus extended in the Roman period to give whole views of cities; and where the head of a deity may earlier have represented the cult and cult image, under the Roman empire the sanctuary and temple itself are illustrated. Many cities adopt as a type the acropolis on which their main cult was enshrined, and one of the most interesting today is perhaps that of Athens (**80**) whose buildings are so well known. The rocks of the hill are clearly differentiated from the walls which were hurriedly erected after the destruction of the city in 480 BC. To the right the great staircase of the Panathenaic Way leads up from the Agora, past the cave sanctuaries of Pan and Apollo, to the monumental entrance way, the Propylaea at the western end of the Acropolis. However, the main temple to be shown is not the Parthenon, but the smaller temple standing to the north, the Erechtheum. The artist has gone to great trouble to show the side of the building as masonry blocks—like the walls of the Erechtheum—and has deliberately avoided the magnificent peripteral colonnades of the larger temple. Surprising though this may seem, the reason probably lies in the greater antiquity of the sacred nature of that particular spot, as well as in the fact that Athena Polias herself shared the building. The great statue of Athena erected between the Erechtheum and the Propylaea is sufficient indication of the importance of her cult, and its gigantic size adds realism to Pausanias' statement[15] that the helmet could be seen by sailors off Cape Sunium. The clear, if unexpected, view of the Acropolis well illustrates how artists could depict considerable detail within the restricting tondo of a coin flan.

It was not only a view of the city and its acropolis which could be used as its 'seal'. At Ephesus, for example, the cult of Artemis was so prominent in the life of the city itself that the temple or cult image could clearly represent the whole citizen body. There was nothing new in this as far as coinage was concerned, and in the Roman period we find many temples so used. It is not only religious buildings which may perform such a function: at Patras, on the gulf of Corinth, the town's activities

80 *The Acropolis, Athens.*
AD 240–267. (1922. 3–17. 82).

centred on its harbour, and it is not surprising to find that from time to time views of this are used as a coin type (**81**). The example illustrated here shows an 'aerial' view. The main jetty carries a stoa of harbour buildings, beyond which three temples are depicted in the city itself. The curve of the harbour wall, with a small spur on its right-hand side, leads out to sea, and in the entrance a large statue acts as a beacon. The distinction of land and sea, essential for the interpretation of the type, is given by the presence of oared galleys rowing past the statue.

81 *The harbour, Patras. Commodus,*
AD 177–192. (1970. 9–9. 15).

82 *The Pharos, Alexandria. Antoninus Pius,*
AD 142/3. (BMC 1206).

Lighthouses, themselves symbols of a city's reliance on the sea for its prosperity, are also commonly used as coin types. The most famous is the great Pharos of Alexandria (**82**). Modern reconstructions commonly misinterpret the details, since coins and other representations which may be compared with them always show round openings in the main rectangular body of the structure. The main watch tower must have been the smaller building on the top, the terrace of which was decorated with statues of Tritons; and the whole is surmounted by a large statue. This provided the model for lighthouses throughout the Mediterranean, and coins illustrate examples from many cities to add to the very meagre information available from excavated sites and other sources.

The town of Antioch in the province of Asia gained prominence in imperial times as the point at which the main road from Ephesus to the East crossed the Maeander. The town therefore owed its prosperity to a bridge, and we are fortunate to possess fine illustrations of the structure on its coins (**83**). In contrast to the aqueduct (**72**), the waters of the river pour through the arches, and the bridge itself is clearly shown to join the two banks, rising from either side towards the centre. The entry from the left is guarded by a gate or triumphal arch. The artist has chosen to include two other details—a heron perched on the gate suggests something of a natural setting, and the river god reclining on 'his' bridge holding a reed, personifies the river to whom the citizens of Antioch owed so much.

In general, however, the reason for the choice of a particular type can only be vaguely related to the life of the city. Sometimes the use of a statue or temple is the only evidence that such a cult existed in the city, and we can only guess whether or not the use of the type coincided with a festival or some such event which would bring the cult briefly into prominence. At Neocaesareia, a city of great importance in the Pontus region,[16] a single issue, surviving in only two specimens, preserves the façade of an ornate gateway in which stands the figure of Tyche, the personification of the city (**84**). Why the type was chosen we cannot know; but the details allow an accurate reconstruction even though the site of the building is not known. The columns of the upper story are indicated in the two planes of a broken façade. The lower columns are set back in receding planes determined more by the round coin flan than by any architectural reality. At roof level even the tiles are sketched in, and over each of the wings a rectangular projection suggests low towers reminiscent of those at Baalbek and Capetolias (**65, 66**).

The connection of the Pontus with oriental architectural forms is also seen at Sebastopolis-Heracleopolis, where a sanctuary of Heracles, patron deity of the city, exhibits a most unusual form (**85**). A barrier, such as we have already seen at other eastern sanctuaries, restricts access to a court flanked with arcades on the other three sides—in plan bearing a marked resemblance to the façade of the British Museum. The figure of Heracles identifies the shrine, of which otherwise nothing is known. Needless to say it was this building, with its veneer of Greco-Roman architecture over a more ancient form, that was the focal point of religious life in the city.

83 *The Bridge across the Maeander, Antioch. Gallienus, AD 253–268.* (BMC 57).

84 *Ornamental gateway, Neocaesareia. Severus Alexander, AD 222–235.* (*1974. 1–2. 23*).

85 *The Sanctuary of Heracles,*
Sebastopolis-Heracleopolis. Caracalla,
AD 198–210. (1974. 1–2. 24).

86 *The scadium, Heraclea*
Pontica. Gordian III,
AD 238–244. (1970. 9–9. 28).

Finally, we may contrast the Greek form of theatre which we have seen at Athens (**72**) with the Roman stadium at Heraclea Pontica, Bithynia (**86**). The front wall can be seen to curve round to the left and right to form the oval of the stadium, and beyond, the rows of spectators watching the games can be discerned. Heracles himself presides, seated at the right-hand end, and a victorious athlete stands crowning himself in the centre of the arena. The architecture of this building can be compared with the better-known Circus Maximus at Rome.[17] The main entrance is at the end, and the outer wall is composed of an arcade with a plain masonry upper story. Above this the artist has carefully cut spikes which must be the awnings that shaded the spectators below from the fierce sun. Like the Circus Maximus the stadium at Heraclea includes a temple building on the inside of the complex reminding us of the link between games and religious festivals. There can be little doubt that the issue of this coin coincided with spectacular games held in honour of Heracles.

The aim of this article has been to reinstate these coins as objects worthy of further research. With such a general theme it has only been possible to skim the surface of the subject in order to show not only the great variety of building types which are depicted on coins, but also how careful the artists were in recording details. Some of the buildings can be checked against their remains uncovered by archaeologists; but for most, the coins are the sole surviving evidence. Of the 24 coins illustrated, 10 have been acquired in the last five years, and this must underline how important it is to have such material gathered together. Each detail should be examined by comparison with other coins and, more important, with actual architectural remains. It should never be forgotten that the artist knew the building that he was depicting, and had to transfer something of its likeness so that those who handled the coins would themselves recognize it. He could abbreviate certain details, or emphasize certain details. With the intelligent appreciation of this, it is more important to study such details as he chose to include than to criticize the overall view as 'unarchitectural'. With the publication of a fuller illustrated account of this material, archaeologists will be able to judge for themselves the great contribution made by the coins to the study of ancient architecture; and it is to be hoped that those responsible for the excavation of Greek cities will make themselves fully aware of the numismatic evidence.

NOTES

1 In collaboration with Professor B. L. Trell the author has compiled an illustrated 'textbook' of architecture on ancient coins, to be published by British Museum Publications Ltd. The only other attempt to gather such material is T. L. Donaldson, *Architectura Numismatica*, London, 1859, reprinted Chicago, 1966. For a bibliography of articles on the subject see T. Hackens, 'Architectura Numismatica; à propos de quelques publications récents', *L'Antiquité Classique*, xli, 1972, pp. 244–54.

2 B. L. Trell, *The Temple of Artemis at Ephesos* (The American Numismatic Society, *Numismatic Notes and Monographs* no. 107), New York, 1945.

3 *Archaeology*, xxvii, 3, July 1974, p. 204.

4 H. Plommer, 'St. John's Church, Ephesus', *Anatolian Studies*, xii, 1962, pp. 119–29.

5 A fourth building, the temple of Venus-Astarte, is not represented in the Museum's collection; cf. D. Winnefeld, 'Zur Geschichte des Syrischen Heliopolis', *Rheinisches Museum für Philologie*, lxix, 1914, pp. 139–59.

6 A. Boethius and J. B. Ward-Perkins, *Etruscan and Roman Architecture*, London, 1970, p. 418, fig. 156.

7 Cf. R. Donceel 'Recherches et travaux archéologiques récents au Liban 1962–1965', *L'Antiquité Classique*, xxxv, 1966, pp. 244–54.

8 I *Kings* 7, 21.

9 Zosimus I, 34 f.

10 M. Gough, 'Anazarbus', *Anatolian Studies*, ii, 1952, pp. 109–110 and plate xi (b).

11 Cf. B. L. Trell, 'Architectura Numismatica Orientalis', *Numismatic Chronicle*, 1970, pp. 29–50.

12 Cf. P. Naster, 'Le pylone égyptien sur les monnaies impériales d'Alexandrie', Antidorum W. Peremans (*Studia Hellenistica* 16), Louvain, 1968, pp. 181–90.

13 Cf. A. Lobbecke in *Zeitschrift für Numismatik*, xxi, 1898, pp. 254–7.

14 Strabo, a native of the city, left us a fine description in his *Geography* III, 39.

15 Pausanias I, 28, 2.

16 F. Cumont, 'Voyage d'exploration archéologique dans le Pont et La Petite Armenie', *Studia Pontica* II, 1906, pp. 267–73.

17 E.g. *Coins of the Roman Empire in the British Museum*, III (Nerva to Hadrian), pl. 32, 2–4; cf. E. Nash, *Pictorial Dictionary of Ancient Rome*, I (London, 1961), pp. 236–40.

Parthian gold from Nineveh

JOHN CURTIS
Assistant Keeper, Western Asiatic Antiquities

The site of Nineveh in North Iraq is chiefly known for the magnificent series of bas-reliefs lining the walls of the Assyrian palaces which were unearthed there in the nineteenth century. These finds, together with similar discoveries at Nimrud some twenty-five miles to the south, created a sensation in Bible-loving Victorian England, and for a time the attention of the public was riveted to the art and history of Assyria. So much was this so, that the discovery of some tombs of Parthian date at Kouyunjik (one of the two mounds within the walls of ancient Nineveh) was largely overlooked. Indeed, the find merited little more than a passing reference in A. H. Layard's classic *Discoveries in the Ruins of Nineveh and Babylon* (London 1853),[1] and was accorded only a footnote (on p. 350) by Rassam in his *Asshur and the Land of Nimrod* (New York 1897). It was left to a German scholar, Otto Benndorf, to publish line-drawings of the two gold masks from the tombs in 1878,[2] and Marshall illustrated one pair of earrings and listed the two finger-rings in his monumental catalogues of Greek, Etruscan and Roman jewellery and finger rings,[3] but he was unaware that they came from Nineveh. The gold necklace and a few of the clothing plaques are illustrated by Perrot and Chipiez as examples of Assyrian(!) jewellery,[4] but otherwise, so far as I know, none of the pieces belonging to this group has hitherto been published, and no details have appeared in print about the circumstances of their discovery.

After his brilliant excavations at Nimrud, in 1847, Layard transferred part of his attentions to Kouyunjik, and he and his young assistant Hormuzd Rassam, an Oriental from a Chaldaean Christian background, worked there intermittently until 1851. In the spring of that year they both returned to England, Layard to be appointed as Under-Secretary for the Foreign Office and later to embark upon a political career as Member of Parliament for Aylesbury,[5] and Rassam to search for some suitable employment. After their departure, excavations on behalf of the British Museum were pursued vigorously in various parts of Mesopotamia under the general surveillance of Colonel H. C. Rawlinson, Her Majesty's Consul-General at Baghdad and the East India Company's Political Agent in Turkish Arabia. Operations at Kouyunjik were watched over by Christian Rassam, Hormuzd's eldest brother and the British Vice-Consul at Mosul, but in view of his many official duties and business interests his supervision was probably little more than nominal. It was during this interim period, before the return of Hormuzd Rassam to Mosul in the autumn of 1852, that the Parthian tombs were discovered. Rawlinson described the finds in two reports[6] to Sir Henry Ellis, the Principal Librarian of the British Museum:

21st April, 1852

In January three tombs were discovered rudely formed of blocks of stone. Two of these had been previously opened and contained nothing but bones. The third, however, and smallest, had escaped spoliation and in it were found among the mouldering remains of what seemed to have been the body of a young female, a considerable number of curious relics. The principal of these were, a thin gold mask for the face—a pair of gold scales laid across the breast—a necklace of small gold beads—two pairs of gold earrings, a number of small gold studs, perhaps belonging to a belt—two rings, an Assyrian cylinder and an *aureus* belonging to Tiberius. The latter article is of interest in fixing the date of the tombs. They belong to the Parthian epoch, and probably date from the 1st century of the Christian era. The mere metallic value of the gold is inconsiderable but the objects are of interest as specimens of Parthian art.

2nd July 1852

I am expecting in a day or two to receive a case containing the produce of the diggings since I left Mosul. Among the relics are another gold mask, a number of gold buttons, some thin gold laminae, four very beautiful glass bottles, and a considerable number of tablets.

Layard was apprised of the discoveries in a series of letters from Matilda Rassam,[7] the wife of Christian and sister of the Reverend George Percy Badger, a chaplain of the East India Company and a distinguished orientalist who is best remembered for his two-volume work *The Nestorians and their Rituals* (London 1852). I have quoted from her letters at length not only because they supplement and enlarge upon Rawlinson's account, but also because they provide an amusing insight into the general conduct of the excavations.

Moossul February 14th, 1852

My dear Mr. Layard,
    Very many thanks for your kind letter of the 23rd December last. However, I really believe were it not for the love which you have for the excavations, that you would forget your old friends entirely . . .

You have our best thanks for the kind interest you have taken in Hormuzd. I hope he will finally get some employment, either in Aden or elsewhere, for it is exceedingly painful to see a young man of his years wandering about England with nothing to do further than paying visits.

What in the name of all patience is the artist to do when he comes here!! There is little or nothing to draw at Kiounjuk. I hope however he will not come to make his grave in Moossul as you so uncharitably predict.[8] You may rely on our doing our best endeavours to make him comfortable, and you may be certain that I will spoil him.

If you promise henceforth to write to me regularly, I will from time to time let you know what is going on at the mound. If not, you shall be kept in utter darkness on the subject. Well, Col. Rawlinson arrived here on the 4th of Dec[b] and immediately began to look over the mound and I believed he was much pleased with the excavations. For 3 days he increased the number of karkhanas [gangs] to 10, afterwards reduced them to 6, now again to two. He is very anxious to get as many of the small tablets as possible, and looked over all those which had been dug up since you left, and requested them to be packed and sent down to Baghdad; they filled three large cases. His further instructions were to forward on to him the accounts monthly together with all the tablets discovered during the month, which I assure you gives me enough to do, and why I do it I cannot tell unless I am possessed with the same philanthropic spirit which inspired you to do so much for the nation . . . We expect the Col. up here again in March to make final arrangements for carrying on the excavations during next summer. I have now the best part of my tale to relate to you. On opening a new trench about three weeks ago to the north of the old trenches, they came down upon a most curious place, which now turns out to be a burial ground.[9] As yet a few stone coffins have been found, some containing ashes showing that the bodies must have been burnt. Others contain human bones; in one of the coffins the remains of a body, i.e. the bones, apparently of a female, were found. All except the teeth, which I have preserved, crumbled to dust at the slightest touch. In this coffin was found the following things: 1 gold coin, in excellent preservation, weighing I should say a little less than a Turkish lira; 2 pairs of gold earrings, 1 pair of which are massive and set with stones, the other pair quite small but exactly like many the women wear here at the present day; 2 gold rings one set with a pretty good ruby with a figure upon it, the other plain; a good number of small gold buttons of different kinds; several gold beads; a fine cylinder, with 2 or 3 lines of cuneiform writing upon it; a gold leaf mask with a perfect impression of a face upon it just as though the leaf had been laid upon the features after death; 2 other pieces of gold leaf but I cannot divine what they were intended for, unless one piece was used as an ornament on the front part of the head—the other seems very much like a pair of spectacles or a covering for the eyes; a number of glass beads; and 2 lovely glass bottles, quite perfect. In the other coffins only a very small quantity of gold was found in the shape of buttons and strips of thick gold leaf which seem to have been bound round the handles of knives or daggers. I fancy the value of all the little articles would amount to about £15 or 20. I have a strong presentiment that we shall ere long find something really valuable, for instance Sennacherib's crown; or some of the gold vessels given by Hezekiah to Sennacherib out of Solomon's Temple; what a glorious discovery such things would be, would they not, under such circumstances I think Her Most Gracious Majesty ought to create a new order, and dub my good Husband Knight of Sennacherib's Crown instead of His Majesty's Garter, for I presume that no such appendages were in vogue at those early times. After all this long rig-ma-roll which I have taken the trouble to give you, I am sure you should be very grateful, and in return send me your new book, which from the papers I see you are publishing.

> . . .
>
> I remain
> My dear Mr. Layard
> Yours very sincerely
> Matilda Rassam.

She continued her account on 19 June 1852:

Last post brought me your nice long letter of the 9th April in reply to mine of the 14th February. Had I known at the moment that I was addressing the Under Secretary of State for Foreign Affairs, I would have been more cautious; however I am persuaded that you are too well acquainted with me and my faults to think evil of what I said.

Since I last wrote to you we have discovered a few more tombs, but the gold ornaments are not so interesting as the first batch, although they are similar; and as I think you have a perfect right to some of them, I have enclosed in the small tin box which Elias is sending to you by this post, containing cylinders, 2 small gold buttons belonging to the gloves of Semiramis, a gold leaf taken from the coronet of the daughter of Ninus and Semiramis, and 2 gold buttons belonging to the gloves of Sennacherib. You ought to have been here when the tombs were found, as I am positive you would have employed a number of karkhanas, and cleared out the whole of the burial ground, as one karkhana can do very little, and that is what is allowed at that particular spot.

Just over a fortnight later (on 5 July 1852) Mrs Rassam wrote with some more information:

Well, since I last wrote we have discovered several tombs all of them empty except one in which we found another gold mask apparently belonging to a man, it being much larger than the first one and considerably heavier; also a few gold buttons similar to those which I sent to you by the last post. It is quite evident that the greater number of the graves were opened some centuries ago, and the bodies stripped of all or most of the ornaments which were upon them, as in most instances the tombs lack one or more of the side stones, some of them also the top slab, and generally speaking the beads and buttons are scattered about, and only by sifting the soil do we find them. Hormuzd writes me that the papers are full of the discoveries, but giving all the credit and honour to Col. Rawlinson, whereas he had nothing to do with it, and it was Rassam who went over to the Mound one day, and ordered a karkhana to work at the very spot where the tombs were found and when we informed Col. Rawlinson of the discovery he seemed to turn up his nose and made out that the tombs were not ancient, and therefore of no importance.

87 *Cat. no. 1. Gold mask.*

88 *Cat. no. 2. Gold mask.*

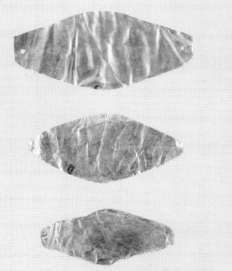

89 *Cat. nos. 3–5. Three gold mouth-pieces.*

90 *Cat. nos. 6–7. Pair of gold eye-coverings.*

91 *Cat. no. 8. Pair of gold earrings set with garnets and turquoise.*

92 *Cat. no. 9. Pair of gold earrings with filigree decoration.*

    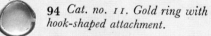

94 *Cat. no. 11. Gold ring with hook-shaped attachment.*

93 *Cat. no. 10. Four gold rings.*

95 *Cat. no. 13. Gold finger-ring, the bezel filled with a garnet engraved with the figure of a nude boy.*

96 *Cat. no. 12. Gold finger-ring.*

The details contained in these two independent accounts accord remarkably well. The only important discrepancy is in the mode of burial, but here Mrs Rassam was perhaps mistaken in thinking that some of the bodies had been cremated as inhumation was the more common practice of the day. It is also curious that she should have referred to the first mask as having 'a perfect impression of a face upon it': the detail cannot be said to be other than crudely executed! It emerges that each coffin was roughly built from slabs of stone forming the sides and the top. Exactly how many were discovered it is impossible to say, but we may surmise that there were perhaps about a dozen. Most of them had been looted, probably in antiquity, but at least three seem to have escaped the attention of the tomb-robbers. The most prolific tomb was that discovered in January 1852, containing a gold face-mask, a gold mouth-piece and 'a pair of spectacles' (a covering for the eyes), two pairs of earrings, two finger-rings, gold buttons and beads and a gold coin of Tiberius. The Assyrian cylinder must of course have been an antiquity when it was buried. Both our sources seem to have thought that the tomb contained only one body, but the recovery of a mouth-piece and a covering for the eyes in addition to a complete face-mask suggests that there must have been two burials in this tomb. This conclusion is endorsed by the finding of two pairs of earrings.

The antiquities from the tombs were despatched from Basra in 1854 in the East India Company's steam frigate *Ackbar*, and were incorporated into the collections of the British Museum in 1856. Unfortunately no information about the tomb-groups seems to have been available to the registrar of the day, as he grouped all the finds together and simply described them as coming 'from the tombs at Kouyunjik'. In the following list of material I have placed LT (Lady's Tomb) after all those items which appear to come from the tomb opened in January 1852, as the presence of the gold coin provides some yardstick for dating the tomb. A full catalogue will be found at the end of this article, but here the material may be summarized as follows: two gold face-masks, each perforated at the corners so that they could be tied to the head of the corpse (**87, 88**; one from LT); three gold mouth-pieces each perforated at either end (**89**; one from LT); two gold coverings for the eyes (**90**; one from LT); a pair of gold earrings inlaid with garnets and with elaborate pendants set with garnets and turquoise (**91**; LT); a pair of gold earrings with filigree decoration (**92**); five simple annular earrings, one with a hook attachment at the base, probably all intended to carry pendants (**93, 94**); gold beads (**101**; some from LT); two gold finger-rings, one set with a garnet on which is engraved a nude boy with arm outstretched (**95**; LT), another with a pear-shaped bezel once filled with a stone now missing (**96**; LT); a large number of small gold plaques of various type equipped with holes or loop fasteners for sewing to clothing (**97–100**; some from LT); an *aureus* of Tiberius (**104**;

LT); sixteen gold leaves (**103**) and four gold-leaf impressions of a coin of Trajan dated to *c.* AD 115 (**105**), probably all part of a funereal wreath; some gold fittings for the handle of a mace or staff (**107**); two small gold caps, perhaps of a bead; three circular pieces of gold overlay, each centrally pierced (**108**); and a hemispherical gold ornament with corrugated sides (**109**). No glass bottles were registered as coming from the tombs, but a glass *unguentarium* from Kouyunjik registered nine months earlier than the material from the tombs is very probably from them (**110**).

It is unclear whether all this material is contemporary or not. The coin of the Emperor Tiberius (dated to AD 16–21) in the Lady's Tomb indicates that these burials (or at least one of them) cannot have been earlier than AD 16, but as the coin may have been in circulation for many years when it was placed in the tomb they could be considerably later. The same applies to the gold-leaf impressions of the coin of Trajan, dated to *c.* AD 115, with which the gold leaves at least are probably associated. Unfortunately none of the other goldwork can be independently dated with any degree of accuracy, but the elaborate earrings from the Lady's Tomb do provide some dating evidence. They find a close parallel at Seleucia-on-the-Tigris where they may have been hidden in the face of Trajan's advance on the city in AD 115/16.[10] Also, earrings with triple pendants hanging from a bar can be seen on Egyptian mummy-portraits mainly dated to the first half of the second century AD,[11] as well as on a funerary bust from Palmyra (BM. 125204; **111**) dated to the early second century AD. On the other hand, this type of earring was popular in the Roman world up to the third century AD.[12] The gold ring with engraved garnet, also from the Lady's Tomb, is loosely dated by Marshall between the first century BC and the second century AD.[13] The contents of a tomb opened at Glinishche near Kerch on the north shore of the Black Sea in 1837 (commonly known as the tomb of the Queen with the Gold Mask) closely resemble those of the Lady's Tomb, and have been dated by coins to the first half of the third century AD.[14] Among the grave-goods from Glinishche were counted a number of garnets mounted in bezels, several hundreds of small stamped plaques in gold, and a gold funerary mask. This mask, however, is much more realistic than our examples, being a faithful representation of the queen's face, and is perhaps later. At present the available evidence seems to indicate a date in the first half of the second century AD for the Kouyunjik burials. The presence of the earring with triple pendants in the Lady's Tomb suggest that it should be dated almost a century later than the reign of Tiberius, to which the gold coin belongs. Such a date is not at variance with that which can be accorded to the glass *unguentarium*.[15] We may conjecture that the burial ground belonged to one community, and the wealth of the burials indicates that they are those of very important members of the settlement at Nineveh,[16] or even perhaps its leaders.

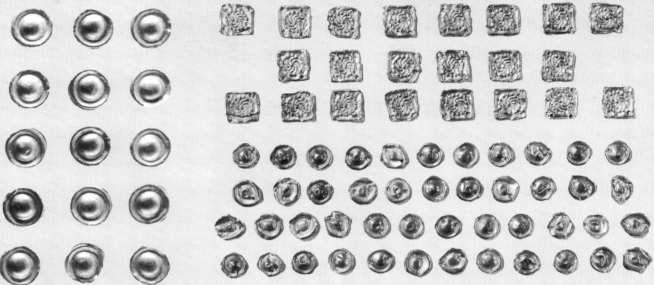

97 *Cat. no. 17. Set of fifteen circular gold plaques.*

98 *Cat. no. 20. Set of forty-six circular gold plaques and twenty-two square gold plaques.*

99 *Cat. no. 16. Set of eight diamond-shaped gold plaques.*

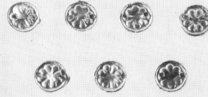

100 *Cat. no. 19. Set of seven circular gold plaques.*

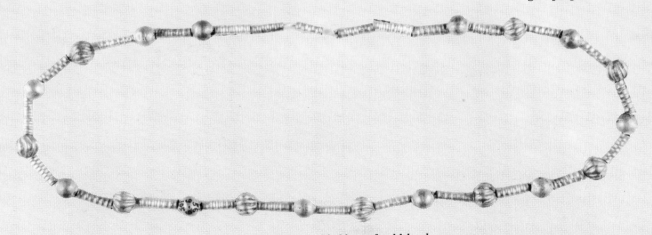

101 *Cat. no. 14. Necklace of gold beads.*

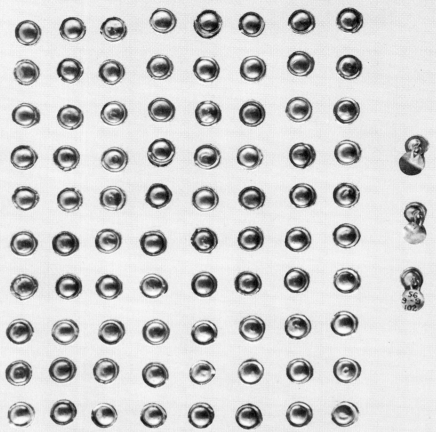

102 *Cat. no. 18. Set of eighty circular gold plaques and three similar plaques with pendant attachments.*

103 *Cat. no. 23. Set of fourteen diamond-shaped gold leaves.*

104 *Cat. no. 21. Aureus of Tiberius* AD *16–21.*

105 *Cat. no. 22. Four gold-leaf impressions of a bronze coin of Trajan.*

106 *Bronze coin of Trajan* C. AD *115 (cf. Cat. no. 22).*

Clearly the tombs date from the Parthian era, but into what sort of cultural context can they be fitted?

In south and central Mesopotamia the most common method of inhumation during the Parthian period was to place the corpse in a slipper-shaped coffin often elaborately decorated in relief and embellished with a blue-green glaze. Stone cist graves of the type we have from Kouyunjik are rare in the western part of the Parthian empire, but they are apparently to be found farther east and in Trans-caucasia.[17] Further, they may be compared with graves constructed from mud-bricks at Nuzi to the south-east of Nineveh and at Seleucia.[18] The use of stone at Kouyunjik may only reflect the ready availability of this material there. In any event, it seems unnecessary to look for parallels with the stone cist graves of the Roman world, as was done for the mud-brick graves of Nuzi.[19]

The custom of covering all or part of a dead person's face has a long history in the ancient world. It is generally thought that the intention was to preserve, or at any rate to conceal the decay of, those organs which would be most needed in the afterlife. As only a completely physical existence beyond the grave was envisaged, it was essential that the deceased would be able to see, eat, breathe and speak. Gold was extensively used as the covering material because of its incorruptible property, but in cases where it was not available some other non-decaying material might be chosen, such as pottery.[20] There may also have been a notion that by blocking the apertures of a corpse its spirit would not have been able to escape from it and haunt the living, nor would demons be able to enter the corpse. In addition, covering the face of the dead person would have made it more presentable at the funeral ceremony and less painful to look upon. It has been suggested that the use of gold funerary masks stems primarily from a Greek tradition,[21] but this is unlikely. The masks from Mycenae are well known, and there are examples of later date such as those from an Illyrian cemetery of the late sixth century BC at Trebenishte in Yugoslavia,[22] but there seems to be no continuous tradition which culminated in their introduction into Western Asia during or before the Hellenistic period. Gold masks from archaeological contexts in Western Asia are rare: they have been found in tombs at Emesa in Syria (modern Homs) dating from the first century AD,[23] and a mask was found in a tomb at Halebiye on the Upper Euphrates by Captain Lynch of the Euphrates expedition in the last century.[24] Otherwise most of the examples in museums and art galleries are without certain provenance, but many are said to come from Syria or Phoenicia.[25] If this is so, we can readily see the Phoenician anthropomorphic sarcophagi of the fifth to third centuries BC (which derive from Egyptian mummy cases) as the forerunners of our gold masks. Elsewhere, gold funerary masks are known from South Russia. We have mentioned above that found in the Queen's Tomb at Glinishche, and another

107 *Cat. no. 24. Set of four gold fittings for a staff or mace-handle.*

108 *Cat. no. 25. Set of three flat gold discs.*

109 *Cat. no. 26. Hemispherical gold disc with corrugated sides.*

110 *Cat. no. 28. Glass unguentarium.*

111 *Funerary bust of a Palmyrene lady, early second century* AD (125204).

was recovered from a tumulus at Olbia.[26] Their presence here may derive from a quite independent tradition, but more probably the practice was borrowed from Western Asia in the late Hellenistic or Roman periods.

The use of gold leaf to cover the eyes and mouth of the corpse is much more common. From the Royal Cemetry at Ur of the Chaldees come strips of gold dating from *c.* 2000 BC which the excavator identified as frontlets[27] but which may well be mouth-pieces. They have also been found at Kültepe in Cappadocia, dating from the early second millennium BC,[28] and there are examples from Tell Halaf in North Syria[29] and Megiddo in Palestine[30] of the late second millennium BC. In Cyprus, mouthpieces were extensively used during the Mycenaean period (*c.* 1400–1100 BC).[31] Their use in Western Asia, however, did not become really widespread until the Hellenistic period, and in burials of this and the succeeding Parthian eras there are many instances of both mouth-pieces and eye-coverings being used. In Mesopotamia the practice may be observed at Warka,[32] Babylon,[33] Nippur,[34] Seleucia,[35] Ashur,[36] Tell Mahuz,[37] and Dura Europos,[38] and in Syria at Emesa.[39] Again there are parallels with South Russia, mouth and eye coverings having been used at Chersonesus on the north coast of the Black Sea. Clearly, the custom as practised in the western Parthian world must be regarded as a direct survival of a Hellenistic tradition.

The same is true of funereal wreaths. Although they do occur in Western Asia in pre-Hellenistic times (e.g. at Ur[40] and probably at Tepe Hissar[41] in Iran) they were never as popular here as in Greece where they were used from the seventh century BC onwards.[42] The significance of the funerary crown is not quite clear; Marshall comments: 'In many cases the crown was clearly a mark of honour, as in the case of the crowns granted to the living. But the custom was so general that some other meaning must have attached to it. Tertullian suggested that the dead were crowned for the same reason that images of the gods were crowned. They became as it were deified. It is possible that some such notion lurked beneath the practice'.[43] At Dura Europos gold leaves from diadems were commonly found,[44] and in burials of the Parthian period at Babylon and Warka the corpse often wore a wreath of gold leaves.[45] In South Russia wreaths, often with impressions of coins placed in the centre, occur frequently in tombs mainly of the Roman period.[46] It seems likely, therefore, that the coin-impressions from Kouyunjik should be associated with the gold leaves.

The gold coin of Tiberius, however, must have served a different function. In most of the burials at the Greek foundation of Seleucia each skeleton was accompanied by a coin, usually placed in the mouth or in the palm of the corpse.[47] At Dura Europos silver coins were sometimes found around the region of the body's pelvis, suggesting that they had originally been placed in a purse attached to a vanished belt,[48] and at Tell Mahuz in graves dating from the end of the third to the beginning of the fourth century AD single coins were placed under the head of the deceased.[49] Perhaps they were intended to pay for entrance to the other world, in which case one is inevitably reminded of the Greek myth in which ferry dues were payable to Charon.

The concept of sewing ornamental discs and plaques on to clothing is well known from both the Greek and Western Asiatic worlds, and gold plaques have been associated with several burials approximately contemporary with the Nineveh tombs. At Nippur, 123 'button-like gold objects for sewing on stuff of some description' were found in a blue-glazed slipper coffin,[50] and from the tomb of the Queen with the Gold Mask at Glinishche several hundred small stamped plaques in gold were recovered.

It emerges that there seem to be few features about the Kouyunjik tombs that can be described as distinctively Parthian. The evidence about their method of construction is inconclusive partly because so little is known about how the dead were interred in the eastern part of the Parthian Empire. On the other hand, many different types of burial custom were practised in Mesopotamia and Syria during the first few centuries AD. About the contents of the tombs we can be a little more specific. The use of gold leaf to cover the eyes and mouth, placing a funereal wreath on the head of the corpse and providing it with a coin are all practices that may be seen as survivals from the Hellenistic period. On the other hand, those items of jewellery which can be regarded as distinctive—the elaborate earrings and the engraved gem—find good parallels in the Roman world. In addition, there are the Roman coins. How, then, can these different elements be reconciled?

After the conquests of Alexander, Western Asia was subjected to a century and a half of Hellenization: Greek cities were founded, the Greek language was widely introduced, laws and administration were based on Greek models, and in the realms of art and architecture Greek influence on Oriental traditions is manifest. Such was the framework into which the Parthians moved. Originally a nomad tribe, they first appear in the region of Parthia, the mountainous country to the south-east of the Caspian Sea, after the death of Alexander the Great. They took over the province in the mid-third century BC, and thence gradually increased their strength until under Mithradates I (*c.* 170–138 BC) they were able to wrest Babylonia from the Seleucids and push the western frontier of Parthia to the Euphrates. This change of ruling dynasty, however, did not signify an abrupt end to Hellenistic influence and culture. Thus in the early Parthian period Greek cities such as Seleucia-on-the-Tigris were allowed to prosper, Greek was retained as the official language, the status of the Parthian king was much the same as that of his Seleucid predecessors, and Mithradates I and some of his successors went so far as to use the epithet 'Philhellene' on their coins. Set against this background, it is not surprising that we should find a considerable Hellenistic influence in the Kouyunjik burials.

Similarly, the presence in the tombs of material that is apparently Roman, either in influence or even in manufacture, as well as the coin and coin-impressions, can be easily explained. Throughout most of the first and part of the second century AD Nineveh was probably within the area controlled by Adiabene, a petty kingdom on the fringe of the Parthian Empire which had been annexed by the Parthians in *c.* 94 BC.[51] It would be going far beyond the limits of our evidence to suggest that during this period Nineveh was an important trading centre (although this was later the case with Mosul on the opposite bank of the Tigris). It is worth noting, however, that Nineveh was situated on an important river crossing and at different periods in her history maintained trade contacts with Aleppo across the Syrian desert, with Babylon to the south, with the Black Sea coast to the north-west, and with the areas to the east and north-east. It is unlikely that all these routes were dormant during the first and second centuries AD, and as Armenia, a vassal state of the Roman Empire, was only a short distance to the north, the settlement at Nineveh probably enjoyed trade contacts with the Roman world and would have been exposed to its material culture. During the reign of Trajan these contacts were to be greatly intensified, for in AD 116 Adiabene was conquered and turned into the Roman province of Assyria. Roman occupation of North Mesopotamia was short-lived, as after Trajan's death in AD 117 his successor, Hadrian, abandoned the policy of maintaining the Roman frontier on the Tigris, and for the next half a century Adiabene seems to have reverted to its former status of a Parthian client-kingdom. Thus we may conclude that during the period in which we have dated our tombs—first half of the second century AD—the settlement at Nineveh would not only have had trade contacts with the Roman Empire but also for a short time been nominally a part of it. It is tempting to propose some connection between the burials and the disaster that overtook Adiabene in AD 116, but until more is known about the internal history of this petty state and until the contents of the tombs can be more securely dated, such speculation must be resisted.

CATALOGUE

Masks, mouth- and eye-pieces

1 56.9.9, 66 (123894). Gold mask. Details of human face crudely indicated by repoussé work. Perforated in four corners. Ht. 16.5 cm., W. 15.3 cm. (**87**).
   BENNDORF, 'Antike Gesichtshelme und Sepulchralmasken', *Denkschriften der kaiserlichen Akademie der Wissenschaften: Philosophisch-historische Classe*, Vienna, 1878, pl. XIV, no. 2.

2 56.9.9, 67 (123895). Another. Ht. 13.9 cm, W. 14.2 cm. (**88**).
     BENNDORF, *op. cit.*, pl. XIV, no. 1.

3 56.9.9, 70. Gold mouth-piece. Perforated at either end. L. 8.25 cm., W. 3.95 cm.
     (**89**).

4 56.9.9, 71. Another. L. 7.15 cm., W. 3.2 cm. (**89**).

5 56.9.9, 76. Another. L. 9.4 cm., W. 4.45 cm. (**89**).

6 56.9.9, 68 (123893). Gold eye-covering. L. 18.5 cm., W. 4.8 cm. (**90**).

7 56.9.9, 69 (123896). Another. L. 13.2 cm., W. 3.9 cm. (**90**).

Earrings

8 56.9.9, 72–3. Elaborate pair of earrings each consisting of a small gold ring from
     which hangs an oval garnet in a gold setting. To this is attached an oblong gold
     plate, from which are suspended three egg-shaped gold settings, the outer pair
     filled with garnets and that in the centre with a turquoise (missing in one earring).
     Semi-elliptical gold pendants, hollow and open at the bottom, hang from the
     egg-shaped pendants. Ht. 5.75 cm., W. 2.0 cm. (**91**).
     MARSHALL, *Catalogue of Jewellery*, 2668–9, HIGGINS, *Greek and Roman Jewellery*, pl. 54, g.

9 56.9.9, 78–9. Pair of gold earrings each with gold wire binding at two ends of
     crescent. Decorated with filigree work. Ring at base for suspension of pendant.
     Ht. 2.55/2.65 cm., W. 1.65/1.5 cm. (**92**).

10 56.9.9, 117–20. Four gold rings. These may have served as earrings independently,
     or been used to hang pendants from, as in the case of 56.9.9, 72–73. Diam. 1.0–
     1.15 cm. (**93**).

11 56.9.9, 116. As above but with hook-shaped attachment at base for pendant.
     Ht. 1.35 cm., W. 1.1 cm. (**94**).

Finger-rings

12 56.9.9, 89. Gold finger-ring with oval bezel once filled with a stone which is now
     missing. Diam. 1.8 cm. (**96**).
     MARSHALL, *Catalogue of Finger Rings*, 739 (not illus.).

13 56.9.9, 90. Gold finger-ring with an oval bezel filled with a garnet engraved with a
     nude boy, standing, with one arm outstretched. Diam. 1.8 cm. (**95**).
     MARSHALL, *Catalogue of Finger Rings*, 441 (not illus.); WALTERS, *Catalogue of Engraved Gems and Cameos*,
     3339 (not illus.).

Beads

14 56.9.9, 105. Necklace comprising the following gold beads (perhaps not all originally associated): 11 plain spherical beads, average diam. 0.6 cm.; 9 spherical melon beads, diam. 0.65 cm.; 26 tubular corrugated beads, L. 0.9 cm., diam. 0.3 cm. (**101**).

15 56.9.9, 124. Flanged gold melon bead. Ht. 0.8 cm., diam. 0.7 cm.

Garment plaques

16 56.9.9, 92. Eight diamond-shaped gold plaques with raised centres and repoussé decoration. Each has a loop fastener at back. Average ht. 1.6 cm., W. 1.3 cm. (**99**).

17 56.9.9, 101. Fifteen circular gold plaques with embossed centres. Each has a loop fastener at back. Average diam. 1.1 cm. (**97**).

18 56.9.9, 102. Eighty-two circular gold plaques as above, but smaller, average diam. 0.75 cm., plus three similar plaques with rings on top to which are attached flat, circular pendants (**102**).

19 56.9.9, 106. Seven circular gold plaques each with embossed rosette in centre and hole on either side. Average diam. 0.95 cm. (**100**).

20 56.9.9, 107. Forty-six circular gold plaques each with embossed centre and hole on either side, average diam. 0.85 cm., plus 22 square gold plaques with repoussé decoration each pierced in four corners, 1.05 cm. square (**98**).

Coin, coin impressions and leaves

21 56.9.9, 77. *Aureus* of Tiberius. Obverse: TI CAESAR DIVI AUG F AUGUSTUS, head laureate, right; reverse: PONTIF MAXIM, female figure seated, right, holding branch and sceptre.

Cf. H. MATTINGLY, *Coins of the Roman Empire in the British Museum*, i, Tiberius, 30ff. AD 16–21. (**104**).

22 56.9.9, 82–5. Four gold-leaf impressions of a bronze coin of Trajan (**105**). Obverse: IMP CAES NER TRAIANO OPTIM AUG GERM, bust, radiate, right, with aegis on left shoulder.

Cf. H. MATTINGLY, *op. cit.*, iii, Trajan, 1100. *c.* AD 115. The coin, a *semis*, is from an unusual series not minted at Rome, but at some unspecified mint in the eastern provinces, possibly Antioch. (**106**). An example in the British Museum collection is illustrated.

23 56.9.9, 93–100, 108–15. Sixteen gold leaves, each diamond-shaped with a repoussé rib. Average L. 1.6 cm., W. 1.3 cm. (**103**).

Miscellaneous

24 56.9.9, 103–4, 122–3. Gold fittings for staff or mace-handle, average diam. 2.5 cm., consisting of three circular bands of gold, one now much distorted, ht. 1.0, 1.55, 1.6 cm., plus a gold cap for the base of the handle, ht. 1.0 cm. (**107**).

25 56.9.9, 86–8. Three flat gold discs, each centrally pierced. Diam. 2.45 cm., 1.95 cm., 1.55 cm. (**108**).

26 56.9.9, 91. Hemispherical gold disc with corrugated sides. Diam. 1.85 cm., ht. 0.9 cm. (**109**).

27 56.9.9, 125–6. Two gold caps, probably for a bead, each centrally pierced. Diam. 0.8 cm., ht. 0.25 cm.

28 55.12.5, 365 (91465). Glass *unguentarium*. Ht. 13.8 cm., diam. 7.0 cm. (**110**).

NOTES

I am indebted to Dr R. D. Barnett for bringing to my attention the letters from Matilda Rassam in the Layard Papers, to Dr Georgina Herrmann with whom I have had several fruitful discussions about the tombs and their contents, to Dr R. A. Higgins and Mr D. M. Bailey of the Greek and Roman Department for locating those items from the tombs in their department, to Mr R. A. G. Carson of the Department of Coins and Medals for identifying the coin and coin impressions, and to Mlle Agnès Spycket of the Musée du Louvre for supplying references to gold masks in the Louvre. The drawing of the engraved gem is by Miss C. A. Searight.

1 Pp. 592–3.

2 'Antike Gesichtshelme und Sepulchral-masken', *Denkschriften der kaiserlichen Akademie der Wissenschaften: Philosophisch-historische Classe*, Vienna 1878, pl. 14, nos 1–2.

3 F. H. Marshall, *Catalogue of the Jewellery, Greek, Etruscan and Roman, in the Departments of Antiquities, British Museum*, London 1911, nos. 2668–9 (pl. LV), and *Catalogue of the Finger Rings, Greek, Etruscan and Roman, in the Departments of Antiquities, British Museum* (London 1907), nos.

441, and 739. No. 441 also included in H. B. Walters, *Catalogue of the Engraved Gems and Cameos, Greek, Etruscan and Roman in the British Museum*, London 1926, no. 3339.

4 *Histoire de l'Art dans l'Antiquité*, ii, Paris 1884, figs 435, 438–9,

5 He was elected on 7 July 1852.

6 These reports are now in the archives of the Trustees, but transcripts are kept in the Department of Western Asiatic Antiquities.

7 Preserved in the Department of Manuscripts, British Museum: Layard Papers, 50–1 (Add. Mss. 38980–1).

8 The last artist, Thomas Septimus Bell, had been drowned while bathing in the River Gomel at Bavian.

9 If by 'the old trenches' the site of Sennacherib's Palace is meant, then the burial ground must have been somewhere in the centre of the Kouyunjik mound.

10 R. J. Braidwood, 'Some Parthian Jewellery', in L. Waterman, *Second Preliminary Report upon the Excavations at Tell Umar, Iraq*, Ann Arbor 1933, pl. XXIV, fig. 1, and pp. 65, 69.

11 See Klaus Parlasca, *Repertorio d'Arte dell'*

Egitto Greco-Romano, Seria B, vol. 1, Palermo 1969, nos. 95, 98, 101, 110, 116, 134, 145.

12 R. A. Higgins, *Greek and Roman Jewellery*, London 1961, p. 185.

13 F. H. Marshall, *Catalogue of Finger Rings*, p. 77, no. 441. See p. 71.

14 See M. Rostovtzeff, *Iranians and Greeks in South Russia*, Oxford 1922, pp. 174–5, 177.

15 Cf. *The Excavations at Dura-Europos*, Final Report IV, Part V: C. W. Clairmont, *The Glass Vessels*, New Haven 1963, pl. XXXV, no. 671, and commentary p. 133. See also C. Isings, *Roman glass from dated finds*, Groningen 1957, form 28b.

16 The size of the settlement at Nineveh during the Parthian period has not been clearly established by excavation, but so far as is known it was restricted to the east bank of the Tigris. Mosul may have been founded or refounded by the Sasanian king Ardashir I: see David Oates, *Studies in the Ancient History of Northern Iraq*, London 1968, p. 77.

17 For references, see M. N. Ponzi, 'Sasanian glassware from Tell Mahuz (North Mesopotamia)', *Mesopotamia*, iii-iv, 1968–9, p. 301 and n. 31, pp. 301–2.

18 R. W. Ehrich, 'The Later Cultures at Yorgan Tepa', in R. F. S. Starr, *Nuzi*, i, Cambridge Mass. 1939, p. 547–8 (baked-brick graves with pitched roofs), and S. Yeivin, 'The Tombs found at Seleucia', in L. Waterman, *op. cit.*, pp. 33–59.

19 Ehrich, *op. cit.*, p. 568.

20 Yeivin, *op. cit.*, p. 46.

21 E.g. by Ponzi, *op. cit.*, p. 304, n. 41.

22 See *Greek-Illyrian Treasures from Yugoslavia*, Sheffield 1974. Catalogue of an exhibition at Sheffield City Museum, pls. 1–2.

23 H. Seyrig, 'Antiquités de la nécropole d'Emèse', *Syria*, xxix, 1952, pp. 209–10 and pl. XXVI.

24 F. R. Chesney, *The Expedition for the Survey of the Rivers Euphrates and Tigris*, i, London 1850, p. 418. See also George Hoffmann, 'Über eine am Euphrat gefundene Mumie mit goldene Gesichtsmaske', *Archäologische Zeitung*, xxxvi, 1878, pp. 25–7.

25 A. de Ridder, *Collection de Clercq : Catalogue*, vii, 'Les bijoux et les pièrres gravées', Paris 1911, pp. 16–18, nos. 17–23; described by the vendors as coming mainly from Syria (p. 17). Nos. 18 and 22 now in Louvre, AO 25065 and 25065 *bis*, published by E. Coche de la Ferté in *L'Oeil*, no. 15, March 1956, pp. 37 ff. Two further examples in Louvre: AO 3988, said to come from Phoenicia, published in *Les merveilles du Louvre* (preface by André Parrot), Paris 1970, p. 46, and MNB 1315, said to come from Tartus, published in *Archeologia*, no. 31, Nov.–Dec. 1969, p. 56. Mask said to come from Sidon: Ludwig Pollak, *Klassisch-antike Goldschmiedearbeiten im Besitze Sr. Excellenz A. J. von Nelidow*, Leipzig, 1903, pl. 7, no. 40. See also G. Krien-Kummrow, 'Maschera' in the *Enciclopedia dell' arte antica, classica e orientale*, iv, Rome 1961, pp. 900–18.

26 Le Comte Alexis Ouvaroff, *Recherches sur les antiquités de la Russie méridionale et des côtes de la Mer Noire*, Atlas, Paris 1855, pl. XIV, no. 1. Date of this piece quite unclear: E. H. Minns, *Scythians and Greeks*, Cambridge 1913, p. 390.

27 C. L. Woolley, *Ur Excavations*, ii, London 1934, pl. 147.

28 Tahsin and Nimet Özgüç, *Kültepe Kazisi Raporu 1949*, Ankara 1953, pl. LVII, no. 588.

29 Baron Max von Oppenheim, *Der Tell Halaf: eine neue Kultur im älteren Mespotamien*, Leipzig 1931, colour-plate III and pp. 192–7.

30 P. L. O. Guy, *Megiddo Tombs* (O.I.P. XXXIII), Chicago 1938, pl. 28, nos. 10, 11, pl. 165, nos. 16, 17, pl. 168, no. 15.

31 See, e.g., F. H. Marshall, *Catalogue of Jewellery*, nos. 151–196.

32 W. K. Loftus, *Travels and Researches in Chaldaea and Susiana*, London 1857, pp. 202–10.

33 R. Koldewey, *The Excavations at Babylon*, London 1914, p. 218.

34 J. P. P. Peters, *Nippur*, ii, New York 1898, pp. 227–8.

35 S. Yeivin, *op. cit.*, pp. 46–9.

36 W. Andrae and H. Lenzen, *Die Partherstadt Assur*, Leipzig 1933, pl. 47, no. a.

37 M. N. Ponzi, *op. cit.*, p. 304 (early Sasanian).

38 *The Excavations at Dura Europos: preliminary report of the ninth season of work 1935–1936*, ii:

N. P. Toll, *The Necropolis*, New Haven 1946, pls. XXXIV, XXXVII, XLI, XLV, XLVIII, and p. 115.

39 H. Seyrig, *op. cit.*, pp. 204 ff.

40 C. L. Woolley, *op. cit.*, pls. 128–9, 135, 144.

41 E. F. Schmidt, *Excavations at Tepe Hissar, Damghan*, Philadelphia 1937, pl. XXXV.

42 R. A. Higgins, *op. cit.*, pp. 101–2, 120–1, 158–9.

43 F. H. Marshall, *Catalogue of Jewellery*, p. xxxii.

44 N. P. Toll, *op. cit.*, p. 115.

45 R. Koldewey, *op. cit.*, pp. 217–19; H. Lenzen, *XV. vorläufiger Bericht über die . . .*

Ausgrabungen in Uruk-Warka, Berlin 1959, pls. 26–27, and *XVI. vorläufiger Bericht . . .*, Berlin 1960, pl. 13.

46 E. H. Minns, *op. cit.*, pp. 388—90.

47 S. Yeivin, *op. cit.*, p. 41.

48 N. P. Toll, *op. cit.*, p. 22.

49 M. N. Ponzi, *op. cit.*, pp. 304–5.

50 J. P. P. Peters, *op. cit.*, p. 127.

51 It has been suggested that Claudius may have made Nineveh into a Roman colony (R. Campbell Thompson, *A Century of Exploration at Nineveh*, London 1929, p. 139), but the evidence is inconclusive.

Gold and silver coin hoards and the end of Roman Britain

R.A.G.CARSON
Deputy Keeper, Coins and Medals

An intriguing feature of the coinage record of the last decades of the province of Roman Britain is the frequency of hoards of silver coins, often of considerable dimensions; for this is in marked contrast to the pattern discernible in other western provinces of the empire. A consideration of the content and pattern of these hoards in particular, and of hoards in general provides evidence bearing on the general circumstances obtaining in the final stages of the history of the province. As always, the difficulty encountered in any consideration of hoards is the defective state of the evidence. There are some 40 hoards which are germane to this enquiry, but of these only about half are recorded with the sufficiency of detail which makes it possible to reconstruct the hoard. For the remainder, the information is restricted to the place of finding, often in most general terms, and the fact that the hoard contained a stated number of coins from a given time period indicated by the names of the first and last emperor represented. Though this information makes it possible to plot the pattern of the hoards, it is very tantalizing where the evidential possibilities of a hoard which has now vanished are seen to be enormous. The extreme case is a hoard from Cleeve Prior in Worcestershire,[1] recorded simply as having contained between 450 and 600 solidi from Valentinian I to Arcadius, and 3000 silver coins from Constantius II to Honorius; but the lost information from other equally imperfectly described but smaller hoards would also have been of great potential use.

By and large the hoards are scattered throughout the length and breadth of the province, inland as well as by the coasts (**112**). The area includes the whole of the civil zone with the exception of the north-west Midlands which, in the Roman period, continued to be thickly forested. The hoards spread into north-east Yorkshire, part of the original military zone, now peaceably settled and defended by a series of signal

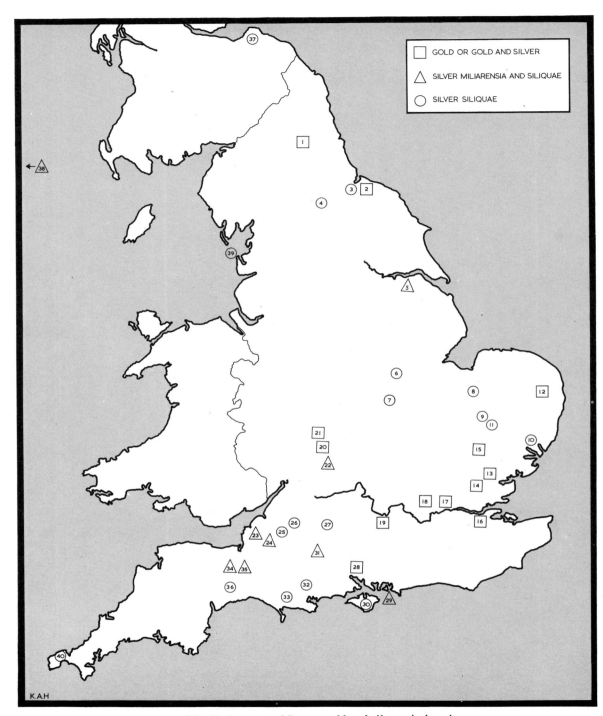

GOLD OR GOLD AND SILVER

SILVER MILIARENSIA AND SILIQUAE

SILVER SILIQUAE

K.A.H

112 *Distribution map of Roman gold and silver coin hoards.*

stations. Apart from a small number of hoards recorded from this area, the bulk of finds comes from the southern part of the province in the area bounded approximately by the Fosse Way running from south-west to north-east. The map of hoard distribution in this part of the province shows one concentration in East Anglia, a second in the Thames Valley, and a third in the south and west. There are left some definite outliers, whose deposition was due to special circumstances which will be considered below.

The defectiveness of information is particularly applicable to the hoards which contain gold. The information ranges in vagueness from '16 gold and 80 silver from Julius Caesar till after Constantine I' for a find at Alcester, Warwickshire, through a conglomerate entry of 26 gold and 400–500 silver from Constantine II to Honorius of a find at Chelmsford in Essex, to specific figures of 4 gold from Gratian to Honorius

113 *Solidus, Magnus Maximus, Corbridge Find.*   **114** *Solidus, Theodosius I, Corbridge Find.*   **115** *Solidus, Gratian, Gravesend Find.*   **116** *Solidus, Arcadius, Terling Find.*

and 10 silver from Julian to Honorius at Carleton St Peter in Norfolk. For only three hoards of gold, or including gold, do we have precise information. The hoard from Corbridge contained 48 solidi from Valentinian I to Maximus, with Gratian most heavily represented with 17 coins and Magnus Maximus with 12. In this hoard 43 of the solidi were struck at the Trier mint in Gaul (**113**), the remaining five coming from Rome, Thessalonica and Constantinople (**114**). The Springhead hoard at Gravesend in Kent was essentially of silver but did contain three solidi, two of Gratian from the Trier and Aquileia mints (**115**) and one of Theodosius, again from Trier. In the find from Terling in Essex there were 25 solidi from Valens to Honorius. Here, while the earlier coins were again from Trier, for Arcadius there was one solidus from the Rome mint and five of the mint of Milan (**116**), and for Honorius again only one solidus of Rome but no fewer than 11 from Milan. In the very much larger number of hoards of silver coins only, again, for a considerable number, we have only the most general information on the content. By and large, these hoards are recorded as containing coins from the time of Constantius II up to Arcadius and Honorius, though a few have a slightly earlier terminal date in the late fourth century.

Fortunately, however, there remains quite a large number of hoards of silver coins of which we have adequate records. Of such hoards there are two principal categories. The first major class, distinguished by the inclusion (in addition to quantities of the smaller coin, the siliqua), of varying amounts of the larger miliarense denomination, comprises the following hoards:

		Miliarensia content
1	South Ferriby	(3 Valens, 1 Honorius)
2	Springhead	(1 Valentinian I, 2 Valens, 5 Gratian, 1 Valentinian II, 1 Theodosius, 2 Magnus Maximus)
3	Willersey	(1 Julian)
4	North Mendips	(1 Constans, 8 Constantius II, 1 Gallus, 1 Julian, 1 Jovian, 5 Valentinian I, 4 Valens, 4 Gratian, 3 Valentinian II, 2 Theodosius, 1 Eugenius)
5	East Harptree	(7 Constantius II, 1 Decentius, 1 Julian, 1 Jovian, 3 Valentinian I, 2 Valens)
6	Southsea	(1 Constantine I, 1 Crispus, 1 Constantine II, 6 Constans, 52 Constantius II, 4 Magnentius 1 Decentius, 3 Gallus, 8 Julian)
7	Grovely Wood	(1 Valens, 2 Gratian, 1 uncertain)
8	Holwel (Taunton)	(2 Constans, 2 Julian, 10 Valentinian I, 4 Valens, 7 Gratian, 2 Valentinian II, 1 Magnus Maximus, 4 Theodosius, 1 Eugenius)
9	North Curry (Taunton)	(1 Gratian)
10	'Mr Wood'	(1 Jovian, 1 Valens, 1 Gratian, 2 Valentinian II, 1 Theodosius)[2]

A simplified analysis of the mints of origin of the miliarensia shows that for the later Constantinian emperors these coins are the products of the Balkan mints of Sirmium (**117**) and Thessalonica (**118**). For the late coinage of Constantius II, of Julian, and of the Valentinianic and Theodosian emperors, the western mints at Arles and, particularly, Trier predominate (**119**), with a lighter representation of Rome (**120**) and Aquileia.

The second major category is that of hoards made up exclusively of siliquae. Of these, there are the two somewhat isolated hoards from Worlton and Richmond in

117 *Miliarense, Julian, Willersey Find.*   **118** *Miliarense, Julian, Southsea Find.*   **119** *Miliarense, Magnus Maximus, Gravesend Find.*   **120** *Miliarense, Valentinian I, East Harptree Find.*

Yorks. Then comes a group which we can term, very generally, East Anglian, with hoards from Sproxton in Lincolnshire, Holyoke in Leicestershire, Fincham in Norfolk, and in Suffolk from Mildenhall, Tuddenham and Icklingham. In a south-western context there are siliqua hoards from Manton Down and Colerne in Wiltshire, from Camerton and Taunton in Somerset, from Dorchester and Shapwick in Dorset, from Shanklin in the Isle of Wight, and one from Honiton in Devon. It should not be forgotten that to this generally 'Wessex' group must be added the hoards from Willersey, East Harptree, North Mendips, Grovely Wood and Southsea which have been already mentioned as containing miliarensia, but which contained substantial siliquae. Reinforced with these additions the patterns of hoards in this area becomes decidedly noteworthy. In the second major category, the span of these hoards as a whole, with some individual variation, is from Constantius II to late Honorius. As for the mint representation, in the siliqua content, which by and large became sub-stantial with the issues of the joint reign of Constantius II and Julian, the more

121 *Siliqua, Julian, Coleraine Find.*   **122** *Siliqua, Constantius II, Gravesend Find.*   **123** *Siliqua, Valentinian I, Shapwick I Find.*   **124** *Siliqua, Valens, Grovely Wood Find.*

eastern mints which were noted for earlier miliarensia make little impact. Only Antioch for Constantius II makes any consistent appearance. For Constantius II and Julian the mints of Arles (**121**) and Lugdunum (**122**) make the heaviest contribution, while, for the house of Valentinian, Trier becomes the predominant mint (**123**) with the other Gallic mints, making some showing, the Italian mints a little (**124**), and more eastern mints scarcely at all. The picture for the Theodosian emperors is somewhat similar in the earlier issues (**125**) but, by the end of the fourth century, a notable feature of the siliquae of Arcadius (**126**) and even more so of Honorius (**127**) is the significant contribution of the Italian mints—Rome to some extent but Milan predominating.

125 *Siliqua,*   **126** *Siliqua,*   **127** *Siliqua,*   **128** *Clipped Siliqua,*   **129** *Clipped Siliqua,*
Theodosius I,   *Arcadius,*   *Honorius,*   *Victor,*   *Honorius,*
Grovely Wood Find.   *Icklingham I Find.*   *Tuddenham Find.*   *Tuddenham Find.*   *Coleraine Find.*

A special feature which distinguishes some of the hoards in both the major categories is the inclusion of siliquae which have been subjected to clipping. This clipping is of varying degree of severity ranging from a very discreet paring of the edge which leaves the inscriptions on obverse and reverse either totally legible or capable of being restored with certainty (**128, 129**), down to such a heavy removal of the outer rim of the coin that nothing but the obverse portrait and the central reverse type are left (**130, 131**). The presence of such clipped siliquae in conjunction with the evidence for the point in time at which this practice of clipping began will be seen below to suggest some modification to the terminal date of hoards of which such pieces are a feature.

The general hoard picture so far described requires to be amplified with more detail of location, content, range, and terminal date to enable the pattern of the hoards to be perceived, and the implications of the evidence to be discussed. The distribution of the hoards is plotted on the accompanying map (**112**), and their details displayed in the table on pp. 74-5.

Some salient features are immediately evident. In the south and west there is a considerable concentration of hoards almost exclusively of silver; along the Thames Valley and into the west Midlands the hoards are mainly of gold as well as silver; in East Anglia is another grouping of hoards exclusively of silver save for one inadequately recorded find allegedly including gold. In the north-east there is a small scatter of hoards, with one exceptional hoard solely of gold solidi at Corbridge. All of these hoards provide a number of patterns but there are left a few hoards which are extraneous to the observed patterns.

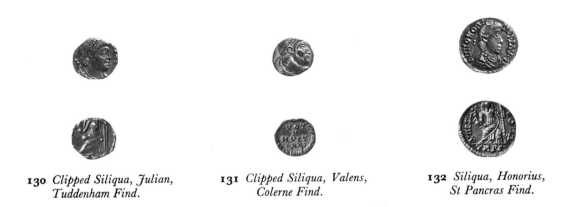

130 *Clipped Siliqua, Julian,*   **131** *Clipped Siliqua, Valens,*   **132** *Siliqua, Honorius,*
      Tuddenham Find.   *Colerne Find.*   *St Pancras Find.*

The four such peripheral hoards are from Traprain Law in Lothian, just south of the Forth, at Coleraine in North Ireland, at Fleetwood in Lancashire, and at Zennor in Cornwall. All of these most probably have a common explanation.[3] In the case of two, Coleraine and Traprain, the explanation is fairly certain. Both of these places lie outside the province in areas where there is no other evidence of a consistent money-using economy at this time, so that these finds represent the simple hoarding of treasure rather than the safe depositing of coins. The evidence of the other material in the Coleraine hoard discovered in 1854 puts this beyond question. In addition to 1506 silver coins there was other silver reported as weighing at least 200 ounces, and comprising pieces of broken embossed silver plate, lumps or ingots of silver, some of which clearly were fragments of the well-known axe-head-shaped late Roman silver ingots. The Traprain find, though much smaller, is of the same nature and both finds seem to represent loot or booty presumably deriving from the province. The other two finds, from Fleetwood and Zennor, admittedly contain only coins. As both are isolated in areas otherwise void of hoards and both have a coastal location they may possibly be genuine instances of the once standard explanation for a hoard as the consequence of barbarian or piratical raids on the province.

Gold and silver coin hoards and the end of Roman Britain

TABLE OF HOARDS

	Find	County	Metal	Quantity	Range	Reference
				NORTH-EAST		
1	Corbridge I	Northumberland	AV	48	Val. I–Maximus	*NC* 1912, pp. 309–12
2	Guisborough	Yorks.	AV	1	Valens–Honorius	Elgee, *Romans in Cleveland*,
			AR	80		p. 14
3	Whorlton	Yorks.	AR	150	Const. II–Honorius	Elgee, *Romans in Cleveland*,
						p. 8
4	Richmond	Yorks.	AR	600 +	Const. II–Victor +	Clarkson, *Richmond*, p. 16
				EAST ANGLIA		
5	South Ferriby	Lincs.	AR	228	Const. II–Honorius	*NC* 1935, pp. 254–74
6	Sproxton	Lincs.	AR	99	Const. II–Honorius	*NC* 1934, pp. 61–73
7	Holyoke	Leics.	AR	230	Julian–Arcadius	*VCH Leics.* i, p. 213
8	Fincham	Norfolk	AR	7	Ant. Pius–Honorius	*NC* 1936, pp. 255–61
9	Mildenhall	Suffolk	AR	*c.* 13	Const. II–Honorius	*NC* 1942, pp. 105–6
10	Tuddenham	Suffolk	AR	114	Const. II–Honorius	*NC* 1946, pp. 169–73
11	Icklingham I	Suffolk	AR	*c.* 337	Const. II–Honorius	*NC* 1908, pp. 215–21
	Icklingham II	Suffolk	AR	32	Const. II–Honorius	*NC* 1929, pp. 319–27
	Icklingham III	Suffolk	AR	318	Const. II–Honorius	*NC* 1936, pp. 257–61
12	Carleton St Peter	Norfolk	AV	4	Gratian–Honorius	*VCH Norf.* i, p. 314
			AR	10	Julian–Honorius	
				THAMES VALLEY		
13	Terling	Essex	AV	30	Const. II–Honorius	*NC* 1933, pp. 145–70
			AR	304		
14	Chelmsford	Essex	AV	26	Const. II–Honorius	*AJ* 1846, p. 162
			AR	300–400		
15	Sturmer	Essex	AV	1	Julian–Honorius	Fox, *Arch. Cambridge Region*,
			AR	29		p. 226
16	Gravesend	Kent	AV	4		
			AR	444	Const. II–Maximus	*NC* 1965, pp. 177–82
17	Maiden Lane	St Pancras, London	AV	?		
			AR	?	Constantine I +	Note in B.M.
18	Great Stanmore	Middlesex	AV	40	Const. II–Honorius	*Gough's Camden* ii, p. 30
19	Reading	Berks.	AV	1	Const. II–Arcadius	*VCH Berks* i, p. 216
			AR	119		
20	Cleeve Prior	Worcs.	AV	450–600	Val. I–Arcadius	*Archaeologia*, lxxiii, 1922–3,
			AR	*c.* 3000	Const. II–Honorius	p. 90
21	Alcester	Worcs.	AV	16	Julius Caesar till	S. Clarke, *Geographical*
			AR	800	after Constantine I	*Description of the World*,
						1871, p. 61

Table of hoards, *cont.*

	Find	County	Metal	Quan. tity	Range	Reference
				SOUTH-WEST		
22	Willersey	Glos.	Æ	56	Const. II–Julian	*NC* 1971, pp. 203–6
23	'North Mendips'	Somerset	Æ	2044	Constans–Honorius	*NC* 1915, pp. 433–519
24	East Harptree	Somerset	Æ	1496	Constantine I–Gratian	*NC* 1888, pp. 22–46
25	Caverton	Somerset	Æ	26	?–Honorius	*VCH Som.* i, p. 292 n.
26	Colerne	Wilts.	Æ	200	Const. II–Honorius	*NC* 1942, pp. 97–104
27	Manton Down	Wilts.	Æ	5	Julian–Honorius	*NC* 1884, pp. 348–9
28	Allington	Hants.	A/	1	Julian–Honorius	*NC* 1869, p. 372
			Æ	50		
29	Southsea	Hants.	Æ	965	Trajan–Julian	*NC* 1936, pp. 292–302 *NC* 1959, pp. 89–91
30	Shanklin	I.O.W.	Æ	6	Gratian–Honorius	*NC* 1844, *Proc.*, pp. 18–19
31	Grovely Wood	Wilts.	Æ	300	Const. II–Arcadius	*NC* 1906, pp. 329–47
32	Shapwick I	Dorset	Æ	120	Const. II–Honorius	*NC* 1936, pp. 245–50
	Shapwick II	Dorset	Æ	125	Const. II–Victor	*NC* 1938, pp. 53–8
33	Dorchester	Dorset	Æ	53	Julian–Honorius	*NC* 1922, pp. 134–9
34	Holwel	Somerset	Æ	318	Const. II–Honorius	*NC* 1844, *Proc.*, pp. 9–14
35	North Cury	Somerset	Æ	150	Constans–Honorius	*Gents. Mag.* 1748, p. 405
36	Honiton	Devon	Æ	16	Julian–Maximus	*NC* 1925, pp. 396–7
				OUTLIERS		
37	Traprain Law	E. Lothian	Æ	4	Valens–Honorius	A. O. Curle, *The Treasure of Traprain*, p. 5
38	Coleraine	N. Ireland	Æ	1506	Julian–Constantine III	*NC* 1855, pp. 101–15
39	Fleetwood	Lancs.	Æ	401	Const. II–Honorius	*NC* 1948, pp. 205–14
40	Zennor	Cornwall	Æ	80	Val. I–Honorius	*VCH Corn..* v, p. 42

In the context of hoards containing gold, the most remarkable is the find of 48 solidi from Corbridge. It is remarkable as the only hoard of this period consisting solely of gold, and as one of the only four hoards of Roman gold in Britain of which we have satisfactory record. It is, however, a hoard in isolation outside any of our patterns, and the circumstances which caused its concealment are not obvious. It contains coins from Valentinian I up to Magnus Maximus who met his end in AD 388. Long gone, however, are the days when a belief that it was under Maximus that the wall defences were abandoned could provide a facile explanation of the deposit; for it has been amply demonstrated that coin finds from the wall generally and from Corstopitum in this particular instance occur later than the Maximus episode.[4] The deposit presumably has some military or official context in view of the place of finding and the quantity of coins, for records of casual finds of gold show nothing from the wall at this time and, from the north of England more generally, only some ten solidi have been noted for the period from Constantius II to Arcadius.[5]

Moving south, the next small group is that from the north Riding of Yorkshire. There are only three hoards of precious metal on record but for none do we have complete detailed information. The hoards are essentially of silver, though the find from Guisborough contained a single gold coin in addition to 80 silver pieces. This Guisborough hoard is recorded simply as covering the period Valens to Honorius, while the much larger hoard from Richmond had 600 coins from Constantius II to Victor 'plus many others of the later emperors', and the find of 150 silver coins from Whorlton was reported to represent emperors from Constantius II to Honorius. The area from which these hoards come had originally been part of the military zone but subsequently it had been more peaceably exploited and defended by a series of signal stations. The examination of the sites of the Yorkshire signal stations revealed no more than a single structural period and their coins, which are not numerous, suggest that these stations ceased to function about 410. Two at least, at Huntcliff and Goldsborough, came to a violent end, and the area became exposed to raids from the sea.[6] The evidence of our three hoards conforms with this general picture. The latest coins mentioned are of Honorius, but as no details are available of the coins' types or their mints we can say only that the coins go on to at least 393. An allowance of time for coins of Honorius to reach the area brings us towards the end of the century which accords with the evidence from the signal stations.

A somewhat larger number of finds has been noted for East Anglia, taken in a rather broad sense. Eleven hoards are recorded, distributed from South Ferriby and Sproxton in Lincolnshire, through Holyoke, Leicestershire and Fincham in Norfolk, to find spots in close proximity at Mildenhall, Tuddenham and Icklingham in Suffolk, the latter in fact having yielded three hoards. All that we know of the Carleton St Peter hoard is that it contained four solidi of emperors from Gratian to Honorius and ten silver coins of emperors from Julian to Honorius; and for the Holyoke hoard we have merely a general report that it contained silver coins up to Honorius. All the others are recorded in detail and make it possible to be somewhat more precise about terminal dates. The 13 coins from the find at Mildenhall represented only a portion of the find. On the assumption that this is a true sample, since Honorius just achieves representation, the hoard closes in 393 or shortly afterwards. In the other hoards the picture is fairly consistent. The latest coins are *Virtus Romanorum* siliquae of the Milan mint. The examples of Arcadius and Honorius far outweigh those of Theodosius I who died in 395. Again the coins of this class of Honorius preponderate over those of Arcadius. The late J. W. E. Pearce, considering this and other features in similar hoards, concluded that the terminal date of such hoards should be placed in the early years of the fifth century.[7]

Farther to the south comes a group of hoards which has a pattern both in composition and location. The common composition feature is that they all contain some gold as well as a substantial quantity of silver coins. In general geographic terms these hoards form a belt which runs along the Thames Valley and into the west Midlands. From east to west there are hoards from Essex at Terling, Chelmsford and Sturmer; south of the Thames estuary there is one from Gravesend in Kent; there is a very confusedly reported find from Maiden Lane, St Pancras in London, of which a portion may have re-appeared in modern times, and another from Middlesex, at Bentley Priory. Farther west is another hoard from Reading, and finally hoards at Alcester in Warwick and from Cleeve Prior in Worcester. Regrettably for only the two hoards from Terling and Gravesend do we have detailed modern records and possibly of a part of the St Pancras hoard. The hoards recorded only in general terms show gold content ranging from a single gold coin in the Reading find to 450–600 at Cleeve Prior but, for gold and silver taken together, the hoards appear consistently to end again with Honorius. Gravesend alone ends somewhat earlier, around 388–9. Both the Terling find and what may be a portion of the St Pancras find contained an example of an unusual siliqua of Honorius of the Trier mint (**132**) which may be as late as 420 when mints in Gaul were once again in the emperor's control after a succession of usurpers from Constantine III on.[8] It would not be safe to assert that all the vaguely recorded hoards are of an equally late date, but those with Honorian content probably can be dated to the first years of the fifth century. The hoards themselves and the consistent presence of gold argues for a continuation of circumstances of some prosperity in this area until quite late.

Of the quite numerous group of hoards from the south and west there are two which require prior and separate mention, for they have a terminal date quite distinct from the general terminus period of the other hoards. One relatively small hoard of 56 silver coins came from Willersey in Gloucestershire, a find made quite recently in 1970. The second was a large hoard of around a thousand silver coins found just at the end of the last century at Southsea, Hampshire. The Willersey hoard consisted of siliquae with the addition of a single miliarense. The Southsea hoard contained some 80 examples of the larger miliarense denomination in addition to the mass of siliquae. The substantial components of both finds were coins of Constantius II and of Julian, and in both hoards the latest coins were of Julian as Augustus providing a terminal date for the content of the hoards of 363. There had indeed been trouble in Britain about this period, but this was occasioned by Pictish and

Scottish incursions in the north of the province and some years before,[9] and so these disturbances can have no bearing on the deposition of these hoards. Despite the coincidence of the terminal date of the hoards, it does seem that here we have to think in terms of local or private circumstances, now quite unknowable, which led to the concealment of the finds.

The remaining hoards in the 'Wessex' area are distributed quite widely. They are all of silver with the single exception of the hoard from Allington, near Southampton, which contained one solidus. In Wiltshire there are hoards from Manton Down, Colerne and Grovely Wood; in Somerset, finds from East Harptree, an unidentified spot in the North Mendips, and from Camerton and Taunton; in Dorset, from Dorchester and two finds from Shapwick; in Devon one from Honiton and, finally, a small find from Shanklin in the Isle of Wight. For this group of hoards there is not the same uniformity of date of deposition as has been observed with some of the other group which we have already considered. One reason for this probably is that for this group we have, for once, a much higher proportion with complete and detailed records. Only for three finds, Camerton, Taunton, and Shanklin do we have to be content with a generalization that the latest coins are of Honorius. For the other hoards about which we have specific information the terminal dates of the coins show quite a range. The earliest is that from East Harptree, concealed before the death of Valens in 378. The next is the find from Honiton where the latest coins are of Magnus Maximus who was executed in 388. A little later are the hoard from Grovely Wood and the second Shapwick find both of which, as they exclude Honorius, must be pre-393. The North Mendips find does include Honorius, but as his representation is quite small compared with that of Theodosius I and Arcadius, its terminus is probably to be dated about 395. For the hoards from Manton Down, Colerne, Dorchester and Shapwick I the terminal date is less easy to establish with complete certainty. The latest coins here, too, are the *Virtus Romanorum* siliquae of the Milan mint, and of these the coins of Honorius preponderate over those of Arcadius. As in the case of one of the categories of the East Anglian group discussed above, the terminal date is probably to be put in the early years of the fifth century.

A modification to the terminal date of some hoards in the groups which have now been considered is suggested by the evidence of the clipping of the silver siliquae found in some hoards. The finds in which clipped siliquae are a feature are those from Colerne and Manton Down in Wiltshire and, in the East Anglian group, at South Ferriby, Fincham, Icklingham II and Tuddenham. It is a feature also of two of the outlying hoards at Fleetwood and at Coleraine. If one leaves aside for the moment the element of clipped siliquae, the evidence of the unclipped pieces suggests that these hoards closed in the early fifth century. The Coleraine hoard is important in this context, for in addition to a high proportion of clipped siliquae it contained at least two coins of Constantine III who met his end in 411. Relevant to the dating of hoards containing clipped siliquae is the evidence of their absence from the East Harptree hoard, ending before the death of Valens. Clipped siliquae are also absent from the hoards, Shapwick II and Grovely Wood which closed before the accession of Honorius in 393, nor are there any in the North Mendips find which, from the small number of coins of Honorius present, closed shortly after 393. The practice, therefore, appears not to have been in operation before the beginning of Honorius' reign. Again, the preponderant Honorian element in the Terling, Sproxton, Icklingham I and III, and Shapwick I hoards, very similar to the unclipped coins in the hoards which do contain clipped coins, suggests a terminus in the first decade of the fifth century, and seems to show that clipping had not yet become a practice. Hoards up to this point, then, show Honorian silver still entering Britain, but the flow must have been checked with the usurpation of Constantine III whose coins do not show up in hoards in Britain proper. Growing scarcity of new coins presumably led to an appreciation in the value of silver and to the practice of clipping. Hoards accumulated or deposited after the separation while necessarily coinciding in composition with the latest pre-separation hoards, since the supply of new coins was effectively interrupted, would contain this element of cut-down coins. On the assumption that the Coleraine treasure originated in Britain, the presence in it of coins of Constantine III dates it to after his usurpation and dates the practice of clipping with it. By how much later in the fifth century clipped siliquae hoards should be dated can only be a matter for speculation. It has been remarked that many clipped siliquae have been cut down to a module very similar to that of the small silver of Valentinian III, but as there is no evidence for the circulation of this silver coinage in Britain it is scarcely evidential value for the date of clipped siliquae.

We can now consider some of the inferences which can be drawn from the coinage picture now presented in some detail. The frequency of late Roman silver coin hoards in Britain in comparison with the relative paucity of such hoards in other areas is no new observation. The chauvinist explanation that this is simply due to more thorough recording in this country, if it ever were true, is certainly now not acceptable. Late silver coins were in circulation in other areas, and there are some hoards on record.[10] Why then did Britain specialize in hoarding late silver when other areas did not, though the coins were there to be hoarded? There are coin hoards enough in Roman Britain in bronze and in silver, but there are remarkably few hoards of gold. Only four substantial gold hoards are on record, Bredgar (Claudius 1), Corbridge I (Antoninus Pius), Water Newton (Constantius II and Constans; see below, pp. 219–220), and Corbridge II (Maximus). There is some small addition of gold to hoards of coins of other metals both in this late period, as we have seen, and in earlier periods. A recent survey of isolated gold finds in Roman Britain[11] shows that there was always some gold in circulation, but for scarcely any emperor other than Nero do the totals from the whole province reach double figures. At the end of the third century the gold coinage of Carausius, to judge from the excessive rarity of surviving examples, must have been limited in quantity, and that of Allectus very little greater.[12] The coinage of Carausius gives us perhaps the clue. Such gold of Carausius as there is, is late in his reign[13] and it would seem that at the outset of the reign, Carausius, having no supply of gold to coin, decided to produce a precious metal coinage in silver as the next most impressive thing. This could explain why a silver coinage was being struck in Britain when it was to all intents and purposes absent from the coinage of the central empire. It would seem that at all periods the economic circumstances of Britain did not require a large circulation of gold coin, and it would then follow that, if precious metal in the form of coinage were required for hoarding, the coins so hoarded would be silver. In Britain in the late period, silver was hoarded because silver coins were available and gold coins were not. In other areas silver, though available, was not hoarded to the same extent, because as finds show, there was more gold available for hoarding.

A second general question which requires examination is why the hoards, and in particular the groups, appear where they do. A fairly obvious but only partial answer is supplied by a comparison of the map of the distribution of hoards with the Ordnance Survey map of Roman Britain. In general there is a coincidence with that part of the province which from quite early in its history had been settled and developed, but the Ordnance Survey map does not yield easy distinction of remains of separate periods. A notable feature, however, is the spread of villa sites with quite marked groupings especially in the South and West, to some extent in the East Anglian area, something less in the Thames Valley belt and a sprinkling in Yorkshire. The *floruit* of the villa was the fourth century, and the view at one time was that the villa culture declined in the latter half of the fourth century, particularly after the raids of 367. A reappraisal of the evidence, however, has produced a map of villas occupied after 367 which bears quite a noticeable resemblance to the map of hoard distribution.[14] There is clearly still much to be done in establishing when particular villas were abandoned or destroyed, but it is possible that many continued in occupation into the fifth century and at some, for instance Hucclecote in Gloucestershire, new mosaic floors were laid down at the very end of the fourth century.[15] It should be emphasized that the coincidence remarked is only that of areas, for very few of the hoards in question are directly associated with villa sites.

The hoards then appear to suggest that up to the beginning of the fifth century circumstances continued to be such that there was still some use of coinage. As increasingly fewer people found it necessary to use coins they were hoarded instead as treasure,[16] and many hoards were never recovered either because their owners perished or simply because coinage no longer had a part to play. The evidence of the clipped siliquae hoards is for some continuation of coinage use even after the separation of Britain from the metropolitan empire, and the examples, admittedly very rare, of Honorian siliquae from Trier in a very few hoards are evidence for some continuation of coinage use down to about 420. To judge from the quite fresh state of these rare late siliquae, they could not have been long in circulation before they were hoarded.

The complementary evidence provided by hoards of bronze coins was last summarized and considered in 1933,[17] but none of the hoards which have been recorded since that date has provided evidence to upset the conclusions reached at that time. In brief, the hoards provide evidence for the continued circulation of bronze coins also into certainly the first years of the fifth century.[18] It has not been possible from a consideration of the internal evidence of the bronze coins themselves to deduce how much later they continued in circulation after the date of the latest coins in the hoards, and it may be that bronze coins continued in use as long as precious metal coinage usage persisted. From the evidence of the late silver coin hoards, the conclusion must be that only a few years after 420 the use of coinage of any kind in Roman Britain came to an end.

NOTES

1 The references for this and for the other hoards discussed are given in the table on pp. 74–75 above.

2 For this hoard of 6 miliarensia and 111 siliquae shown to the British Museum and recorded in 1954 there is no certain provenance or date of finding.

3 Cf. B. H. St J. O'Neil, 'A hoard of late Roman coins from Northamptonshire; its parallels and significance', *Archeological Journal*, 1933, p. 291.

4 J. P. C. Kent, 'Coin evidence and the evacuation of Hadrian's wall', *Transactions of the Cumberland and Westmorland Antiquarian and Archeological Society*, 11, 1952, pp. 4–15.

5 P. Isaac, *Finds of Roman gold coins in Britain*, 1970 (unpublished M.A. thesis, University of Durham).

6 Sheppard Frere, *Britannia. A history of Roman Britain*, London, 1967, p. 373.

7 J. W. E. Pearce, 'A second find of siliquae from Shapwick', *Numismatic Chronicle*, 1938, pp. 57–8.

8 In 1958 a small group of seven siliquae of Valens, Maximus, Arcadius and Honorius was found in the earth filling of a window-box of a flat in St Pancras, but it was not possible to discover whether the earth had come from the area of the Maiden Lane, St Pancras, find. Cf. R. A. G. Carson, 'Roman Coins acquired by the British Museum', *NC* 1959, p. 15 and n. 1.

9 Frere, *op. cit.*, p. 350.

10 E.g. Limoges (Haute Vienne), France: A. Blanchet, *Les trésors de monnaies romaines*, Paris, 1900, p. 240; San Genesio, near Pavia, Italy: *Atti dell' Accademia Nazionale dei Lincei*, Ser. viii,

1954, pp. 166–84; Lower Danube: *Wiener Numismatische Monatshefte*, 1868, p. 248.

11 Isaac, *op. cit.*

12 P. H. Webb, *Roman Imperial Coinage* V2, ed. H. Mattingly and E. A. Sydenham, London, 1933, pp. 463, 516–17, 558–9.

13 R. A. G. Carson, 'The Mints and Coinage of Carausius and Allectus', *Journal of the Archaeological Association*, 3rd. ser., xxii, 1959, p. 38.

14 Graham Webster, 'The future of villa studies', *The Roman Villa in Britain*, ed. A. L. F. Rivet, London, 1969, p. 230.

15 Frere, *op. cit.*, p. 373.

16 The association of other objects in precious metal in a number of finds lends some support to this view: Whorlton—ingots, broken spoons, and a silver ring; Terling—two gold rings; Willersey—a silver ring; East Harptree—five pieces of cast silver and a silver ring; Grovely Wood—six silver rings; Dorchester—two silver spoons; Manton Down–12 pewter dishes.

17 See n. 3.

18 J. P. C. Kent, 'From Roman Britain to Saxon England', *Anglo-Saxon Coins. Studies presented to F. M. Stenton*, ed. R. H. M. Dolley, London, 1961, p. 4.

The Malcolm celestial globe

R.H.PINDER-WILSON

Deputy Keeper, Oriental Antiquities

In the Islamic cosmology the ninth sphere was the vault of the heavens to which were attached the stars. These were seen to revolve with the sphere in its daily revolution round the earth. Ptolemy, following in the footsteps of Hipparchus, had observed and recorded the positions of the stars for his own time and the Islamic astronomers continued this tradition.

The Arabs inherited the constellation figures from the ancient world. This transmission took place early in the history of Islam. In the desert, about 50 miles east of 'Amman in Jordan, the Umayyad Caliph Walīd I built a small palace known as Quṣayr 'Amrā, comprising an audience hall and bath, all richly decorated with mosaics and frescoes. The hemispherical dome of the *calidarium* was painted with the constellations of the firmament.[1] The shortcomings of the rendering are many; not least the figures were transferred direct from a plane to the curving surface of the dome and are depicted back to front. Nevertheless, the thirty-seven figures which survive bear a remarkable resemblance in all essentials to those of the Farnese Globe, the most famous representation of the constellations surviving from the classical world.

The work of recording the star positions was begun in the following century when Greek scientific works were being systematically translated into Arabic. The first star catalogue was prepared for the 'Abbasid Caliph al-Ma'mūn in AD 829.[2] This was intended to establish the difference between positions of the stars in that year and those recorded in Ptolemy's Almagest of AD 138 due to the precession of the equinoxes. This intense interest in astronomy during the ninth century stimulated the production of scientific instruments. Chief amongst these was the astrolabe, but we also know from literature of the period that celestial globes were also constructed.[3] The purpose of such globes was both demonstration and the solving of problems of star positions. We know, too, that these globes were illustrated with the constellation figures.

The most notable work describing the star constellations is the *Book of the Fixed Stars* by the Persian astronomer 'Abd al-Raḥmān al-Ṣūfī who composed it in AD 964 for 'Aḍud al-Dawla, the greatest of the Buyid dynasty.[4] Each constellation and its stars are described in great detail and accompanied by drawings. Each constellation is paired; the one figure of the constellation being depicted as seen from outside the firmament, that is, on the globe; the other as seen in the vault of heaven by the observer. 'Abd al-Raḥmān al-Ṣūfī had himself constructed a silver globe for 'Aḍud al-Dawla and according to his own declaration the illustrations were traced from the constellation figures of a globe.[5]

Based on the work of his predecessors as well as on accurate observation, 'Abd al-Raḥmān's book was to have a lasting influence on astronomy in the Islamic world. The earliest surviving version was copied and illustrated by his son in AD 1009–10 and is preserved in the Bodleian Library, Oxford.[6] Thereafter, the book was copied continuously in the Islamic world down to the nineteenth century, the astronomical data of each version being adjusted for the precession.[7] The constellation figures, too, of each successive version, while retaining the exact star positions of the original, are rendered in the style current in the period when they were executed. The figures—in particular the human ones—became orientalized and divorced from their classical prototypes because, unlike their Christian contemporaries in the West, the Muslims had little or no interest in Greek and Roman mythology. While western astronomy sacrificed scientific accuracy to this mythological element in their delineation of the constellations, the Muslims observed a strict adherence to the astrothetic aspect; and thus remained truer to the scientific spirit of the Greco-Roman world.[8]

I

There are thirteen celestial globes surviving from the medieval Islamic world, that is, from the fifteenth century or earlier.[9] That their makers based their delineations on the *Book of the Fixed Stars* is highly probable since in the case of four of the globes it is explicitly stated that the star positions are those described by al-Ṣūfī.[10] Two of the ten globes were made in Spain in the eleventh century, the remaining eight in the eastern Islamic world. All have been described—many in the greatest detail—but the published reproductions of the constellation figures have been limited to hand-drawn copies or, at best, photographs of a few details. A comparative study of the style and iconography of the constellation figures might well provide the solution of the problem where each globe was made; but this can only be undertaken when each is reproduced photographically in its entirety. It is hoped that this article on the

Malcolm celestial globe in the British Museum will encourage the detailed publication of the other celestial globes (Plate II, p. 288).

The Malcolm celestial globe is named after its one-time owner, the distinguished soldier and statesman, General Sir John Malcolm (1769–1833).[11] He had been presented with the globe by the leader of the Bohora community—Shi'a Muslims belonging to a branch of the Isma'ili sect—whose ancestors had brought it to India from Persia when they sought refuge in that country from persecution.[12] Malcolm deposited the globe with the Royal Asiatic Society of Great Britain and Ireland, probably in 1829, when it was the subject of a learned paper delivered by Dorn to the Society on 21 February.[13] Dorn subsequently published his paper in the Transactions of the Society and accompanied it with two admirable lithographed plates of the globe (**133, 134**). On 25 February 1871, the Trustees of the British Museum sanctioned the purchase of the globe from Sir John's only son, General George Malcolm.

The globe, 24 cm. in diameter, is of brass cast in two hemispheres, the junction

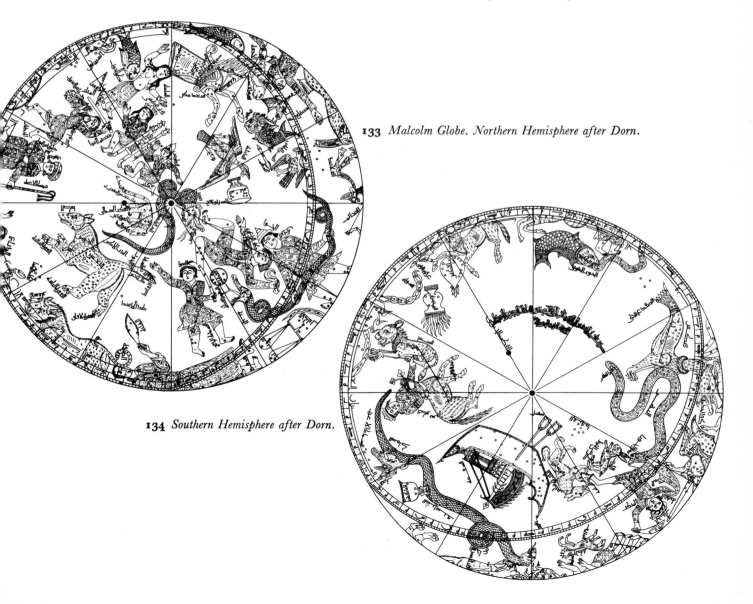

133 *Malcolm Globe. Northern Hemisphere after Dorn.*

134 *Southern Hemisphere after Dorn.*

coinciding with the ecliptic. The ecliptic and celestial equators are graduated in single degrees with every fifth labelled. In accordance with the usual practice in medieval Islamic astronomical instruments, the figures are indicated by Kufic letters of the equivalent numerical value. The ecliptic repeats every 30°; the celestial equator beginning at the vernal equinox is divided into three segments, each of 100°, and one of 60°. The circles of longitude are relative to the ecliptic. Forty-eight constellation figures are traced on the surface; and the stars—about one thousand—are indicated by inlaid silver dots of varying size according to the magnitude of the star.[14] The names of the constellations and the principal star groups or stars are traced in Kufic characters.

The maker's name and date are inscribed in Kufic and inlaid with silver below the Southern Fish in the southern hemisphere (**158**):

Ṣana'ahu al-faqīr 'ilā Allāh ta'ālā Muḥammad ibn Hilāl al-munajjim al-Mawṣilī fī sanah 674 *hijrīyah.*

Made by him who is in need of God—may He be exalted—Muḥammad ibn Hilāl the astronomer of Mosul in the year 674 H [AD 1274–5].

The stand, also of brass, consists of a horizon ring supported by a hemispherical frame of two crossing members. This rests on four legs, concave in profile, which are attached to an eight-lobed base frame. Four bars radiate inwards from the latter and meet in a small circular tray. This stand is later than the globe and certainly not earlier than the sixteenth century since the horizon ring is marked with the four points of the compass in *naskhi* script, a feature unknown in instruments of the fifteenth century and earlier.[15]

It is not possible to know what was the form of the original stand. The globe itself is complete except for the meridian rings which would have encompassed it, being attached to the two poles by pins.[16]

In the description of the constellations which follows, the reader should refer to Dorn's two planometric projections in order to see the figures in their relation one with the other and with the equator and ecliptic circles (**133, 134**). In the northern hemisphere (**133**) the graduated circle in the lower half is the ecliptic, and in the upper half the equator. In the southern hemisphere, the positions of the ecliptic and equator are reversed.

The constellations of the Northern hemisphere:

1 Ursa Minor (*al-dubb al-aṣghar*), the Lesser Bear (**135**). The Pole Star at the end of the tail is known in Arabic as *al-jady*, 'the kid'. The hole bored in the globe to the right of the Pole Star is the North Celestial Pole.

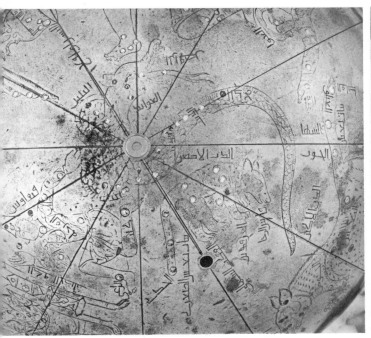

135 *Ursa Minor, Draco and Cepheus.*

136 *Ursa Major.*

137 *Boötes and Corona Borealis.*

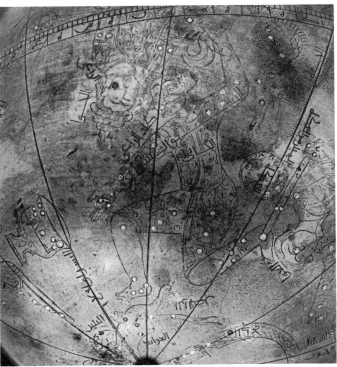

138 *Hercules and Lyra.*

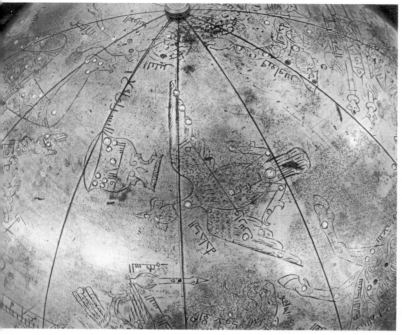

139 *Cygnus.*

140 *Cassiopeia, Andromeda and Triangulum.*

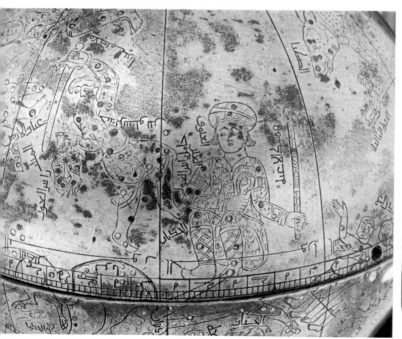

141 *Perseus and Auriga.*

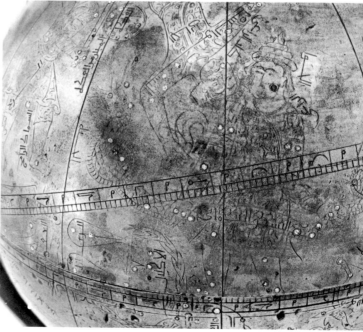

142 *Ophiuchus and Serpens.*

2 Ursa Major (*al-dubb al-akbar*), the Greater Bear (**136**). In this spirited drawing of a bear, the fur is rendered naturalistically by tiny hatched lines.

3 Draco (*al-tinnīn*), the Dragon (**135**), which curls about the northern pole of the ecliptic is represented as a snake with open jaws and forked tongue.

4 Cepheus (*qīfā'ūs*) (**135**). This, Cetus and Centaur (see **153** and **157** below) are the only constellations for which the Muslims retained the Greek names. The kneeling youth is beardless with hair parted in the middle under a pointed hat. His tunic, reaching to just above the knees, is decorated with a *ṭirāz* band below each shoulder and held in at the waist by a belt with a cable design. The scrolling lines on this garment represent not a textile pattern but folds—a stylized rendering which occurs in all the clothing worn by the human figures on the globe.

5 Boötes (*al-'awwā'*) (**137**). The Arabs called this constellation 'the Crier', evidently mistranslating the Greek 'Ploughman' by associating it with the Greek βοάτης, 'crying'. On the globe he stands with legs apart and with right hand raised, the left arm close to the body and holding a stick. Beneath a tunic with revers at the neck, he wears breeches reaching below the knees. His head with hair parted in the middle, is bare.

6 Corona Borealis (*al-fakkah*), the Northern Crown (**137**) is to the right of the Crier and is shown as a simple circlet.

7 Hercules (*al-jāthī*), the Kneeler (**138**). The Arabs knew this constellation under its alternative Greek name ἐν γονάσιν. The kneeling figure with right arm extended down and left arm held aloft wielding a sickle is beardless and bare-headed. His tunic, tight fitting around the thighs like breeches, is partially open at the front to reveal an undershirt.

8 Lyra (*al-shalyāq*), the Lyre (**138**), would appear to be represented as a footed bowl. The reading of the word *al-shalyāq* is disputed. Some of the *al-Ṣūfī* manuscripts, including the Bodleian copy, have *al-silyāq*. The meaning of both words is obscure. The representation is probably intended for a lyre which is rendered in a highly stylized manner in the *al-Ṣūfī* manuscripts. In support of this, certain of the latter use the alternative description *al-lūrā*, an obvious borrowing from the Greek.[17]

9 Cygnus (*al-dajajah*), the Chicken (**139**). The flying bird is seen from below. The legs are bent forwards in order to accommodate the stars at the tips of the claws.

10 Cassiopeia (*dhāt al-kursī*), the Enthroned Woman (**140**). The woman with hair arranged in tresses falling on her shoulders, wears a crown. The right forearm is

raised, the left hand grasps one of the upright supports of the throne. These upright supports are united by a carved back and decorated with trilobed finials and clawed feet.

11　Perseus (*ḥāmil ra's al-ghūl*), the Bearer of the Monster's Head (**141**). Again, the awkward posture of the bearded figure is determined by the star positions. The monster head which the figure grasps by its hair appears to be that of an animal with projecting fangs. In the Bodleian version of *al-Ṣūfī*, however, the monster's head is human and bearded.[18]

12　Auriga (*mumsik al-a'innah*), He who Holds the Reins (**141**). The youthful figure is squatting on his haunches, holding the rein in his right hand and a whip in his left. Unusual features are the shoes and the cross-gartered legs.

13　Ophiuchus and Serpens (*al-ḥawwā* and *al-ḥayyah*), the Serpent Charmer and the Serpent (**142**). The two constellations are combined. The curious conical headdress of the Serpent Charmer seems to consist of three layers of cloth surmounted by a topknot. He grasps the writhing form of the Serpent in his two hands.

14　Sagitta (*al-sahm*), the Arrow (**143**), lies below the Eagle.

15　Aquila (*al-nasr al-ṭā'ir*), the Flying Eagle (**143**), is represented standing with wings outstretched.

16　Delphinus (*al-dulfīn*), the Dolphin (**143**), appears to the left of the Eagle.

17　Equuleus (*qit'at al-faras*), the Part of the Horse (**143**), lies above the Dolphin and consists of the head and neck of a horse.

18　Pegasus (*al-faras al-a'aẓam*), the Greater Horse (**144**), is beautifully rendered as the protome of a winged horse.

19　Andromeda (*al-mar'at al-musalsala*), the Woman Enchained (**140, 144**), stands to the left of, and below, Pegasus. Bare-headed, her tresses fall over her shoulders. She wears a skirt but is naked above the waist. In some versions the two outstretched arms are joined by a chain which is more often omitted as on the globe.[19]

20　Triangulum (*al-muthallath*), the Triangle (**140**).

The Signs of the Zodiac

The names of the constellations in the Zodiac are inscribed immediately above the ecliptic.

21　Aries (*al-ḥamal*), the Ram (**145**), is shown in the act of running with head turned backwards.

143 *Sagitta, Aquila, Delphinus and Equuleus.*

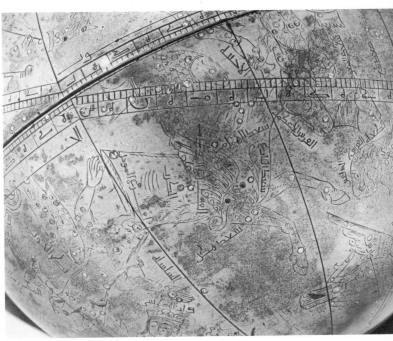

144 *Pegasus, Andromeda and Pisces.*

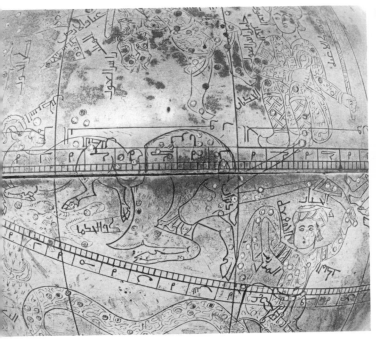

145 *Aries and Taurus.*

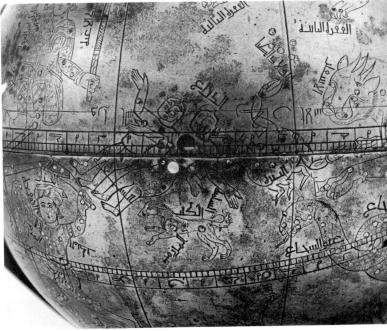

146 *Gemini, Cancer and Canis Minor.*

147 *Leo.*

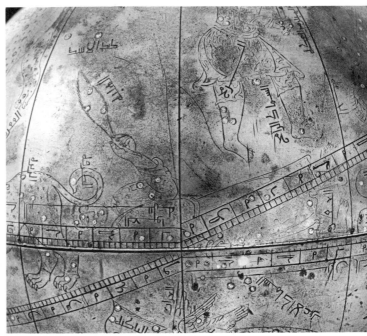

148 *Virgo.*

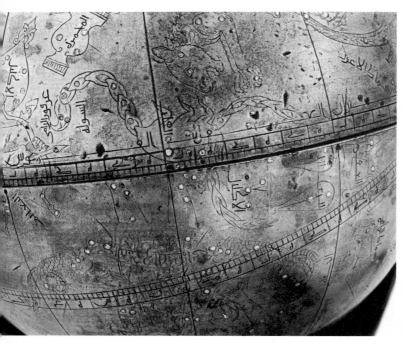

149 *Libra and Scorpio.*

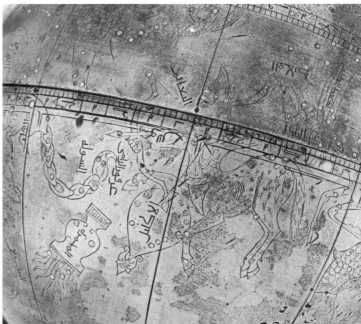

150 *Sagittarius, Ara and Corona Australis.*

22 Taurus (*al-thawr*), the Bull (**145**). The protome of the Bull is shown charging with lowered head and straight horns.

23 Gemini (*al-jawzā'*), the Twins (**146**), are shown as youths naked to the waist and wearing knee-length breeches. Both have outstretched arms, one arm crossing the chest of the other.

24 Cancer (*al-saraṭān*), the Crab (**146**), can be seen to the right of the Twin and consists of carapace, six legs and articulated mandibles.

25 Leo (*al-asad*) the Lion (**147**) advances majestically to the left, its tail curled and three curious spikes of tufted hair growing from the top of its head.

26 Virgo (*al-sunbulah*), the Ear (the Virgin), (**148**), is shown as an excessively tall woman clothed in a garment reaching nearly to the ankles. She grasps in her left hand a tuft of hair. Her right arm hangs down, the hand being only partially visible owing to the junction of the two hemispheres.

27 Libra (*al-mīzān*), the Balance (**149**), is represented by two pans suspended from a horizontal beam.

28 Scorpio (*al-ʿaqrab*), the Scorpion (**149**), to the left of the Balance, has six legs, long articulated tail and mandibles.

29 Sagittarius (*al-qaws*), the Archer (**150**), is represented as a centaur according to classical iconography. His head, rendered in profile is crowned with a Phrygian type of head-dress from the back of which are attached streamers fluttering in the wind. He grasps a double bow in his right hand, drawing back the bow string and shaft with his left hand.

30 Capricornus (*al-jady*), the Kid (**151**), is represented as the forepart of a goat with long slightly curving horns and the hind part in the form of a fish's tail; and is based on the classical prototype.

31 Aquarius (*al-dalw*), the Bucket (**152**), appears in the form of a standing woman bare-headed with long hair and wearing an ankle-length garment. Her right arm is extended; her left grasps a narrow vase from which issues an undulating stream of water.

32 Pisces (*al-ḥūt*), the Fish (**144**), the one immediately to the left of Andromeda, the other between the mane and wing of Pegasus.

The Southern Hemisphere

33 Cetus (*al-qīṭus*), the Whale (**153**). This fantastic creature is composed of the fore-part of an animal and the hindpart of a fish. The head on an elongated neck seems to be that of a barking dog; the feet, those of a feline creature. A corded collar is wound around the neck.

34 Orion (*al-jabbār*), the Giant (**154**), is shown as a turbaned youth in the act of running. He wields in his left hand a club while the sleeve of the raised right arm is extended well beyond the hand in order to accommodate the nine stars.

35 Eridanus (*al-nahr*), the River (**153**), is rendered in the form of a curling snake, the water being indicated by small hooks attached to an undulating line.

36 Lepus (*al-arnab*), the Hare (**154**), runs with ears erect below Orion.

37 Canis Major (*al-kalb al-akbar*), the Greater Dog (**154**), can be seen to the right of the Hare.

38 Canis (*al-kalb*), the Dog (**154**), appears above the equator and to the right of Orion.

39 Argo (*al-safīnah*), the Ship (**155**), is a schematized view of a ship in full sail with a running wind. The patterning on the square sail may be intended to indicate the texture of the medieval sail which was woven from the leaves of the coconut tree or the palm tree. The two side rudders in the form of oars were the common means of steering but are here shown mistakenly at the bows instead of the stern.[20]

40 Hydra (*al-Shujāʿ*) the Serpent (**156**). The skin of the snake is treated in the manner as in Draco.

41 Crater (*al-bāṭiyah*), the Bowl (**156**).

42 Corvus (*al-ghurāb*), the Crow (**156**) is perched on the Serpent behind Crater. The partially extended wings were necessitated by the star positions of the constellations. According to *al-Ṣūfī*, the star in the beak, the star on the head and the star on the right wing of the bird form a more or less straight line.[21]

43 Centaurus (*qantūrīs*), the Centaur (**157**). The Greek ancestry of the figure is striking if confronted with the centaur of the Farnese Globe.[22] There is a close resemblance in the movement of the figure. The *thyrsos* held in the right hand of the Greek original has been replaced by three flowers. Nor does the centaur of the Farnese Globe grasp the neighbouring constellation Lupus by its hind leg—a feature belonging to the Sassanian art of Persia.

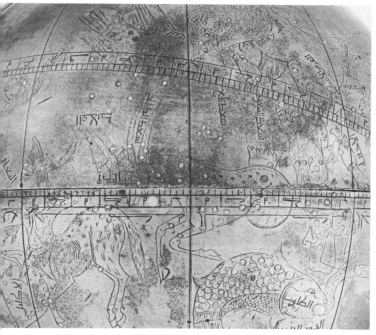

151 *Capricornus and Piscis Australis.*

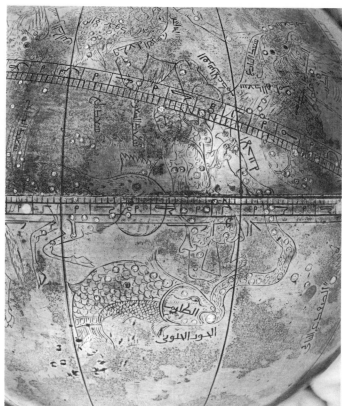

152 *Aquarius.*

154 *Orion, Lepus and Canis Major and Canis Minor.*

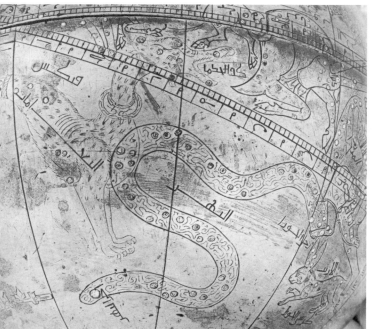

153 *Cetus and Eridanus.*

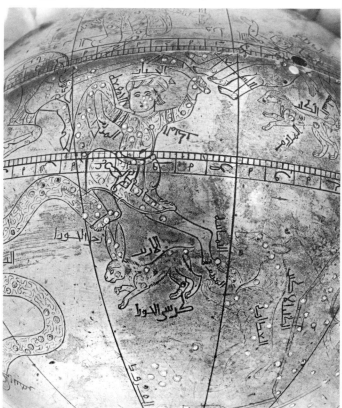

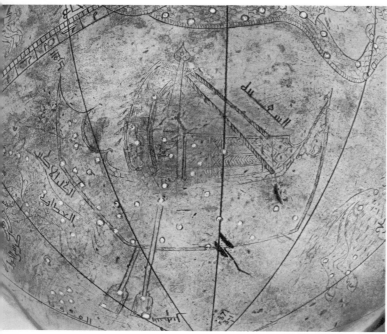

155 *Argo Navis.*

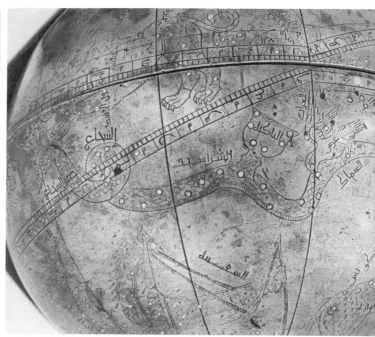

156 *Hydra, Crater and Corvus.*

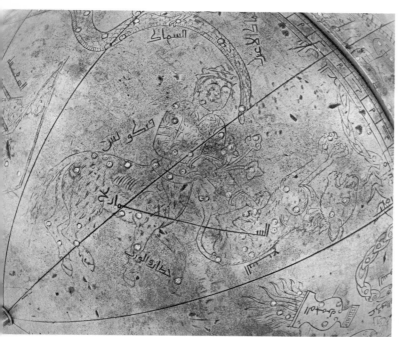

157 *Centaurus, Lupus and Ara.*

158 *Signature of maker and date, inlaid in silver.*

44 Lupus (*al-sab'*), the Wild Beast (**157**).

45 Ara (*al-mijmarah*), the Censer (**157**), is represented as a vase from which issues flames.

46 Corona Australis (*al-iklīl*), the (Southern) Crown (**150**), lies between the forelegs of Sagittarius. The intention of this curious figure is not clear; but it is the usual form of the Southern Crown in the *al-Sūfī* manuscripts.[23]

47 Piscis Australis (*al-ḥawt al-janūbī*), the Southern Fish (**152**), lies below Aquarius.

II

Save for a few details, the Islamic iconography of the constellations is remarkably uniform. In so far as it diverges from the classical, their representation results from a difference in artistic language. Naturalism was the main preoccupation of the artists of the classical tradition; the human body, whether naked or draped, formed the centre of their vision. The human figures in the constellations are shown often with their backs to the viewer, their faces turned away or in profile in order to indicate movement. In the *al-Sūfī* manuscripts, the naked form is generally avoided; figures are so arranged that the upper part of the body is turned to the viewer and the head is rendered frontally or in three-quarters. The exceptions are Centaurus, Sagittarius and Perseus who are sometimes represented in profile.[24] There are, too, divergences such as the substitution of Medusa's head by that of a monster in Perseus;[25] of the lion skin by an elongated sleeve in Orion;[26] of the club by a sickle in Hercules.[27] Such changes were due to a failure to understand the mythology of the original.

Nevertheless, there are certain differences in the iconography of the Malcolm celestial globe and the *al-Sūfī* manuscripts which are significant enough to suggest that the *Book of the Fixed Stars* was not the sole source of the images on the globe. Virgo in the Bodleian *al-Sūfī* manuscript stands with the arms hanging down close to her side, the left elbow close to the body and the forearm and hand pointing down and slightly to her left.[28] The posture of Virgo on the Malcolm globe (**148**) is similar except that her left forearm is raised and her left hand grasps a switch of horse hair. That this is a switch of hair is indicated by the inscription to the right which reads *al-hulbah*. Now according to al-Sūfī, the group of three stars above *al-ṣarfah*, the brilliant star at the tail of Leo, is called *al-ḍafīrah* and by the Arabs *al-hulbah*.[29] In a manuscript of the *Book of the Fixed Stars* in the Public Library, Leningrad, copied in 1015 H (AD 1606) in Nayin in central Persia, there is a description written alongside this group of three stars which reads '*al-hulbah* which Ptolemy calls *al-ḍafīrah* and which is outside the figure of Leo'.[30] *Al-ḍafīrah* ('tress') is the constellation Coma Berenices, the Hair of Berenice, which Ptolemy describes as an ivy leaf.[31] In a manuscript of Ptolemy in the Vatican Library made at the beginning of the ninth century, this ivy leaf is represented just above the tail of Leo.[32] It also appears in the vault at Quṣayr 'Amrā where it seems to be held by Virgo.[33]

The constellation Aquarius is represented in the *al-Ṣūfī* manuscripts as a male figure;[34] but on the globe as a female figure (**152**). The Aquarius of the Farnese Globe is in the form of a naked woman with her back to the viewer.[35] At Quṣayr 'Amrā and in the Vatican manuscript of Ptolemy, the constellation is a man as it is in western manuscripts until Dürer reintroduced the Farnese model in his celestial map of 1515.[36]

Muḥammad ibn Hilāl, the maker of the Malcolm celestial globe, is not recorded in literature. That a professional astronomer should have made the globe is no cause for surprise since Muslim astronomers were accustomed to make their own instruments.[37] We may infer from the toponym al-mawṣilī that he was born in Mosul; and although we do not know where he pursued his studies in astronomy, it is very probable that he acquired his skill in metalwork in his native city which, under the rule of Badr al-Dīn Lu'lu' (1218–59), became famous as a centre for the production of inlaid brass vessels.[38] The industry was still flourishing in 1250 but probably declined after the city was sacked by the Mongol Hulāgū in 1262. Metalworkers, originally of Mosul, are known to have carried on their craft as far from their native city as Damascus and Cairo.[39] Besides Muḥammad ibn Hilāl, two other Mosul metalworkers are recorded as having produced astronomical instruments: in 1241/2 Muḥammad ibn Khutlukh made the beautiful geomantic instrument, now in the British Museum,[40] and in 1318/19 'Abd al-Raḥmān ibn Burhān made a celestial globe, at one time in the Chadenat Collection.[41]

There are two celestial globes close in date to the Malcolm celestial globe. The first is a globe in the Musée du Louvre made in 1084 H (AD 1285/6) by the astrolabist Muḥammad ibn Maḥmūd ibn 'Alī who states that he based the constellation figures and the star positions on 'Abd al-Raḥmān al-Ṣūfī's *Book of the Fixed Stars*.[42] The second globe, in the Mathematisch-Physikalischer Salon, Dresden, was made by Muḥammad ibn Mu'ayyad al-Dīn al-'Urḍī, probably between 1278 and 1310.[43] On both these globes the figure of Virgo is winged but the left arm is in the same position as on the Malcolm globe, the hand grasping the switch of hair, which is also inscribed *al-hulbah*.[44] Other points of similarity between the Dresden and Malcolm globes are the hair style in which the hair parted in the middle falls down straight to the ears, the curious headgear of Ophiuchus already noted (**142**)[45] and the squatting posture of

Auriga (**141**).[46] In the Dresden globe, the legs of Auriga are cross-gartered in precisely the same manner as on the Malcolm globe.

The maker of the Dresden globe was the son of Mu'ayyad al-Dīn al-'Urḍi, one of the distinguished group of astronomers brought together by Naṣīr al-Dīn al-Ṭūsī. He played a prominent part in the creation of Hulāgū's astronomical observatory at Marāgha, the Ilkhanid capital in Azerbaijan; and made or designed many of the instruments.[47] The observatory was begun in 1257 and completed probably by 1262. It continued in use until about 1316. Mu'ayyad al-Dīn has left us a description of the instruments he made.[48] In this there is no mention of celestial globes. But since the Marāgha observatory was an institution for teaching as well as for observation, it is quite possible that the son made the globe for use in the observatory. It is against this background of intense activity in astronomical studies that we have to consider the Malcolm globe and the globe in the Musée du Louvre. It may be that one result of this activity was a renewed attempt to return to the classical sources of the constellation figures.

Whether or not he worked at Marāgha, there can be no doubt of Muḥammad ibn Hilal's artistic affiliation. His style is in direct succession to that of the miniaturists who were working at Mosul in the reign of Badr al-Dīn Lu'lu'. It is naturally in the rendering of human figures that his artistic origins are most apparent. His facial type, when beardless, is round, the eyes not over-narrow beneath delicately arched eyebrows, and the mouth small; it is similar to the facial type found in a manuscript of the *Book of Antidotes* (*Kitāb al-Diryāq*) executed probably in Mosul about 1250.[49] His other type of face with heavy jowl and small pointed chin (**138**) is, however, more characteristic of the *al-Ṣūfī* figures.[50] The hair style in which the hair, parted in the middle, falls behind the ears is found not in the miniatures but in the silver inlaid metalwork of Mosul.[51]

Most characteristic of the Mosul style is his treatment of costume, more particularly his rendering of folds by convoluted tubes which assume a decorative effect far removed from the naturalism of classical drapery. This feature was already defined by the Mosul artists who contributed the frontispieces to the six surviving volumes of a twenty-volume set of the *Book of Songs* (*Kitāb al-Aghānī*) by Abu'l-Faraj al-Isfahāni completed in 1219.[52]

His drawing owes little or nothing to the art of eastern Asia which was to make such a powerful impact on Persia from the closing years of the thirteenth century. Indeed, the head-dress worn by Ophiuchus is the only feature which may possibly be traced to a Far Eastern if not to a Central Asian source (**142**).

Muḥammad ibn Hilal's artistic achievement is incontestable. He delineated the constellation figures with an assurance and an unerring eye and hand that makes his incomparably the finest of the surviving Islamic celestial globes. His status as astronomer is harder to assess. His is the earliest of the three globes discussed above but all the related material—globes and astronomical literature—needs to be further studied before we can determine what part he played in restoring the link with Greek tradition.

NOTES

1 F. Saxl, 'The Zodiac of Qusayr 'Amra', in K. A. C. Creswell, *Early Muslim Architecture*, ii, London 1932, pp. 338–50.

2 M. Destombes, 'Note sur le catalogue d'étoiles du Calife Al-Mamoun', *Actes du VIIIe Congrès International d'Histoire des Sciences*, 1956, pp. 309–12.

3 M. Destombes, 'Un globe céleste arabe du XIIe siècle', *Comptes rendus des séances, Académie des inscriptions et belles lettres*, 1958, p. 308.

4 H. C. F. C. Schjellerup, *Description des étoiles fixes composée au milieu du dixième siècle de notre ère par l'astronome persan Abd-al-Rahman al-Sûfî*, St Petersburg 1874.

5 This declaration is preserved by al-Biruni (see S. M. Stern, 'Abd al-Raḥmān b. 'Umar al-Sufî', *Encyclopaedia of Islam* (new edition), i, Leiden–London 1960, p. 86 f.

6 E. Wellesz, 'An early al-Sûfî manuscript in the Bodleian Library in Oxford, a study in Islamic constellation images', *Ars Orientalis*, iii, 1959, pp. 1–26.

7 A. Hauber, 'Zur Verbreitung des Astronomen Sufi', *Der Islam*, viii, 1918, p. 48 ff; J. Upton, '"A manuscript of the book of fixed stars", by Abd al-Raḥmān Al Ṣûfî', *Metropolitan Museum Studies*, iv, 1933, pp. 179–97; K. Holter, 'Die islamischen Miniaturhandschriften vor 1350', *Zentralblatt für Bibliothekswesen*, liv, 1937, pp. 4–5; H. Buchtal, R. Ettinghausen and O. Kurz, 'Supplementary notes to K. Holter's checklist of Islamic illuminated manuscripts before 1350', *Ars Islamica*, vii, 1940, p. 148; C. Brockelmann, *Geschichte der Arabischen Literatur*, Suppl. i, p. 398.

8 E. Panofsky and F. Saxl, 'Classical mythology in mediaeval art', *Metropolitan Museum Studies*, iv, 1933, pp. 228–80.

9 E. L. Stevenson, *Terrestrial and celestial globes, their history and construction*, i, New Haven, 1921, pp. 26–34; M. Destombes, 'Globes célestes et catalogues d'étoiles orientaux du Moyen-Age', *Actes du VIIIe Congrès International d'Histoire des Sciences*, 1956, pp. 313–24; M. Destombes, n. 9 above, pp. 308–12.

10 Globe dated 684 (1284–5 AD), Musée du Louvre; globe dated 764 (1362–3 AD), Museum of the History of Science, Oxford; globe, dated 834 (1430–1), British Museum (see Destombes, 'Globes célestes . . .', pp. 7–9, nos. 5, 9 and 10): and globe, dated 785 (AD 1383–4), Astronomical Observatory, Istanbul (see M. Destombes, 'Les chiffres coufiques des instruments astronomique arabes', *Physis, Rivista di Storia della Scienza*, ii, 1960, p. 206).

11 For bibliography see L. A. Meyer, *Islamic Astrolabists and their Works*, Geneva, 1956, p. 68, with the following additions: Destombes, 'Globes célestes', p. 7; Wellesz, 'An early al-Ṣûfî manuscript . . .', p. 25; Destombes, 'Un globe céleste arabe . . .' p. 306 f; U. Scerrato, *Arte Islamica a Napoli, Opere delle Raccolte Pubbliche Napoletane, Istituto Universitario Orientale di Napoli*, Naples 1967, p. 33.

12 This information, for which I am indebted to Mr John Hansman, is recorded in the Proceedings of the Anniversary Meeting of the Royal Asiatic Society, 7 June 1830. Malcolm most likely received the globe from the leader of the Bohora community in Bombay, not, I think, when he was Governor (1827–30) but during an earlier stay from 1810 to 1812 during which he was engaged in writing his *History of Persia* (London 1815).

13 B. Dorn, 'Description of the Celestial Globe belonging to Major-General Sir John

Malcolm, GCB, KLS, deposited in the Museum of the Royal Asiatic Society of Great Britain and Ireland', *Transactions of the Royal Asiatic Society*, ii, 1830, pp. 371–92.

14 I have followed Dorn in listing forty-seven constellations. He combines Ophiuchus and Serpens under number 13. Al-Ṣūfī, however, lists them as two separate constellations.

15 Destombes, 'Les chiffres coufiques ...', p. 200.

16 Such as on the celestial globe in the Musée du Louvre; see *Arts de l'Islam des origines à 1700 dans les collections publiques françaises* (catalogue of exhibition held in the Orangerie des Tuileries, Paris 1971), p. 142, no. 190 and plate on p. 190.

17 Schjellerup, p. 75.

18 Wellesz, 'An early al-Ṣūfī manuscript ...', fig. 7.

19 The enchained arms are represented on the celestial globe in the Musée du Louvre (S. Assemani, *Globus coelestis cufico-arabicus Veliterni Musei Borgiani*, Padua 1790, Tab. II).

20 G. F. Hourani, *Arab seafaring in the Indian Ocean in ancient and early medieval times*, Princeton Oriental Studies, xiii, pp. 98 and 100.

21 Schjellerup, p. 240.

22 Panofsky and Saxl, p. 233, fig. 6.

23 Schjellerup, pl. IV, fig. 46.

24 Wellesz, figs. 7, 14, 17, 56, 65, and 66.

25 Schjellerup, pl. I, fig. 11.

26 Wellesz, figs. 16 and 45.

27 Wellesz, figs. 5 and 46.

28 Wellesz, fig. 13.

29 Schjellerup, p. 50.

30 Schjellerup, pl. II, fig. 26.

31 Saxl, 'The Zodiac of Quṣayr 'Amra', p. 292.

32 Saxl, 'Zodiac', p. 293, fig. 343 left.

33 Saxl, 'Zodiac', p. 293, fig. 343 right.

34 Wellesz, fig. 15; Schjellerup, pl. III, fig. 32, pl. VII, fig. 32.

35 Saxl, 'Zodiac', p. 295, fig. 374.

36 Saxl, 'Zodiac', p. 295, fig. 374; Panofsky and Saxl, 'Classical Mythology', p. 245, fig. 20.

37 Mayer, *Islamic Astrolabists*, p. 13 f.

38 D. S. Rice, 'The Brasses of Badr al-Dīn Lu'lu'', *Bulletin of the School of Oriental and African Studies*, xiii, 1950, pp. 628–34. For Badr al-Dīn Lu'lu' see M. Sobernheim in *Encyclopaedia of Islam*. From 1218 to 1233 he ruled as Atābek in the name of three Zengid princes; and from 1233 until his death, as an independent prince.

39 D. S. Rice, 'Inlaid brasses from the workshops of Ahmad al-Dhakī al-Mawṣili', *Ars Orientalis*, ii, 1957, p. 326.

40 D. Barrett, *Islamic Metalwork in the British Museum*, London 1949, pl. 16 and 17.

41 Mayer, *Islamic Astrolabists*, p. 31.

42 Mayer, p. 72.

43 Mayer, p. 72 f; Destombes, 'Globes célestes', p. 8.

44 *Arts de l'Islam des origines à 1700*, fig. 190; A. U. Pope (ed.), *Survey of Persian Art*, London 1939, vi, pl. 1403.

45 A. Drechsler, *Der arabische Himmels-Globus angefertigt 1279 zu Maragha von Muhammed bin Muwajid Elardh zugehörig dem Königl. mathematisch-physikalischen Salon zu Dresden*, Dresden 1873, pl. III. Centaurus, who is represented on the Dresden globe as a woman, also wears the same head-dress, cf. *Survey of Persian Art*, pl. 1403.

46 Drechsler, pl. I. *Survey of Persian Art*, pl. 1403.

47 A. Sayili, *The Observatory in Islam and its place in the General History of the Observatory*, Publications of the Turkish Historical Society Series, vii, no. 38, Ankara 1960, pp. 189–223.

48 H. J. Seemann, 'Die Instrumente der Sternwarte zu Marāgha', *Sitzungsberichte der Phys.-Med. Sozietät*, lx, Erlangen, 1928.

49 K. Holter, 'Die Galen-Handschrift und die Makamen des Harīrī der Wiener Nationalbibliothek', *Jahrbuch der Kunsthistorischen Sammlungen in Wien*, xi, 1937, pp. 1–15; R. Ettinghausen, *Arab Painting*, Geneva 1962, p. 91.

50 Wellesz, figs. 4, 5 and 48.

51 Rice, 'Inlaid Brasses', pp. 301–11, fig. 33a, c, pl. 8a, d, e.

52 Ettinghausen, *Arab Painting*, pp. 61–5.

The writer wishes to thank Mrs Emilie Savage Smith for her advice and information.

A Bacchic sarcophagus in the Renaissance

RUTH OLITSKY RUBINSTEIN

Warburg Institute, University of London

The Bacchic sarcophagus in the British Museum came into the collections with the Townley sculptures in 1805.[1] It remained almost continuously on view until the Second World War when it was put into the storerooms, where it is now. The plan to open the storerooms so that visitors to the Museum can see the Roman sculptures is now in progress; and, there, several other important works which inspired Renaissance artists will again be revealed.[2]

The history of the sarcophagus is obscure until the fifteenth century when it was first drawn by Renaissance artists, possibly before the end of Martin V's pontificate (1417–31). From then until the late sixteenth century, it was visible at Santa Maria Maggiore in Rome, where it was much admired. No other sarcophagus relief, and there were many in Rome at this time, was so often drawn to judge from the number of representations of it noted so far.[3] It was probably restored when Sixtus V (1585–90) removed it from Santa Maria Maggiore to his new Villa Montalto nearby. The restorations are first reflected in the engravings by François Perrier (1645). From the Villa Montalto the sarcophagus was bought in 1786 by Thomas Jenkins, one of Charles Townley's agents.

On the following pages I shall first describe the sarcophagus as it is now and as it was, unrestored, in the Renaissance; then, as an introduction to the Catalogue, I shall consider the influence of the sarcophagus on the visual arts in the Quattrocento and in the Cinquecento, and its restoration reflected in seventeenth-century engravings. This will be followed by an illustrated catalogue of the drawings of the sarcophagus arranged chronologically in so far as uncertainty of attributions and other information allows. The drawings will be referred to in the text by catalogue number.

159 The Triumphal Procession of Bacchus and Ariadne, *Roman sarcophagus front, second century A.D. London, British Museum 2298.*

160 *The Triumphal Chariot of Bacchus and Ariadne, detail of front. London, British Museum 2298.*

I. THE SARCOPHAGUS

The front (159)

The sarcophagus relief of the front gives the impression of excessive length in relation to its diminutive height. Within the frame, the relief is 1 ft. 4 ins. (41 cms.) high and 7 ft. ½ in. (2.14 m.) long. It contains twenty-five figures of which six have either been replaced or added. These new figures, probably of the late sixteenth century, from left to right, are: the body of the cupid on the centaur's back, the dancing satyr in the middle looking over his shoulder at Silenus, and the standing child. The elephant's forequarters and the two satyrs on the extreme right, except for the *pedum* hung with a tympanum in the background, have been added, at a point where the sarcophagus, as it was known in the Renaissance, must have been broken off, since none of the drawings show figures to the right of the satyr with a child on his shoulders. The restorations of the reliefs, perceptible in the detailed photographs, are noted by Matz in his description of the sarcophagus. The additions of noses, arms, legs, bunches of grapes, and entirely new figures, are in a marble lighter in colour, slightly pinkish, and smoother than the weathered greyish marble of the original; the contrast has been emphasized by a recent cleaning.

The figures of the front can be divided into four groups. The figure types, often represented in antique art, have been classified, discussed, and illustrated by Matz.[4]

The Triumphal Chariot of Bacchus and Ariadne (160)

The chariot is drawn by two centaurs playing triumphal music on the lyre and the double pipes, each wearing a crescent. They are guided by Cupid, who, as the god of love, also presides over the bridal couple. Bacchus lounges with voluptuous ease on the chariot under a small parasol, drowsy with wine and love. Ariadne bends over him, touching the garland that falls diagonally across his torso, while he languidly pours wine into the bowl of the following satyr. The goat, sacred to Bacchus, is represented carved on the side of the chariot, hauled by the horn by a satyr. Another satyr bounds on the obliquely-represented front of the chariot. A woman carrying the *liknon* filled with fruit advances in the background; the fringed cover of the *liknon* has blown back. Most of the artists of the Renaissance have wrongly interpreted this flying drapery as a banner held by Cupid.

The Quartet of Dancers (161)

Shaggy Pan, dancing in an exuberant twist has kicked off the lid of the *cista mystica*, thus liberating the uncoiling sacred snake. His hand has been restored holding Pan's pipes; sometimes this type of dancing Pan holds grapes. The ecstatic male satyr on

161 *The Quartet of Dancers : Pan, ecstatic satyr with a wineskin, maenad in a chiton, new satyr. Detail from front. London, British Museum 2298.*

tiptoe facing front is flourishing, with his left hand, a large wineskin. The maenad next to him is also facing us in her dance, but only for a moment as she whirls around, her soft chiton swinging out only to curve under in agitated folds at the hem. Her incorrectly restored hand holds grapes, the other is broken, but she belongs to a well-known type of maenad with cymbals. In the reversed engraving of 1549 by Battista Franco (**173**) she strikes a tambourine, but both hands were missing in the Renaissance (**162**).

The fourth dancing figure, the satyr balancing curiously back towards Silenus is completely new.[5] That another figure had once been broken off here is apparent from the deep chipping under the shoulder of the maenad in the background, invisible in the photograph. What was there before? A satyr appears twice on the earliest of the Quattrocento drawings of the two sarcophagus ends (Cat. 1–2; **182** and **183**). In both drawings he is seen from the back and twists around so that his head and upper

162 *Anonymous Italian, mid-sixteenth century, front and two ends of British Museum 2298.*
Munich, Staatliche Graphische Sammlung 2536.

torso turns towards the left, his right leg crosses behind his left leg, and his hands are held up in front of his face to the left as he blows the double pipes. The assumption that this was the figure in the centre of the front is supported by the appearance of just such a figure in the middle of the frieze of the *Camino* of Iole in the Palazzo Ducale in Urbino, which is wholly inspired by this sarcophagus (**169** and p. 117). Furthermore, if this satyr and the new figures are drawn and juxtaposed, their bodies and legs roughly fit the same area and only the raised arms are at variance. The mid-sixteenth-century drawing in Munich (Cat. 23; **162**) shows a broken-off hand holding a pipe, and the surface of the relief's background reveals reworking to the left of the raised arm of the new satyr. The drawing in Erlangen by a South German artist of the mid-sixteenth century does not seem to be connected with this figure, as thought

163 *Silenus's Group. Detail of front. British Museum 2298.*

by Matz, but with an unknown prototype shared by the lilting bronze satyr playing the pipes attributed to Camelio (see Cat. 28; **208**).

Silenus's Group (**163**)

The maenad in profile running in the background visually connects with, but is otherwise independent of, the dancing quartet which she leaves behind and Silenus's group which she is about to overtake beyond the ass. Only the Munich drawing (**162**) and Naldini (**206**) show her; Aspertini (**192**) draws her as an old man. Her left arm is curved up beyond her head, and her right arm is stretched out behind, her right hand holding the *thyrsos* (Cat. 13; **194**).

Next comes the much repeated motif of Silenus, too relaxed by the wine to sit upright on the ass which stands waiting, head down, ears depressed and back.[6] A satyr with one foot on a rock does his best to support Silenus's sagging weight, while a

164 *The Nude Maenad's Group with ithyphallic satyr, draped woman, and satyr with a child on his shoulders. Detail of front. British Museum 2298.*

nimble satyr with a *pedum* in the background impatiently urges the stalled procession forward.

The Nude Maenad's Group (164)

The whole procession comes about-face towards the dance of the nude maenad facing us in a state of ecstasy, holding a tympanum above her head. Her long veil flies upward with the movement, twines round her arm, billows out to the right, catches her knee, and flutters down against the advancing foot of an ithyphallic satyr who dances towards her from the right, his right arm upraised, the other caught up in drapery behind his back.

The hideous child holding grapes is new, and that nothing was there in the Renaissance is clear from Franco's engraving (**173**) and Naldini's drawing (**206**) which show the figure of a draped priestly female in her entirety. Who is she, so quietly regarding the ithyphallic satyr to the left? The sinuously beautiful satyr,

165 *Left end: Drunken Pan carried by two cupids and a satyr. British Museum 2298 B.*

166 *Right end: Two satyrs punishing Pan. British Museum 2298 C.*

holding on his shoulders, with one hand, an infant who reaches towards the partly original grapes in his other hand, is again a traditional motif. In the background, ranging behind his legs are the hindquarters of a panther resuming the original direction towards the right recorded only in Naldini's drawing (Cat. 26; **206**). An irregular vertical break of the sarcophagus occurred at this point, which left the bottom of the panther's garland and the *pedum* and tympanum above. The elephant's head and two satyrs to the right are new.

The ends
The two ends of the sarcophagus both show Pan, a fertility god, in contrasting circumstances. The reliefs are Hellenistic in inspiration, and probably are intended to have some symbolic relationship with the triumphant *thiasos* of Bacchus and Ariadne on the front. The fascination of the Renaissance artists for these sensitively carved reliefs of nude figures in poses of relaxation or stress is reflected by the number of drawings after them. The measurements of each end (within the relief field) are 1 ft. 4. ins (41 cms.) high by 2 ft. ½ in. (62 cms.) long.

The left end (**165**). The relief is continuous with the front of the sarcophagus, as the original hoof of Pan, now broken off, touched the shoulder of the tipsy satyr terminating the sarcophagus front, and the trained vine or tree framing the left side and the top extends almost to the terminal satyr's head as reflected in the Munich drawing and by Naldini (Cat. 24; **162** and **204**).

The drunken voluptuous Pan is carried by two cupids who bear his entire weight, helped by a satyr wearing the *nebris* and supporting Pan's length from the background, his legs in the lunging pose. Together they carry Pan towards the procession on the front. Pan is melting into a blissful somnolence induced by the sacred wine. The muscles of his upper right arm have dissolved to a relaxed hollow; his hands are already heavy. His supporters seem to sympathize with his voluptuous state, and the scene imparts more a feeling of affection than of mockery.

The right end (**166**) strikes another note. Pent-up energy is revealed in every muscle and stance. Here Pan is astride the back of a bearded satyr who grasps Pan's wrists before him and bends with a dedicated expression over an altar piled with fruit suggesting fecundity, including pomegranates, surmounted by the pine cone, and hung with a garland. The altar stands under a tree or trained vine similar to the one on the other end, but not extended to frame all of the top. A younger satyr, taut and alert behind Pan, turned to the left in the lunging position, looks back towards Pan and pulls up his tail with the intention of beating him with a scourge he held in his other hand, which has broken off. The drawings show different interpretations of the missing weapon: club, reeds, or possibly goatskin thongs, which suggest the absence of the satyr's hand in the later Renaissance, confirmed by the Munich drawing (**162**). Whether the end reliefs represent purification through wine and flagellation, or the cycle of the seasons symbolized in Lupercalian rites in which Pan, fig trees, and flagellations played a part, or various forms of ecstasy, is not known.[7]

These possibilities, unsupported here, but connected with death and the afterlife appropriate to a sarcophagus, bring us to a consideration of the symbolism of the scene on the front, the triumphal procession of Bacchus and Ariadne.

THE MYTH

The story of Bacchus and Ariadne can be pieced together from a number of contradictory classical sources. The sarcophagus relief presupposes the story that Bacchus, the wine god, on his travels with the half-divine, half-human companions of his childhood, nymphs, satyrs, Pan, and Silenus, had discovered Ariadne on the island of Naxos, abandoned by Theseus. There Bacchus rescued her and made her his immortal bride. Many Roman sarcophagi celebrate Bacchus's discovery of Ariadne, asleep on Naxos, her elbow over her head, while a satyr lifts her drapery.[8] This sarcophagus instead shows the subsequent triumphal procession or *thiasos* of the wedded pair: Bacchus and Ariadne in their chariot being conveyed by the centaurs, guided by Cupid, to the other world to live happily ever after, accompanied by Bacchus's rejoicing companions.[9] Of this *cortège*, Pan and the dancing maenads and satyrs, transported by wine and music and the presence of the god, reveal their ecstasy, that wild physical freedom, which enters those who participate in the Bacchic mysteries. Panofsky, referring to the *orgia* or worship of Bacchus in which Bacchanalia were enacted, and following Cumont's interpretation,[10] summarizes what the Bacchic *thiasos* evokes:

an overpowering joy remembered by the votaries of Dionysus as a transitory experience in life and accepted by them as a promise of unending felicity after death.[11]

Such a concept helps to explain the popularity of the Bacchic cults, and the large proportion of surviving sarcophagi in the Renaissance with Bacchic themes.[12]

The sarcophagus, carved on three sides, was intended to be placed against the wall inside a family tomb chamber which would have had to be outside the walls of Rome, probably along a road.[13] Although it could have been seen by the family of the deceased, it was never intended for public display, nor for all the admiration it was destined to have some thirteen centuries later until its present obscurity.

II. THE SARCOPHAGUS IN THE RENAISSANCE

The Quattrocento. Amico Aspertini inscribed his drawings (*c.* 1500) of the sarcophagus: *a santa maria magiore* (**191–3**), and this is the sole evidence of the location of the sarcophagus. We can only assume that it was already there when drawn in the Quattrocento, that it was probably in the portico of that basilica or in the piazza, and that, if the earliest drawings are as early as 1420–30, it came to the attention of artists and humanists while Martin V was in residence at the papal palace at Santa Maria Maggiore part of each year from 1421–24.[14]

Any artist trained in the Trecento tradition of craftsmanship[15] which still prevailed in the Quattrocento, and whose work was chiefly religious in content, would find these reliefs outside his artistic experience. They offered him a strange variety of upward movements reflecting joy and primitive sensuality, contrasting with relaxed voluptuousness. Here he could study the nude body in action, draperies in motion, and the mythical creatures part man, part animal, centaurs, Pan and satyrs with horns. But how could he use this imagery for which Christian art had no need? To judge from his drawings (Cat. 1–3; **182–4**), the first Quattrocento artist to copy the sarcophagus was not as interested in the meaning of its reliefs as in the opportunity they offered to draw the nude figure in action. These sheets, thought to be from a model book of drawings of motifs to be used out of context in other compositions, are works of art in themselves. He has arranged the figures in decorative patterns, taking the nude piping satyr, now lost from the centre of the sarcophagus, to complete the compositions of the two ends (**182** and **183**). The lucidly balanced movement of the lunging position of the satyrs on both ends is carefully observed by this artist. The stance is like a fencer's lunge, with the diagonal line of the body continuing through the back leg, the knee of which turns out while the advancing knee bends forward. It is varied by pivoting the torso and arms. This clear example of the pose may have opened the eyes of the artists to its many other available representations in battle sarcophagi and other Greco-Roman and Etruscan reliefs and statues, and the motif became widespread in Renaissance art. The sinuous satyr from the front of the sarcophagus forms part of a pattern with figures from various other reliefs (**184**). This figure, too, entirely intact in the Renaissance, was later used in Quattrocento works of art (see p. 115 and n. 30). These small drawings are delicately shaded, and carefully finished. They show the skill of a miniaturist, or perhaps a goldsmith, in their detailed perception of three-dimensional form. A study of the drawings themselves might help to solve the problem of whether they were directly drawn from the antique reliefs, or were copies from another model book (see Cat. 3).

The only other Quattrocento drawings known to be directly of the sarcophagus

167 Adam. *Lorenzo and Vittorio Ghiberti,*
c. 1452–64. Bronze frame of Andrea
Pisano's doors, Florence, Baptistry.

168 Eve. *Lorenzo and Vittorio Ghiberti,*
c. 1452–64. Bronze frame of Andrea
Pisano's doors. Florence, Baptistry.

were done somewhat later; a date of *c.* 1460 has been proposed, and they seem to be by a North Italian artist (Cat. 4–6; **185–7**). His understanding of the form of the figures from the sarcophagus has resulted in distinct shading within firm outlines to emphasize the volume. But the real difference between his approach and that of his predecessor is that he is moved by the subject matter; he has interpreted the feelings motivating the action of these figures in a personal way. The principles which he learned here were probably transferred to his own works of art, but the motifs copied from antique reliefs by our first artist and his contemporaries, Pisanello and Gentile da Fabriano, perhaps thirty years earlier, did not change the International Gothic style in which they had been brought up. Their Florentine contemporaries, innovators of the new style, Masaccio, Donatello, Luca della Robbia and Ghiberti, sought in antique art not isolated motifs so much as the principles underlying the naturalistic portrayal of form and movement. Their drawings of antique sculpture have not survived.

Ghiberti seems to have kept a model book, now lost, in which he recorded figures from the Bacchic sarcophagus at Santa Maria Maggiore. In his panel of the *Genesis*, probably designed before 1429, on the east doors of the Florentine Baptistry, the nude maenad from the front of the sarcophagus has been detected in the figure of Eve in the Expulsion on the right, and hidden behind her, in the lunging position of the satyr pulling Pan's tail, from the right end of the sarcophagus, is Adam.[16]

Two splendid adaptations, one of the sinuous satyr carrying a child on his shoulders, reversed (**167**), the other of the same nude maenad dancing with her veil (**168**), appear on either side of the bottom of the bronze frame of Andrea Pisano's south doors of the same Baptistry. Here they have become Adam and Eve after the Fall. Cain and Abel as infants wrestle at Adam's feet; he holds the vase on his head, from which springs upward the floral decoration of the frame, with a gesture reminiscent of the ithyphallic satyr's right hand. Eve, in her upward movement, needs the two children to anchor her to earth, a movement *in alto verso l'aëre* most gratifying to Alberti.[17] She holds a spindle with a broken shaft in her left hand, and her veil, encircling her in a spiral, billows out like Fortuna's sail. It was Lorenzo Ghiberti's last major project, assumed to have been designed by him from his earlier drawings of the sarcophagus, and executed after his death by his son Vittorio and his workshop from 1456–64.[18] Vasari described the ornament of the frames finished by Ghiberti's son as:

la più rara e maravigliosa cosa che si possa veder di bronzo[19]

It was in this way that Ghiberti translated Bacchic motifs into the context of the Old Testament. Towards the end of the Quattrocento Bacchic imagery became popular

169 Camino della Iole, *Urbino, Palazzo Ducale.*

in poetry,[20] works of art, and in the decorative arts which furnished the palaces and villas of Renaissance collectors and patrons.

An early example is the marble chimney piece in Urbino, the *Camino della Iole* (**169**) carved for one of Federigo da Montefeltro's new rooms in the palace, decorated *c.* 1460.[21] The *Camino* reflects Federigo's love of antiquity.[22] The identity of the sculptor has never been proved,[23] but Federigo himself evidently took a lively interest in the project, according to his biographer, Vespasiano da Bisticci:

. . . e a udirlo parlare con uno scultore, pareva che l'arte fusse sua; in modo che ne ragionava![24]

On either side of the fireplace in niches carved out of its sides, stand nude statues of Hercules and Iole, similar to the figures of Hercules and Abundantia in the marble frames of the Porta della Mandorla of the Florentine Cathedral.[25] Above them, the lower of the two friezes repeats the entire front relief of the Bacchic sarcophagus at Santa Maria Maggiore. The significant changes are that the shallow rectangular space in which the scene takes place has been substituted for the curved recession of the sarcophagus front, giving a clearer definition of space in which the figures are less crowded as those in the background have been omitted. The maenad in the chiton now has room to spin around, and the lost piping satyr can be seen in his original position (see Cat. 2; **183**). Two additional satyrs and a tree hung with shields have been added at the right where the sarcophagus had been broken, utilizing the surviving *pedum* and tympanum. One of the lunging satyrs may be an adaptation from Pan's tormentor on the right end.[26] Furthermore, all references to the Bacchic cult have been suppressed, and an animated scroll or ribbon replaces the snake. The sarcophagus relief has been interpreted here as a joyful celebration of the Triumph of Love, and Cupid's stance on the rump of a centaur, looking towards the lovers, with his arms flung wide, is a spirited reconstruction from the remaining fragments. It has been suggested that the *Camino* is a wedding allegory for Federigo and his wife Battista Sforza, married in 1460.[27]

If the Bacchic relief can be seen here as an allegorical Triumph of Love as a natural and fertile force, it is love moderated by all the cardinal and theological virtues which triumphs on the back of the portraits in the Uffizi of Federigo and his wife Battista painted by Piero della Francesca some years later.[28]

Extremes of fantasy were also sparked off by such sarcophagus reliefs at about the same time in Venice and Padua. Jacopo Bellini's transformation of antique sources is so poetic and imaginative that one has to be equally imaginative to see the Bacchic sarcophagus at Santa Maria Maggiore as an inspiration for his otherworldly triumphs of the Pans, the spellbinding beauty of Silenus and a youth on a donkey, and the whirling maenadic skirts of the splendid Judith in his sketchbook in the British

Museum.[29] Works of art will continue to be found that reflect the fusion of multiple inspirations including motifs from this sarcophagus. Certainly such transformations are more revealing of the creative process than direct copies, but in a study which focuses on the antique object rather than on the artists' achievements, such examples would be out of place except to reveal the far-reaching influence of the object.[30]

The Cinquecento. The drawings of the sarcophagus were done between 1500 and 1560, when an increasing number of antique sculptures came to light during the building of new villas and palaces. Artists came to Rome from other parts of Italy and north of the Alps to draw the antique ruins and works of art ancient and modern as part of their training in their own craft. Later in the century, the more antiquarian-minded artists dedicated themselves to recording antique reliefs and sculptures more or less systematically. They included such artists as Dosio, Pighius, Pirro Ligorio, and the engravers of antique statues, Lafrery and Cavalieri in the latter half of the century.[31] If the greatest Cinquecento artists, Michelangelo, Leonardo, Raphael, Parmigianino, and Correggio kept sketchbooks of drawings of antique works of art, only a few sheets of this sort remain. Some of the artists who copied the Bacchic sarcophagus at Santa Maria Maggiore seem to have done so when they were young, as though it belonged to the canon of antique reliefs to be studied.

Two drawings of the sarcophagus are in the sketchbook at the Ashmolean Museum, Oxford, attributed to Jacopo Ripanda (Cat. 8–9; **189–90**). He worked on the decorations with Pinturicchio for Alexander VI in the *Appartamenti Borgia* in the Vatican Palace where the *grotteschi* decorations of the recently discovered Golden House of Nero were imitated.[32] These detailed but somewhat weak pen and wash drawings of the left end and the triumphal chariot show something of his decorative antiquarian interests.

His contemporary and fellow Bolognese is the bizarre Amico Aspertini, sympathetically characterized by Phyllis Bober as a law unto himself.[33] His taste is for antique reliefs showing figures in violent action, but he was also fond of the capricious *grotteschi* which he used in his own work in Bologna. His early sketchbook, in Wolfegg Castle, is similar to the early model books as it includes antique objects like sacrificial instruments, armour and decorative motifs to be used by painters. As in the well-known *Codex Escurialensis*,[34] whole sarcophagus reliefs are copied, but Aspertini tends to mix up the sequence, transpose and alter the figures, and introduce motifs from other reliefs, with *invenzioni all'antica* (Cat. 11; **192**). His interpretation of Silenus on the ass (**192**) has been connected with Baldassare Peruzzi's version of the motif in a fresco in the Farnesina (**170**).[35] Aspertini returned to Rome to draw his favourites of thirty years before in a later sketchbook in the British Museum datable *c.* 1532–4,

170 *Silenus. Baldassare Peruzzi, detail of fresco decoration, Sala de' Fregi, Rome, Villa Farnesina.*

171 *Bacchus and Ariadne. Giovanni da Udine, stucco of vault iii, Logge Vaticane.*

but he drew them with a greater compression of form, as can be seen in a comparison of his two versions of the right end (Cat. 12 and 14; **193** and **195**).

In the meantime, the sarcophagus was drawn by one of Raphael's assistants, probably Giovanni Francesco Penni. A group of Pan and two dancing bassarids from the front are drawn in the Fossombrone Sketchbook (Cat. 13; **194**) with ease and accuracy. The value of this unpublished and recently discovered sketchbook is that it may reflect Raphael's antiquarian interests, which otherwise are very little known and still to be reconstructed. Raphael's own creative transformations in his paintings of the antique works of art he studied make his sources often untraceable, but in the decorations of the Vatican *Logge* which he supervised (1518–19), identifiable motifs from Roman sarcophagi and other antique sources were used. Of the stucco reliefs there based on motifs from the Bacchic sarcophagus at Santa Maria Maggiore, the most beautiful is Bacchus and Ariadne (**171**).[36] The adaptation, by Giovanni da Udine, Raphael's assistant, is inspired by the antique *stucchi* in the Colosseum, which in turn often isolated motifs from sarcophagi.[37]

As in the Quattrocento, the sarcophagus was considered as a source for *invenzioni* based on combinations of motifs, and this can be seen in engravings by Marcantonio Raimondi and his school. The closest that any of them come to a figure from the sarcophagus is the engraving which is sometimes printed as *Two Sibyls and the Zodiac* (B. xiv, 397; **172**).[38] The figure on the left is based on a statue or relief of a victory writing on a shield, while the other is the maenad in a chiton, now with a book, looking up to the left, her long hair flying, but otherwise almost identical with the figure on the front of the sarcophagus. Such engravings, adapted as various symbols in books, were widely disseminated, as we shall see when we come to Franco's engraving of the sarcophagus (see below).

In the 1530s and the '40s the Dutch painter Marten van Heemskerck, Lambert Lombard from Liège (Cat. 17), Frans Floris (Cat. 18), and other Northerners came to Rome. The Heemskerck sketchbooks (Cat. 15 and 16), which, however, probably contain drawings by other hands, provide the most comprehensive record up to that time of reliefs and statues to be seen in private collections and in the Vatican, on the Capitoline, on Monte Cavallo and the Lateran, wherever there were antique works of art to be seen.

Vasari describes Battista Franco working with Heemskerck and his assistants[39] and also preparing a book of drawings after the antique.[40] His drawing of the drunken Pan from the left end is done with a facility of which Vasari would have approved (Cat. 19; **200**). His engraving of the whole front and right end of the sarcophagus reversed and 'restored' has already been referred to in the description of the sarcophagus (p. 106; **173**). It is said to have been done in 1549 and shows a stylized elegance in comparison with the original relief, and a certain freedom of interpretation particularly in the Silenus group where the supporting satyr is wearing more clothes, and the maenad behind him is converted into another supporter. This group, after Franco's engraving, is the subject of a woodcut illustrating Vincenzo Cartari's *Imagini degli Dei* (**174**) and was also used by Natale Conti in his *Mythologia*, Venice 1567.[41] Cartari's handbook was intended to be useful for artists looking for mythological themes, and indeed Lomazzo recommended the *Imagini* to painters in his influential treatise on painting.[42]

The tendency to see the sarcophagus as a whole, and reconstructed, is reflected in Girolamo da Carpi's drawing in Düsseldorf (Cat. 20; **201**) in which more than half the front of the sarcophagus is portrayed with the completed figures. Girolamo's drawing style is sometimes confused with Franco's (Cat. 19; **200** and Cat. 21; **202**). He was in Rome from 1549–54 and made a large number of drawings of antique reliefs and statues at the time when Dosio[43] and the German, Stephanus Pighius,[44] were making theirs, which included complete sarcophagus reliefs. Among them is also a sketch of a detail of the right end (Cat. 21; **202**) and another version of the same subject (Cat. 22; **203**), both of which may depend not on the sarcophagus itself but on another drawing.

An unattributed drawing in Munich (Cat. 23; **162**), formerly attributed to Polidoro da Caravaggio, shows the sarcophagus without any restorations. This is unique because, even in the Quattrocento drawings (Cat. 1–2; **182** and **183**), the artists replaced arms and legs of the figures on the ends which some later artists copied as broken. It is not to be excluded that the damage was done after the mid-Quattrocento, perhaps when the satyr was removed or destroyed. Only Raphael's assistant, Penni, showed complete self-control in copying exactly, but broke down when it came to interpreting the *thyrsos* (Cat. 13; **194**). It can be assumed that the Munich drawing was correct, as the breakages shown are made up by the present restorations. It may

172 *The Maenad in the chiton, Marcantonio Raimondi or his school, engraving of an allegory. Bartsch, XIV, 397.*

come from the circle of Dosio, whose approach to the antique sculpture he drew was more objective than Girolamo da Carpi's (Cat. 20; **201**), but that is guesswork and so is the date, which could be *c.* 1550.

Taddeo Zuccaro's beautiful pen and wash drawing, which would date from the same period, *c.* 1550 according to Mr Gere,[45] of Diana running with hounds, is an example of an *invenzione* inspired by the Bacchic sarcophagus at Santa Maria Maggiore. Diana, on tiptoe, is running forward and slightly to the left, her soft chiton fluttering in her rapid movement. She holds two hounds at her right side with their leads held in her right hand at her left side. From her raised left hand, she holds a third lead for an invisible hound behind her. Her skirts billow out and curve under at the hem in agitated scallops, as do the maenad's on the sarcophagus relief. This tenuous resemblance of Taddeo's Diana to the maenad might seem a coincidence, were it not for the smaller male figure in the background, drawn only in pen. He is also running in the same direction on tiptoe, his left leg slightly in front of the other, head turned up to the right, and his left arm raised. He is perhaps a shepherd holding

173 *Bacchic sarcophagus, front and right end, reversed. Battista Franco, engraving,*
1549. Bartsch, XVI, 134, 45.

a staff, his movement emphasized by a piece of drapery wound diagonally around
his body and fluttering down behind him, not unlike the spiralling drapery of the
nude maenad of the sarcophagus. His pose echoes that of the ecstatic satyr with the
wineskin who stands to the left of the maenad in the chiton on the relief (**161**).
Taddeo has caught the exhilaration of movement of these two figures, but although
he has freed them from their background so that they might bound forward in space,
he has drawn them running with their feet still close together. These figures were
known to Taddeo: an *invenzione* from the right end of the sarcophagus appears in a
group of Pan carrying a satyress on his back in Taddeo's *Bacchanale* at Caprarola,
painted in the early 1560s, in which multiple prototypes have been transformed.[46]

Another drawing, appended to the Catalogue (Cat. 28, p.151), is also datable *c.* 1540–
50. This is the splendid study in Erlangen of two views of a piping satyr with the Torso
Belvedere (**208**). Seen in this chronological context with the other drawings of the
sarcophagus, it seems even more unlikely that it could still refer to the satyr missing
from the front (**169**, **182** and **183**).

The last known drawings of the sarcophagus are by the young Florentine pupil of Pontormo, Giovambattista Naldini, who went to Rome in September 1560 for a few months, furnished by Vasari, at Vincenzo Borghini's request, with a letter of instruction on the most important things for a painter to see. Marco da Ravenna was asked by Vasari to show him modern works of art by Raphael's school, and among the antiquities Naldini drew were the reliefs from the Arch of Titus, Bacchic reliefs at the Villa Borghese, the Torlonia Bacchic vase, and the Bacchic sarcophagus at Santa Maria Maggiore which he drew in four views (Cat. 24–7). A number of Naldini's drawings after the antique are at Christ Church, Oxford, and it should be possible to

174 *Silenus's group after Battista Franco's engraving (173). Vincenzo Cartari,* Le vere e nuove imagini degli dei antichi, *1615, p. 559.*

reconstruct from these and drawings in other collections the sketch book which he made in Rome. Apart from the interest this would have for the formation of Naldini's style, it would serve as an illustrated guide to those works of art, both ancient and modern, considered by Vasari in his lost letter of 1560 to be most worthy of study in Rome. It would also put in perspective the stylistic importance of the Bacchic sarcophagus as an object of study at this time.

EPILOGUE

The Restorations. With the drawings of Naldini, the visual record of the sarcophagus in the Renaissance comes to an end, although more drawings will probably come to light. The spell of the sarcophagus seems to have faded after it was restored. It is not known when that was, or exactly when the sarcophagus was moved to the garden of the Villa Montalto, laid out in the 1570s by Domenico Fontana. Its high wall ran along the northern flank of Santa Maria Maggiore. It seems possible that it was moved *c.* 1585, shortly after Cardinal Felice Peretti became Pope Sixtus V (1585–90), and before the obelisk was erected (1587) at Santa Maria Maggiore with an inscription below and the cross on top, signifying the triumph of Christianity over paganism.[47]

If it was restored at this time, the most likely restorer to supervise the work would

175 *Bacchic procession. Relief from a Neo-Attic marble krater. First century A.D. Pisa, Campo Santo.*
(*From Paolo Lasinio figlio*, Raccolta di sarcofagi, urne e altri monumenti di scultura del Campo
Santo di Pisa, *Pisa 1814, pl. lxi.*)

176 *Bacchic sarcophagus, left half of front. London, British Museum 2298.*

177 *Bacchic sarcophagus, right half of front. London, British Museum 2298.*

have been Flaminio Vacca (1538–1600). He worked for Sixtus V as a sculptor in Santa Maria Maggiore and on the Acqua Felice. His biographer, Baglione, stresses his role as a restorer of antique sculpture, explaining that for this reason he made few original works of his own.[48] He is also known for his lively and delightful memoir of the archaeological discoveries in Rome, which deserves a new edition.[49] Although circumstances point to Vacca as the restorer of the sarcophagus, the restorations do not.

The restorations as we see them today, apart from some later damage, have been referred to on p. 105. According to Matz the restorer used as a source for two of the new figures the large marble krater with a continuous Bacchic relief, which had stood on a column on the back of a lion in front of the Cathedral at Pisa until 1598, and is now in the Campo Santo (**175**).[50] The satyr in the centre of the sarcophagus, replacing the lost one (**176** and **177**), and the second satyr from the right playing the double pipes (**177**) are both from the krater, as noted by Matz. The terminal satyr on the right might be a free adaptation of the fifth figure in Lasinio's engraved projection (**175**).

If the restorer had visited Pisa himself, however, he would have noticed in the Campo Santo a very similar Bacchic sarcophagus[51] which preserved the piping satyr seen from the back in the centre of the relief, in much better repair than it is now, as can be seen from Dosio's drawing of it, wrongly thought by Hülsen to be of the Santa Maria Maggiore sarcophagus.[52]

The restorer also shows misplaced antiquarian enthusiasm in converting the panther, midway, to an elephant, changing the iconography of the original triumphal *thiasos* of Bacchus and Ariadne to an Indian Triumph, and as such it is described by Bellori in his captions for Perrier's engravings (**178** and **179**). The proportions of the new figures are not those of the second century ones, and they are too sober to participate in the spirit which animates the rest of the group.

François Perrier engraved the sarcophagus front when it was in the garden of the Villa Montalto. He was a French painter, in Rome on a second visit from 1635–45, and his book of over fifty engravings after famous reliefs in Rome was published in Rome in 1645.[53] A few years after the publication of Perrier's book, the Dutch painter and engraver, Jan de Bisschop, also known as Episcopius, copied some of the motifs from it, including four from the sarcophagus. The album containing these drawings is in the Victoria and Albert Museum in London.[54] In 1693, Pietro Santi Bartoli published his *Admiranda*[55] with clearer plates of the sarcophagus than Perrier's (**180, 181**). Bellori's captions, now in capital letters, with a numbered key to each figure, explain the myth with utmost clarity. Yet this antiquarian approach, combined with its restoration, perhaps robbed the sarcophagus of the magic it had held for the artists of the Quattrocento and Cinquecento. Realizing how much it meant to them may help us to see it with new eyes when it is again on view.

subacta India, atq; Elephantibus ad pompam deductis Dionysius ad Insulam Dium appulit, ostriadnæ misertus eam a Theseo derelictam sui recepit curru, super que ipse pone stratus, e cantharo in sauni poculum fundit, e vase eiecit, famus, mittit Apotheosin iris memoriam; Pentheus discerpsi, stat ad pedes cista, in qua occultantur Liberi sacra senesia in Here Noristhia, et fauolis lubrici, iustum qui se furosij proæbebant Habet apolo in hortis Montaltis 9

178 *Right half of front of the Bacchic sarcophagus, reversed.* François Perrier *and* G. Bellori, Icones et segmenta illustrium e marmore tabularum quae Romae adhuc extant, *Rome 1645, pl. 8.*

hilarem liquorem Ariadna eum amplectitur, pampineos, monili eburneum, alligat pectus, erecta umbella ad arcendas soles, Amor uolitat cum uexillo, sopitum; excitat deq; triumphante triumphat satyrus ebrius merum Bacchi sanguis, quem titubantem sauius sustinet, Idemq; duplicem tybiam inflans ludere Bassaridas pueros sauiosi, docet, hic dicitur Ariadnæ Chorus unde Catullus plurimis in locis in hortis Montaltis 9

179 *Left half of front of the Bacchic sarcophagus, reversed.* F. Perrier *and* G. Bellori, Icones et segmenta . . . tabularum, *Rome 1645, pl. 9.*

BACCHI ET ARIADNÆ CHORVS

SVBACTA INDIA BACCHVS ARIADNAM A THESEO DERELICTAM SVO RECEPIT CVRRV IPSE E CANTHARO IN GENVNI POCVLVM HILAREM FVNDIT LIQVOREM, ARIADNA SMYLACIS SERTO EIVSDEM PECTVS ALLIGAT ET AMPLECTITVR, AMOR VOLITAT CVM FLABELLO SEV VEXILLO DEVM EXCITAT SATYRVS EBRIVS MERVM EFFVNDIT FAVNVS QVATIT AFRI CRES IN MEMORIAM PENTHEI DISCERPTI BACCHVS IPSE CVRRV INVECTVS EST A CENTAVRIS CVM ISTI PLVRIMVM VINO INCALESCANT ACLYRA PRÆCIPVE EXCELLANT

In hac, et sequentibus habes Saltationes thimelicam et Satyricam apparatum In hortis Montaltis 48

180 *Left half of front of the Bacchic sarcophagus.* P. S. Bartoli *and* G. Bellori, Admiranda Romanarum antiquitatum ac veteris sculpturae vestigia, *Rome 1693, pl. 48.*

181 *Right half of front of the Bacchic sarcophagus. P. S. Bartoli and G. Bellori*, Admiranda,
Rome 1693, pl. 49.

III. CATALOGUE OF FIFTEENTH AND SIXTEENTH-CENTURY DRAWINGS OF THE BACCHIC SARCOPHAGUS AT SANTA MARIA MAGGIORE IN ROME

This list is in chronological order, as far as dates are known or can be approximated by knowledge of the artist's presence in Rome or, in the case of anonymous artists, on the basis of style.

The purpose of this catalogue is to show the drawings as visual records of the impression which the sarcophagus made on the artists.

When there is more than one drawing by an artist, they are arranged in the sequence of the sarcophagus reliefs: left end, front, left to right, right end, except where the drawings are on the recto and verso of the same sheet; in that case they have not been separated.

Bibliographical notes

Most of the drawings after the sarcophagus have been listed by the following:

Christian Hülsen, *Das Skizzenbuch des Giovannantonio Dosio im Staatlichen Kupferstichkabinett zu Berlin*, Berlin 1933, p. 10, no. 37. The list is valid for our sarcophagus, but the Dosio drawing is of another one in Pisa (Matz, ii, no. 89 as Matz points out, ii, p. 204.) Hereafter, Hülsen, *Dosio*.

Bernhard Degenhart, 'Michele di Giovanni di Bartolo: Disegni dall' antico e il camino "della Iole" ', *Bollettino d'Arte*, xxxv, 1950, pp. 208–15. Hereafter, Degenhart, 1950.

Phyllis Pray Bober, *Drawings after the Antique by Amico Aspertini. Sketchbooks in the British Museum*, London 1957, p. 47. Hereafter, Bober, *Aspertini*.

Ulrich Middeldorf, 'Su alcuni bronzetti all'antica del Quattrocento', *Il mondo antico nel Rinascimento, Atti del V Convegno Internazionale di Studi sul Rinascimento (1956)*, Florence 1958, pp. 169–70, and especially 170, n. 1, which contains a long list of additional works of art inspired by the sarcophagus. See Cat. 20 and n. 30. Hereafter, Middeldorf, 1958.

Annegrit Schmitt, 'Gentile da Fabriano und der Beginn der Antikennachzeichnung', *Münchner Jahrbuch der bildenden Kunst*, xi, 1960, pp. 121–2, no. 6. Hereafter, Schmitt, 1960.

Bernhard Degenhart and Annegrit Schmitt, *Corpus der italienischen Zeichnungen 1300–1450, I, Süd- und Mittelitalien*, i, Berlin 1968, nos. 136–7, and a list on p. 248. Hereafter, Degenhart and Schmitt, *Corpus*.

Friedrich Matz, *Die dionysischen Sarkophage, II* (Die antiken Sarkophagreliefs, iv), Berlin 1968, no. 88, p. 204–5. Hereafter, Matz and the number of his drawings list. See Cat. 28.

To Matz's list, which is the most complete, the following drawings are added: Cat. 13 (identified by A. Parronchi), 19 (identified by P. Bober for the Census), 20 (indicated by U. Middeldorf, 1958), 22 (see Cat. 21), 26 (photograph in Mr and Mrs Pouncey's files), and 27 (published by P. Barocchi).

1   Central Italian, *c.* 1420–30 (**182**).

Left end: Pan carried by his supporters. Front: Piping satyr (lost).

Paris, Louvre, 5611 recto.

Silver point on grey-green prepared parchment. 12.6 × 17.3 cms.

Bibl. DEGENHART, 1950, pp. 208–15, as Michele di Giovanni di Bartolo.
   MIDDELDORF, 1958, pp. 169–70, n. 3, not by Michele.
   SCHMITT, 1960, pp. 122, 134, 146, as Michele.
   DEGENHART and SCHMITT, *Corpus*, no. 136 p. 245, present attribution (see Cat. 3 for discussion), pp. 247–8, and p. 249, n. 5 summarizes the literature on the relation of Cat. 1 and 2 (satyr piping) to the *Camino* in Urbino (see above, p. 117).

See comments on p. 106. The piping satyr is seen from the right, a view which shows his legs to be separate. He has a tail which is missing in Cat. 2; and his hair is straighter and longer. Apart from these differences the pose is basically the same, and it has always been assumed that the same figure has been drawn twice.

In the scene of the left end, the tension and stress of carrying Pan is emphasized.

2   Central Italian, *c.* 1420–30 (**183**).

Right end: Two satyrs punishing Pan. Front: Piping satyr (lost).

Paris, Louvre, 5611 verso.

Silver point on grey-green prepared parchment. 12.6 × 17.3 cms.

Bibl. See Cat. 1.

The view of the piping satyr is from the left and shows him as he appears on the *Camino* in Urbino (**169**) with his legs crossed and apparently close together. He has short curly hair as in the Urbino relief.

3   Central Italian, *c.* 1420–30 (**184**).

Front, right: Nude satyr with a child on his shoulders.

Paris, Louvre, R.F.38.

Brown silver point on grey-green prepared parchment. 15.9 × 21.8 cms.
Bibl. DEGENHART and SCHMITT, *Corpus*, no. 137, pp. 248–9.
　　See Cat. 1.

The other figures are from three different reliefs in Rome. On the left is a maenad from a Bacchic sarcophagus now at Hever Castle in Kent (Matz i, no. 44). Cf. Pisanello drawing, Oxford, Ashmolean (Parker, ii, 41 verso), attributed by Degenhart and Schmitt to Gentile da Fabriano (*Corpus*, no. 132). Cat. 3 omits the maenad's left leg to make room for the other figures on the sheet. This suggests that Cat. 3 includes a copy after the Oxford drawing and may not be directly after the sarcophagus. Gentile was in Rome in 1427; Pisanello in 1432. This could therefore suggest a later date than the one assigned it in the *Corpus*.

4　North Italian, *c.* 1460 (**185**).
Left end: Drunken Pan carried by supporters.
Milan, Biblioteca Ambrosiana, 1707 verso.
Metal point, pen with brown ink on paper. 31 × 20.8 cms.
Bibl. A. SCHMITT, *Disegni di Pisanello e di maestri del suo tempo*, exhibition catalogue. Fondazione Cini, Venice 1966, no. 33 verso, as Milanese, *c.* 1460.
　　Matz, ii, p. 204 no. 3.

182 *Central Italian artist, c. 1420–30. Left end, and satyr (lost) from the front. Paris, Louvre 5611 recto.*

183 *Central Italian artist, c. 1420–30. Right end, and satyr (lost) from the front. Paris, Louvre 5611 verso.*

184 *Central Italian artist.*
c. 1420–30. Front (detail)
satyr with child on his shoulders.
Paris, Louvre R.F.38.

185 *North Italian, c. 1460. Left end. Milan, Biblioteca*
Ambrosiana, 1707 verso.

186 *North Italian, c. 1460. Front (detail) : The two*
dancing maenads and the ithyphallic satyr. Milan,
Biblioteca Ambrosiana, 1707 recto.

The artist of Cat. 4–6 has also been called the Ambrosiana Anonymous (Schmitt, 1960, p. 122). For the earliest attributions to Pisanello or School of Mantegna, see C. Vincenzi, 'Di tre fogli di disegni quattrocenteschi dall'antico', *Rassegna d'arte*, x, 1910, pp. 6–11. According to Degenhart, 1950, p. 209, the drawings were later outlined in a Mantegnesque hand. Like Cat. 1–3, Cat. 4–6 formed part of a model book (the figures along the top of Cat. 4 are copied from the Medea sarcophagus, much drawn in the Quattrocento at SS. Cosma and Damiano; now in the museum at Ancona. Schmitt, 1960, p. 118, no. 1; C. Robert, *Mythologische Cyklen* (Die antiken Sarkophagreliefs, ii), Berlin 1890, no. 199).

The technique of modelling with fine parallel lines within firmly defined contours is used to create an impression of solidity of form. The source of light in the three drawings varies. In Cat. 4 it comes from above and from the right.

Compared with the stiffness of the figures in the earlier drawings, those of Cat. 4–6 show a certain fluidity and lightness of movement. The emotions expressed by the faces in the reliefs are made milder. The artist is accurate in copying the damaged marble, but Pan's right hand, later restored, is a weak invention, and the satyr's hand-hold of Pan's leg from below is contrary to the original one.

5 North Italian, *c.* 1460 (**186**).
Front: Maenad in a chiton; nude maenad and ithyphallic satyr.
Milan: Biblioteca Ambrosiana, 1707 recto.
Bibl. See Cat. 4. Schmitt, no. 33 recto.
The bronze lion's head with ring in two views at the top of the sheet might be connected with the heads from the Roman ship found in the Lago di Nemi in 1444 by Cardinal Prospero Colonna (Martin V's nephew) who later tried to excavate it. Although it greatly excited the humanists, Alberti, Flavio Biondo and Pius II, this is the only Quattrocento drawing I know of it (see Biondo, *Italia illustrata*, written 1448–53, in *Roma Triumphante*, Basle 1559, pp. 325–6; cf. Pius II, *Commentarii*, Bk. XI, p. 307, written 1463). This, or a similar head, was later drawn in the so-called Peruzzi sketchbook in Siena, and another ten heads were excavated in the nineteenth and twentieth centuries, now in the Terme Museum in Rome. Not noted by Schmitt, 1966. F. Dionisi, *Le Navi Sacre di Claudio del Lago di Nemi*, Rome 1956, pp. 18–23 and O. Kurz, 'Lion-masks with Rings in the West and in the East', *Studies in Art*, Scripta Hierosolymitana, XXIV, 1972, pp. 27–8, and n. 30. The drapery of the two maenads falls in the crisp frozen runnels inherited from the Gothic tradition, but the use of reflected light within the outlines gives an impression of volume.

188 *Attributed to School of Mantegna. Late fifteenth century? Front (detail): Pan, frontal satyr, and maenad in the chiton. Present owner unknown.*

187 *North Italian, c. 1460. Right end. Milan, Biblioteca Ambrosiana, F. 214 inf., no. 2.*

6 North Italian, *c.* 1460 (**187**).
Right end: Two Satyrs punishing Pan.
Milan, Biblioteca Ambrosiana, F. 214 inf., no. 2 recto.
Metal point and pen with brown ink on paper. 31 × 20 cms.
Bibl. See Cat. 4. Schmitt, no. 29 recto.

(The drawing at the top is from a Nereid sarcophagus at Grottaferrata. See N. Dacos, 'A propos d'un fragment de sarcophage de Grottaferrata et de son influence à la Renaissance', *Bull. de l'Inst. Hist. Belge de Rome*, xxxiii, 1961, pp. 143–50; A. Rumpf, *Die Meerwesen* (Die antiken Sarkophagreliefs, v, i), Berlin 1939, no. 151.)

The torso and hip of the satyr pulling Pan's tail lack both the tautness of the original and the straight alignment of the contour from waist to ankle. It is possible that the right hand of the satyr on the left was broken off later. Cf. Cat. 3. A softer expression is given to the eyes.

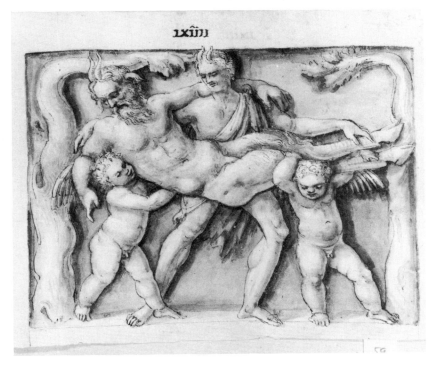

ıxĩĩĵĩ

189 *Style of Jacopo Ripanda, early sixteenth century. Left end. Oxford, Ashmolean, 668, f. 59.*

7 Attributed to School of Mantegna, late fifteenth century (**188**).

Front: Pan, frontal satyr faintly indicated, and maenad in a chiton.

Present owner unknown.

London, Poynter Sale, 24–25 April, 1918.

Bibl. Matz, ii, p. 204, no. 15.

The figure of Pan has been drawn with particular attention to the torsion of his dance, and the curls of his fleecy legs. The ecstatic satyr did not interest the artist, and the maenad's drapery, by contrast to the treatment of Pan, seems to be stony without the appearance of softness that the marble gives.

8 Style of Jacopo Ripanda (active 1490–1530), early sixteenth century (**189**).

Left end: Pan carried by his supporters.

Oxford, Ashmolean Museum, 'Ripanda Sketchbook', f. 59.

Quarto size sheet.

Bibl. K. T. PARKER, *Catalogue of the Collection of Drawings in the Ashmolean Museum*, ii, Italian Schools, Oxford 1972, no. 668, p. 360.

The artist has interpreted this relief freely, framing it with flanking trees, restoring breakages, and changing details such as the direction of the satyr's eyes. The result,

190 *Style of Jacopo Ripanda, early sixteenth century. Front (detail) : the triumphal chariot of Bacchus and Ariadne.* Oxford, Ashmolean 668, f. 58.

in a technique of pen and wash, is a compact, decorative composition which betrays certain weaknesses such as Pan's parallel legs and the satyr's and cupid's parallel hands supporting them.

9 Style of Jacopo Ripanda (active 1490–1530), early sixteenth century (**190**).
Front: Left side, the triumphal chariot of Bacchus and Ariadne.
Oxford, Ashmolean Museum, 'Ripanda Sketchbook', f. 58.
Quarto size sheet.
Bibl. See Cat. 8.
Not only have the missing parts been restored, but existing motifs have been enlarged or embellished. The full-length woman in the background carrying the *liknon* is emphasized, and now carries a large wicker tray of fruits; the parasol is bigger, the satyr on the cart pulls a bull by the tail rather than a goat by the horn. These decorative antiquarian additions cannot contribute to the festive atmosphere the artist might have intended. Bacchus is insecure on his chariot; the participants all seem lacklustre.

10 Amico Aspertini (*c.* 1475–1552), *c.* 1500–1503 (**191**).

Left end: Drunken Pan carried by supporters.

Schloss Wolfegg, Germany. Wolfegg Sketchbook, f. 48 verso.

Folio: 22.5 × 17 cms.

Bibl. P. BOBER, *Aspertini*, pp. 5–12 for attribution and date. Cat. 10–12 from this sketchbook are the only drawings which give the location of the sarcophagus: 'a santa maria magiore'.

With the use of strong shading, Aspertini has animated Pan's originally relaxed figure, and with the turn of the head, the eyes looking up, and the legs carried splayed, a more sensual element is emphasized which may have inspired later engravings. (Cf. H. Zerner, *École de Fontainebleau: Gravures*, Paris 1969, L.D.82.)

Instead of showing the lunging position of the legs of the satyr in the background, Aspertini has shown both knees bent in almost the same direction (cf. Cat. 12).

191 *Amico Aspertini, c. 1500–03. Left end. Wolfegg sketchbook, f. 48 verso.*

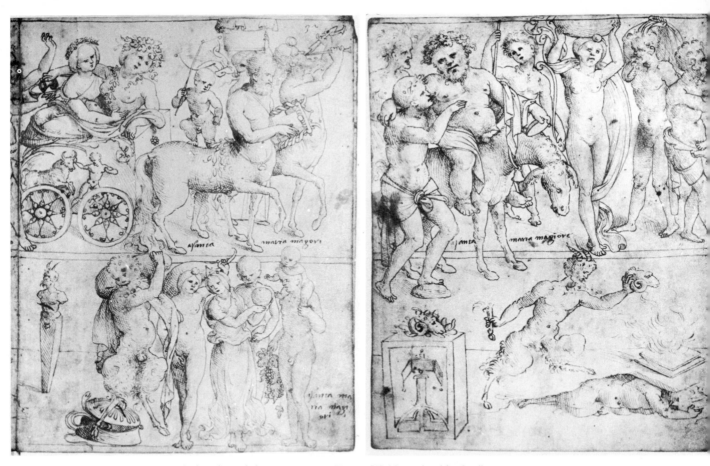

192 *Amico Aspertini, c. 1500–03. Front. Wolfegg sketchbook, ff. 31 verso–32 recto.*

11 Amico Aspertini (*c.* 1475–1552), *c.* 1500–03 (**192**).

Front: Confused sequence.

Schloss Wolfegg, Germany, Wolfegg Sketchbook, ff. 31 verso.–32.

22.5 × 17 cms.

Bibl. See Cat. 10.

Top of f. 31 verso: Silenus on ass, nude maenad, ithyphallic satyr, satyr following triumphal chariot; top of f. 32: triumphal chariot drawn by centaurs; bottom of f. 32: Pan, ecstatic frontal satyr with wineskin, now a Venus *pudica*, maenad with the chiton, and the two figures transposed from the right of the front. (The satyr on the bottom part of f. 31 v. is a free interpretation of a relief in the Villa Borghese: Reinach, *Répertoire de Reliefs*, iii, Paris 1912, 168.)

Aspertini has captured some of the drunken confusion of the relief, and in the extraordinary instruments of the centaurs, the neatly covered *liknon*, the languid pose of the maenad in the chiton, and other extravagances, he demonstrates his imaginative independence.

193 *Amico Aspertini, c. 1500–03. Right end. Wolfegg sketchbook, f. 47 verso (detail).*

12 Amico Aspertini (*c.* 1475–1552), *c.* 1500–03 (**193**).
Right end: Two satyrs punishing Pan.
Schloss Wolfegg, Germany. Wolfegg Sketchbook, f. 47 verso. (detail).
Bibl. See Cat. 10.
Aspertini has emphasized the pulling of Pan's tail by taking his viewpoint from the
left of centre and changing the satyr's pose to one of outright tugging. The whip seems
to be composed of a few reeds or straws. Cf. Cat. 14.

13 Workshop of Raphael: Giovanni Francesco Penni? (1496–1536?), *c.* 1520 (**194**).
Front: Pan, frontal satyr, and maenad in a chiton.
Fossombrone, Biblioteca Passionei, 'Giulio Romano Sketchbook', f. 89 recto.
Folio: 33 × 25 cms.

Bibl. Unpublished. The sketchbook of about 100 sheets drawn on both sides, contains copies after
antique architecture and sculpture and a few details of Giulio Romano's paintings. It was
photographed by Mr Howard Burns and by Professor A. Parronchi independently.

Pan and the satyr were badly blotted when a drawing on the opposite sheet was
later cancelled and the book closed when the ink was still wet.

The drawing shows an appreciation for the lightness of the dancing figures, the
crisp carving of the marble before it was worn down (Pan's legs), and the exact
proportions. The *cista mystica* is correctly drawn, but the *thyrsos* of the running
maenad (right) has been interpreted as a kind of trumpet. Otherwise the group is
copied faithfully without any attempt to restore missing pieces.

194 *Workshop of Raphael, G. F.
Penni? c. 1520. Front (detail): Pan,
frontal satyr and maenad in the chiton.
Fossombrone sketchbook, f. 89 recto.*

14 Amico Aspertini (*c.* 1475–1552), 1531–34 (**195**).
Right end: Two satyrs punishing Pan.
London, British Museum, Dept. of Prints and Drawings, 197. b. 1, Aspertini Sketchbook,
I, f. 2.
Pen, brown ink, light brown wash, heightened with white.
Bibl. P. BOBER, *Aspertini*, p. 47.
Compared with Cat. 12 of the same subject drawn by Aspertini some thirty years
before, the action is compressed so that the three figures form a vertical, rather than a
horizontal composition. The tail-pulling satyr is more Hellenistic in form, hair

flying back, bearded of chin and shin, with powerful shoulders and chest; he is no longer the slight figure of the Wolfegg Sketchbook. His stance is at variance to the relief, his right leg is seen frontally and not in profile.

The satyr carrying Pan is almost standing up, his face now hidden. Pan's features are almost simian. He seems to consider being flogged by three harmless-looking reeds a rather novel experience.

195 *Amico Aspertini. 1531–4. Right end. London, British Museum, Aspertini sketchbook I, f. 2.*

15 Marten van Heemskerck? (1498–1574); Heemskerck was in Rome 1532–*c*. 1536 (**196**).

Left end: Drunken Pan carried by his supporters (right). Front: Nude Maenad (left).

Berlin, Dahlem, Staatliche Museen, Kupferstichkabinett.

Bibl. C. HÜLSEN and H. EGGER, *Die römischen Skizzenbücher von Marten van Heemskerck*, ii, Berlin 1916, f. 65 v. p. 40, pl. 93.

It has been pointed out by Mr Gere that not all the drawings in these sketchbooks are by Heemskerck, therefore this attribution may need revision. (Degenhart, 1950, p. 214, n. 3 rejects the attributions to Giulio Romano; bibliography.) Cat. 15 and 16 can be compared in technique with a drawing attributed to the Studio of Giulio Romano, illustrated in the *Catalogue of the Ellesmere Collection, Part II, Drawings by Giulio Romano and other sixteenth-century masters*, Sotheby Sale, 5 December 1972, lot 41. On Heemskerck drawings, see J. Garff, *Tegninger af Maerten van Heemskerck*, Den Kongelige Kobberstiksamling, Statens Museum for Kunst, Copenhagen 1971.

In the drawing of the drunken Pan, the artist has taken his viewpoint from right of

196 *Marten van Heemskerck? 1534–6. Front (detail), nude maenad, and left end. Berlin sketchbook,
f. 65 verso.*

centre so as to emphasize the diagonal recession of Pan's body and the gentle torsion
of the upper chest and shoulders. The relaxed expression of Pan in his transport is
most amiably defined. There is no attempt to supply missing pieces.

The nude maenad is drawn without regard to sequence; her satyr is on the recto
of this sheet (Cat. 16). Her heavier figure could indicate the taste of a Northern artist.

16 Marten van Heemskerck? (1498–1574), in Rome 1532–*c*. 1536 (**197**).
Front: Ithyphallic satyr.
Berlin, Kupferstichkabinett.
Bibl. See Cat. 15, ii, f. 65, pl. 92.
This figure, on a sheet with two statues, could pass for a third. The satyr's upraised right arm is not drawn, the phallus ends in a fanciful loop, and instead of the weight balanced evenly though precariously on the toes of both feet, only his right leg takes the weight. The left leg has been missing and has only been outlined in the drawing without regard to the surviving foot. The whole effect of this muscular figure in isolation is impressive, and the original spirit of the relief is stressed.

197 *Marten van Heemskerck? 1534–6. Front (detail), ithyphallic satyr. Berlin sketchbook, f. 65 recto.*

17 Lambert Lombard (1506–66), in Rome 1537–8 (**198**).

Left end: Drunken Pan carried by supporters.

Liège, Musée, Cabinet des Estampes. Album of Lambert Lombard (formerly in the Collection of the Duke of Arenberg, Brussels), f. 121.

Bibl. See N. DACOS, *Les peintres belges à Rome au XVIe siècle*, i, Brussels and Rome 1964 for further bibliography on L. L., p. 31.

The album also contains drawings by a follower, *c.* 1570. This spirited little sketch may be in the later hand.

18 Workshop of Frans Floris I (1516–70), in Rome 1542–7 (**199**).

Left end: Drunken Pan carried by his supporters.

Basle, Kunstmuseum, Kupferstichkabinett, Cod. U. IV, f. 26 verso.

Pen and ink. 18.2 × 23.7 cms.

Bibl. For attribution and inventory, see CARL VAN DE VELDE, 'A Roman Sketchbook of Frans Floris', *Master Drawings*, vii, 3 (1969), pp. 255–86. Matz, p. 204, no. 9.

This is reproduced here to show by contrast an uninspired copy, perhaps a copy not from the sarcophagus itself. Frans Floris was a pupil of Lambert Lombard. In any case it shows that the sarcophagus was copied by Northerners and drawings of it must have circulated north of the Alps.

198 *Lambert Lombard c. 1538? Left end.*
Liège, Museum. Album, f. 121.

199 *Workshop of Frans Floris I. c. 1542–7. Left end.*
Basle, Kunstmuseum, Cod. U. IV, f. 26 verso.

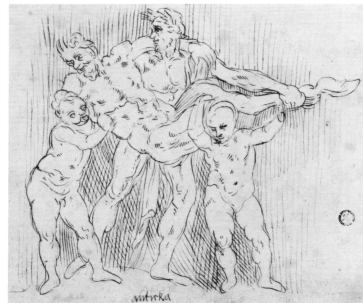

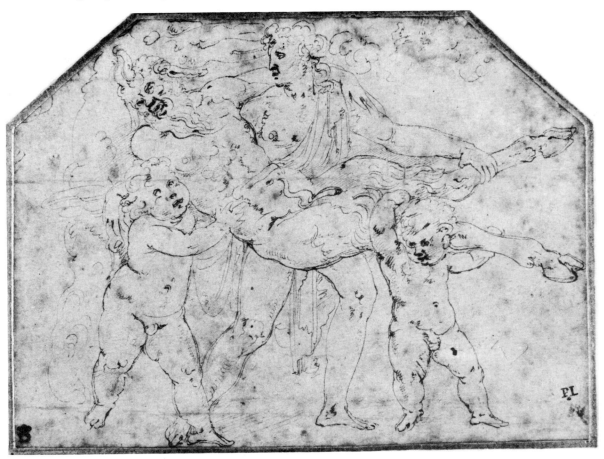

200 *Battista Franco. 1540s. Left end. Chatsworth, 292.*

19 Battista Franco (1510–1561), 1540s (**200**).

Left end: Drunken Pan carried by his supporters.

Chatsworth, Devonshire Collection 292.

Bibl. None. Originally attributed to Battista Franco, it was reattributed to Girolamo da Carpi by
A. E. Popham. Now Mr Gere thinks the original attribution more likely.

The scene is drawn, it seems, more as an exercise in Franco's characteristic calligraphic line, light, wiry and graceful, than as an attempt to discover new depths in
the relief. The restoration of Pan's broken leg is a happy solution (cf. **191**).

A copy of this drawing is illustrated by F. Malaguzzi Valeri, *I disegni della R.
Pinacoteca di Brera*, Milan 1906, fig. 2 as Battista Franco. Noted by Bober, *Aspertini*,
p. 47; Matz, p. 204, no. 10.

20 Girolamo da Carpi (1501–57), *c.* 1549–54 when Girolamo was in Rome (**201**).

Front: All existing figures from the maenad in the chiton to right, including the satyr with a child on his shoulders.

Düsseldorf, Kunstmuseum, Kupferstichkabinett, FP. 126.

Bibl. Exhibition catalogue: *Meisterzeichnungen der Sammlung Lambert Krahe* (Nov.–Jan. 1969–70)
    Kunstmuseum, Düsseldorf 1969, pp. 23–4, no. 18 (entry by E. Schaar), fig. 24.
    Noted in connection with the sarcophagus by Middeldorf, 1958, p. 170, n. 1.
    The attribution to Girolamo was first made in 1964 by Dr Konrad Oberhuber.

Girolamo has supplied the missing arms and legs (cf. Cat. 23 and 26; and existing restorations). The maenad in profile running behind Silenus is not recorded, nor are the attributes of the ithyphallic satyr who appears as a male nude with one undraped arm behind his back. His free interpretation of this figure is an unreliable indication of the condition of the sarcophagus. He seems captivated by the lightness of movement and the sinuosity of the figures.

201 *Girolamo da Carpi.* c. *1549–54. Front: right side. Düsseldorf, Kunstmuseum, FP. 126.*

21 Girolamo da Carpi (1501–57), between 1551–4 when Girolamo was in Rome: see water mark (**202**).

Right end: Pan carried by a satyr.

Providence, Museum of Art, Rhode Island School of Design, no. 22.229 verso.

Pen and ink on brown paper. 28.5 × 18.5 cms.

Bibl. Listed by A. SCHMITT, 1960, p. 122; DEGENHART and SCHMITT, *Corpus*, I, 1, no. 136, p. 248, n. 2 as Battista Franco.

The following information was kindly supplied by the Curator of Prints and Drawings at the R. I. Museum, Mrs Diana L. Johnson.

Watermark: Pascal Lamb (Briquet, 51: Vicenza 1551–60).

202 *Girolamo da Carpi, c. 1551–4. Right end. Providence, Museum, Rhode Island School of Design, 22.229 verso.*

Attributions: An old inscription (eighteenth century?) to 'Hieronimo da Carpi' on lower right. Since then it has been attributed at the Museum to Polidoro and to Battista Franco. The present attribution was made *c.* 1960 when P. Bober reattributed drawings in the so-called Giulio Romano Album in the Rosenbach Foundation, Philadelphia, to Girolamo da Carpi. (See W. Vitzthum's review of A. Bertini's Catalogue of Turin drawings in the *Art Bulletin*, XLIII, I, 1961, p. 72, for Mrs Bober's attributions.) See Cat. 22.

The relationship between this drawing and the variant in the Rosenbach Sketchbook (Cat. 22) is puzzling. Neither seems to refer so much to the sarcophagus itself as to some common prototype. Neither of them shows the satyr who pulls Pan's tail, and they both restore in the same way the satyr gripping Pan's arm, instead of his wrist, a peculiar solution not seen elsewhere.

22 Girolamo da Carpi (1501–57). Date: see Cat. 21 (**203**).

Right end: Pan carried by a satyr.

Philadelphia, Rosenbach Foundation. Girolamo da Carpi Sketchbook, f. 144.

Norman Canedy's edition of the sketchbook is in the press and will be published soon by the Warburg Institute. This drawing, with its modelling with line shading, gives more of an impression of the form of the relief than Cat. 21 which could be a copy.

203 *Girolamo da Carpi. c. 1551–4. Right end (detail). Philadelphia, Rosenbach sketchbook, f. 144.*

23 Anonymous Italian, *c*. mid-sixteenth century (**162**).

Complete sarcophagus, ends and front.

Munich, Staatliche Graphische Sammlung, 2536.

Bibl. DEGENHART, 1950, fig. 14; DEGENHART and SCHMITT, *Corpus*, p. 247, fig. 353; MATZ, p. 204, no. 7.

Formerly attributed to Polidoro da Caravaggio.

The value of this drawing is documentary. It shows the state of the sarcophagus before its restoration in the sixteenth century. It can therefore be used as a yardstick to see how much the artists were inventing their reconstructions, as the real restorations were made later than any of the drawings. Its accuracy can be measured by comparing it with photographs of the sarcophagus which show the restorations clearly.

It is the only drawing which shows the pipe of the missing satyr (indicated by an arrow in the *Corpus*, fig. 353), and a bit of the back of his heel. Degenhart and Schmitt, *Corpus*, p. 247 saw traces of two hands, but the lower hand belongs to the maenad running behind Silenus (see **194**).

It is possible that the figure of the satyr was removed in one piece (probably *c*. 1450?), perhaps for a collector. I am grateful to Professor Sir Ernst Gombrich for this suggestion. The damage to the rest of the sarcophagus, the breaking of noses, arms and legs, may have been the result of a single attack rather than the gradual effects of time. The likely time for this to have taken place would have been between the first drawings (Cat. 1–3) and the second (Cat. 4–6), in the mid-Quattrocento.

24 Battista Naldini (1537–91), 1560 (**204**).

Left end: Drunken Pan carried by supporters.

Oxford, Christ Church.

Bibl. C. F. BELL, *Drawings by the Old Masters in the Library of Christ Church Oxford*, Oxford 1914, p. 51, Z 21, as anonymous Italian 1500–50.

In the forthcoming catalogue of the Christ Church drawings by J. Byam Shaw, Bell Z 21 will appear as Inv. no. 0832 and Cat. no. 195. The attribution of Cat. 24 and 25 to Naldini was made by A. E. Popham and Philip Pouncey independently. I am grateful to Mr Byam Shaw and to Mr John Christian for this information.

P. BAROCCHI, 'Itinerario di Giovambattista Naldini', *L'Arte Antica e Moderna*, xxi, ii, 1965, pp. 246–8, and 269, n. 35; fig. 91 c.

(For exchange of letters between Borghini and Vasari (reprinted by Barocchi, pp. 246–7), see K. FREY, *Der Literarische Nachlass Giorgio Vasaris*, i, Munich 1923, pp. 582 and 586.)

Naldini's drawings of the sarcophagus (Cat. 24–27) are done in the special pen and ink technique he used to copy antique reliefs. They are dashed off quickly with verve and boldness after accurate study. With a bold outline and quick, sure shading with parallel strokes and hatching, he gives a lively impression of the *musculatura* of the

204 *Battista Naldini. 1560. Left end. Oxford, Christ Church, 0832.*

figures. His characteristic exaggeration of knees was deplored by his biographer, R. Borghini, *Il Riposo*, Florence 1584, p. 198.

In No. 24, which omits the feet, Naldini records the exact condition of the relief, and includes the tree or vine, and the back of the terminal satyr following the triumphal chariot on the front (cf. Cat. 23). He has emphasized the modelling and relaxed torsion of Pan's body.

25 Battista Naldini (1537–91), 1560 (**205**).
Front: Left half, omitting terminal satyr, and including the maenad in a chiton. Oxford, Christ Church.
Bibl. Bell, Z 25. Byam Shaw, inv. no. 0836, Cat. no. 199. Barocchi, fig. 91 d.
   See No. 24.
Apart from the invention of the cupid waving a banner, the breakages are faithfully recorded.

205 *Battista Naldini. 1560. Front: left half. Oxford, Christ Church, 0836.*

26 Battista Naldini (1537–91), 1560 (**206**).

Front: Right half, from Silenus's group and including the satyr carrying a child.
Present ownership unknown. Sotheby Sale of Old Master Drawings, 24 May 1966,
lot 18.

Naldini has included the figures of the maenad in profile to right in the background,
and the hind quarters of the panther moving towards right, a unique representation
of this animal which the restorers interpreted as an elephant. He has carefully noted
the long slice off the thigh of the satyr supporting Silenus, but as in Cat. 20, the other
missing pieces have been supplied. Naldini gives a *serpentinata* reconstruction of the
lower right leg of the nude maenad, with knee forward and ankle back.

206 *Battista Naldini. 1560. Front: right half. Owner unknown.*

27 Battista Naldini (1537–91), 1560 (**207**).

Right end: Two satyrs punishing Pan.

Florence, Uffizi, Gabinetto dei Disegni, 14443 F verso.

Pen and brown ink. 32 × 22 cms.

Bibl. P. BAROCCHI, 1965, fig. 92 b.
  Attributed to Battista Naldini by Keith Andrews in 1964. See Cat. 24.

This drawing, in which the attention is focused on Pan and the satyr carrying him, shows that the relief was broken on the left, as Naldini has not attempted to show its connection with the front as he did in Cat. 24. The broken forearm of the satyr on the left remains as it was and as it is now, but Naldini has supplied the satyr carrying Pan with a mighty arm. The altar and part of the tree trunk are included, as in No. 23.

28 Anonymous South German, *c.* 1540–50 (**208**).

Front: Thought to be of the missing satyr originally in the centre of the relief.

Erlangen, Universitätsbibliothek, B. 908.

Brush and ink on reddish yellow prepared paper. 44.7 × 30.2 cms.

207 *Battista Naldini. 1560. Right end. Florence, Uffizi, 14443 F. verso.*

208 *Two views of a piping satyr with the Torso Belvedere. c. 1540–50. Erlangen, Universitätsbibliothek, B. 908.*

Bibl. Exhibition catalogue: DIETER KUHRMANN, *Altdeutsche Zeichnungen aus der Universitätsbibliothek Erlangen*, Munich 1974, pp. 103–4, no. 97, with further bibliography and comparisons, including a Passarotti drawing in Munich, 2237 v; fig. 73.

Matz, p. 204, no. 14.

The drawing shows two views of a satyr striding forward, his upper body curved back as he tilts his head and lifts his arms to play the double pipes raised almost straight up before him. Between the two views, on the edge of plinth, is a model of the Torso Belvedere. The pose of the satyr is reflected in a lyrical sixteenth-century bronze, the example in the Louvre illustrated side by side with the drawing in profile view by H. R. Weihrauch, *Europäische Bronzestatuetten*, Brunswick 1967, figs. 150 and 151 as possibly by Francesco da Sant'Agata. The literature on the bronze is assembled and the model attributed to Camelio (*c.* 1455/60–1537), by Sir John Pope-Hennessy, assisted by Anthony F. Radcliffe, *Italian Sculpture, The Frick Collection Illustrated Catalogue*, iii, New York 1970, pp. 158–62, with 3 plates of the Frick example, including the back view.

The essential character of the pose, the freedom of the lilting, forward stride, often repeated in sixteenth-century paintings and drawings of Bacchanalia (for examples, see F. Antal, 'Observations on Girolamo da Carpi', *Art Bulletin*, xxx, 2, 1948, figs. 15–17, pp. 93–4) seems to depend on a model less necessarily constricted than a figure pressed towards the background in a sarcophagus relief (**169, 182, 183**, Cat. 1 and 2). A closer prototype may still be found perhaps in a variant of the bronze dancing satyr in the Bibliothèque Nationale, Paris (M. Bieber, *The Sculpture of the Hellenistic Age*, revised edition, New York 1961, fig. 561 and p. 139).

Acknowledgments

I should like to thank my friends in the Warburg Institute, London University, for their help and advice, and especially Mr Stanley Parker Ross, the photographer of the Warburg Institute, and his assistants who have re-photographed the sarcophagus. I particularly wish to acknowledge Phyllis Bober's Census of Antique Works of Art known to Renaissance Artists, sponsored by the Warburg Institute and the Institute of Fine Arts, New York University, which has provided most of the visual material on which this study is based.

I am grateful to Mr Denys Haynes, Keeper of Greek and Roman Antiquities in the British Museum, and Mrs Haynes for their help, and particularly to Mr Brian Cook, who read the typescript and was generous with his knowledge of Roman sculpture, as was Mr William Cole. Warm thanks go to Mr John Gere, Keeper of Prints and Drawings in the British Museum, for reading the first draft, and making valuable suggestions.

Others I should like to thank for information and photographs are Dr Alessandro Bettagno, Miss Shaunagh FitzGerald, Mrs Laurie Fusco, Miss Jane Low, Professor Ulrich Middeldorf, Mr and Mrs Philip Pouncey, and Dr Peter Spring. Others are acknowledged in the notes and catalogue. Finally I should like to express my thanks to my husband for all his advice, to Sir John Pope-Hennessy, who suggested this article, and to Mr Richard Camber for his constructive encouragement.

After this article went to press, I learned that several striking North Italian borrowings from the sarcophagus have been recently discovered by Professor Gunter Schweikhart whose findings will soon appear in the *Mitteilungen des Kunthistorischen Institutes in Florenz*, xx, 1976, and in his forthcoming book on Falconetto as a painter. See now his 'Un rilievo all'antica sconosciuto nell' Odeo Cornaro a Padova', *Padova e la sua Provincia*, xxi, 7–8, 1975, pp. 8–11.

Photographic Credits. Kunstmuseum, Basle: 199; Madame Nicole Dacos-Crifo, Brussels: 171; Fürstliche Sammlung, Schloss Wolfegg, Germany: 191, 192, 193; Staatliche Museen, Berlin–Dahlem: 196, 197; Devonshire Collection, Chatsworth: 200; Landesbildstelle Rheinland, Düsseldorf: 201; Graphische Sammlung, Erlangen: 208; Brogi Collection, Florence: 167, 168; Soprintendenza alle Gallerie, Florence: 207; Professor Alessandro Parronchi, Florence: 194; Fratelli Alinari, Florence: 169, 170; Musée des Beaux Arts, Liège: 198; Courtauld Institute of Art, University of London: 188, 200; Sotheby & Co., London: 206; Fondazione Cini, Venice: 185, 186, 187; Staatliche Graphische Sammlung, Munich: 162; Musée du Louvre, Paris: 182, 183, 184; Museum of Art, Rhode Island School of Design: 202; Rosenbach Foundation, Philadelphia: 203.

All other photographs reproduced by courtesy of the Warburg Institute, University of London.

NOTES

1 A. H. Smith, *A Catalogue of Sculpture in the Department of Greek and Roman Antiquities, British Museum*, iii, London 1904, pp. 301–4, no. 2298. F. Matz, *Die dionysischen Sarkophage*, ii (Die antiken Sarkophagreliefs, iv), Berlin 1968, pp. 204–7, no. 88 (hereafter Matz). I am grateful to Mr B. F. Cook, Assistant Keeper in the Department of Greek and Roman Antiquities, for this information from his study of the Townley Collection to be published in a later issue of the *Yearbook*. See Matz, ii, p. 205 for a

bibliography which includes the later history of the sarcophagus.

2 Among them is a neo-Attic relief, *Dionysus and his Retinue visiting Icarius* (Smith, iii, no. 2190), much drawn in the Renaissance and also from the Villa Montalto.

3 See Phyllis Pray Bober, *Drawings after the Antique by Amico Aspertini : Sketchbooks in the British Museum*, London 1957, pp. vii–viii for a statement of the scope and aims of her Census of Antique Works of Art known to Renaissance

Artists, which is a collection of documentation and photographs of antique works of art known before 1527 in Italy, including fifteenth and sixteenth century drawings of them. Matz, i, pp. viii–xii, lists 385 extant Bacchic sarcophagi. Forty so far are in the Census. Of these, at least eight, as far as we know, were in Rome before *c.* 1450. I am grateful to Dr Peter Spring for his useful index, extracted from the Census and other sources, of antique sculpture and reliefs known in Rome before 1447, deposited in the Warburg Institute.

4 The references in Matz's description of no. 88 to TH (*thiasos*) types are explained in his first volume: (left to right) centaur musicians, p. 72, TH 119; Pan, p. 63, TH 108; ecstatic satyr with wineskin (Askophorus B), p. 47, TH 70; maenad in chiton (Kymbalistria B), p. 31, TH 30; missing satyr from centre (Aulistrios H), p. 43, TH 60; group with Silenus on ass, p. 71, TH 118; nude maenad (Tympanistra A), p. 27, TH 21; satyr carrying child (Kinderträger A), p. 48, TH 75.

5 The restorations are discussed in more detail below, pp. 123–5 and n. 52.

6 For other examples in antique and Renaissance art, see O. Kurz, 'Begram et l'occident gréco-romain', in J. Hackin, *Nouvelles recherches archéologiques à Begram* (Mémoires de la Délégation Archéologique Française en Afganistan xi), Paris 1954, pp. 111–12.

7 Other examples of the left end (Pan carried by cupids) are from sarcophagi in S. Scolastica, Subiaco (Matz, ii, no. 78) and in the Fitzwilliam Museum, Cambridge (Matz, ii, no. 129; L. Budde and R. Nicholls, *A Catalogue of the Greek and Roman Sculpture in the Fitzwilliam Museum Cambridge*, Cambridge 1964, no. 161). Another scene from the right end (the satyr pulling Pan's tail) is on a sarcophagus front from Ostia in Munich (Matz, ii, no. 85). Various interpretations of the scene are presented by M. J. Vermaseren, 'Fragments de sarcophage de Sainte-Prisque: Pan enfant corrigé par un Satyre', *Latomus*, 1959, pp. 742–50.

8 Matz, iii, no. 218.

9 Cf. Propertius, *Elegiae*, iii, xvii, 7–9; Ovid, *Fasti*, iii, 510.

10 F. Cumont, *Afterlife in Roman Paganism*, New Haven 1922, p. 35; cf. M. P. Nilsson, *The Dionysiac Mysteries of the Hellenistic and Roman Age*, Lund 1957, p. 131. See also Cumont, *Recherches sur le symbolisme funéraire des Romains*, Paris 1942.

11 E. Panofsky, *Tomb Sculpture*, London 1964, p. 34.

12 R. Turcan, *Les sarcophages romains à représentations Dionysiaques. Essai de chronologie et d'histoire religieuse*, Paris 1966.

13 J. M. C. Toynbee, *Death and Burial in the Roman World*, London 1971, pp. 270–5. See also J. Kirchmann, *De Funeribus Romanorum Libri Quatuor* (first published in 1604), 4th ed., rev., Frankfort 1672, book ii, especially chapter xxv.

14 Peter Spring, 'The Topographical and Archaeological Study of the Antiquities of the City of Rome, 1420–1447', Ph.D. Thesis, University of Edinburgh 1972, pp. 102–14; Appendix B, pp. 422–8. For a view of the Basilica and Palace *c.* 1550, see R. Krautheimer, S. Corbett, and W. Frankl, *Corpus Basilicarum Christianarum Romae*, iii (Eng. ed.), Vatican City 1967, fig. 17. This volume includes a full bibliography and list of views.

15 As described by Cennino d'Andrea Cennini, *The Craftsman's Handbook. The Italian 'Il Libro dell'Arte'*, trans. D. V. Thompson, Jr., New Haven, Conn. 1933.

16 Richard Krautheimer, in collaboration with Trude Krautheimer-Hess, *Lorenzo Ghiberti*, Princeton, N.J., rev. ed., i, 1970, p. 288 (on hypothetical drawings made in Rome); ii, pl. 84 (*Expulsion*); p. 344, Handlist of Antiques, no. 26. Hereafter, Krautheimer, *Ghiberti*.

17 Leon Battista Alberti, *On Painting*, trans., introd., and notes by J. R. Spencer, rev. ed., New Haven, Conn., 1966, p. 74: 'The most graceful movements and the most lively are those which move upwards into the air'. For the Italian quotation see L. B. Alberti, *Il Trattato della Pittura*, ed. G. Papini, Lanciano 1913, Bk. ii, p. 62.

18 Krautheimer, *Ghiberti*, i, pp. 211–13.

19 G. Vasari, *Le Vite de' più Eccellenti Pittori Scultori ed Architettori*, ed. G. Milanesi, ii, Florence 1906, p. 245: 'this ornament, I say,

which is the most rare and marvellous thing which one can see in bronze'. Hereafter, Vasari, ed. Mil. Degenhart, 1950, p. 213, was the first to notice the connection between the Ghiberti reliefs and the sarcophagus.

20 Perhaps the most famous Renaissance poem to celebrate Bacchus, and which almost seems to describe the sarcophagus, is the *Canzona di Bacco* by Lorenzo de' Medici, in the Canti Carnascialeschi, in *Tutte le Opere, Scritti Giocosi,* Milan 1958, pp. 153–4. I am grateful to Jill Kraye for pointing out this, and also Poliziano's *Orfeo.*

21 P. Rotondi, *The Ducal Palace of Urbino. Its Architecture and Decoration,* London 1969 (trans. from 1st ed. 1950), pp. 20–1. For bibliography and most recent discussion on the Palace, see L. H. Heydenreich and W. Lotz, *Architecture in Italy 1400 to 1600* (Pelican History of Art), Harmondsworth 1974, chapter 7: 'Urbino', pp. 71–9. Hereafter, Heydenreich and Lotz, *Architecture.*

22 C. H. Clough, 'Federigo da Montefeltro's Patronage of the Arts, 1468–1482', *Journal of the Warburg and Courtauld Institutes,* xxxvi, 1973, p. 141. Hereafter, Clough, *JWCI,* 1973.

23 Clarence Kennedy was the first to suggest an attribution to Michele di Giovanni di Bartolo, a pupil of Bernardo Rossellino, in 'Il Greco aus Fiesole', *Mitteilungen des Kunsthistorischen Institutes in Florenz,* iv, 1932–4, pp. 25–40. Hereafter Kennedy, *Flor. Mitt.,* 1932–4; cf. Degenhart, 1950; Middeldorf, 1958 (see bibliographical note, p. 127); M. Salmi, in *Encyclopedia of World Art,* xii, McGraw-Hill, New York, Toronto and London 1966, p. 18, s.v. 'Renaissance'; and C. Seymour Jr, *Sculpture in Italy, 1400–1500* (The Pelican History of Art), Harmondsworth 1966, pp. 144 and 241, n. 27. The earlier attribution to Francesco Laurana by L. Venturi, 'Studi sul Palazzo Ducale di Urbino', *L'Arte,* xvii, 1914, pp. 415–73 gains some support from M. d'Elia, 'Appunti per la ricostruzione delle attività di Francesco Laurana', *Annali della Facoltà di Lettere e Filosofia,* (Studi e contributi dell'Istituto di Archeologia e storia dell'arte dell'Università di Bari), v, 3, 1959, p. 9. Cf. John Pope-Hennessy,

Italian Renaissance Sculpture (rev. ed.), London and New York 1971, p. 314, who cites Venturi's attribution to Laurana (1459–60), without comment, and gives this attribution a question mark in the index.

24 Vespasiano da Bisticci, *Vite di Uomini Illustri del Secolo XV,* ed. P. d'Ancona and E. Aeschlimann, Milan 1951, pp. 208–9: '.... and to hear him talk with a sculptor, it seemed that the art was his, such was the way that he discussed it!'

25 Krautheimer, *Ghiberti,* ii, figs. 6 and 5.

26 Degenhart and Schmitt, *Corpus,* I, 1, p. 248, n. 5, discuss the right end of the *Camino* frieze in terms of the original undamaged sarcophagus.

27 Kennedy, *Flor. Mitt.,* 1932–4, p. 36; Salmi in *Encyclopedia of World Art,* p. 18. In 1464 the poet Filelfo hailed Federigo as Hercules in an eulogy, see Clough, *JWCI,* 1973, p. 134.

28 E. Battisti, *Piero della Francesca,* ii, Milan 1971, pp. 57–8 for bibliography and discussion of whether or not Battista's portrait was painted *post-mortem.* Battista died in 1472. The elaborate frame in the Uffizi uniting the two portraits preserves the imagery of the two *Camino* reliefs and of the *Sala della Iole.*

29 F. Saxl, *A Heritage of Images. A Selection of Lectures,* ed. H. Honour and J. Fleming, with an introd. by E. H. Gombrich, Harmondsworth 1970, p. 65, and pls. 83–6; B. Degenhart and A. Schmitt, 'Ein Musterblatt des Jacopo Bellini mit Zeichnungen nach der Antike', *Festschrift Luitpold Dussler,* Munich 1972, pp. 153–4 and p. 164, n. 21. For illustrations from the facsimile edition, see V. Goloubew, *Les Dessins de Jacopo Bellini au Louvre et au British Museum,* i, Brussels 1908–12, xxxix, cxxvi, cxxxii.

30 Middeldorf, 1958 (see bibliographical note, p. 127) has pointed out further transformations of this sort: Botticelli, *Calumny of Apelles,* Florence, Uffizi, no. 1496, figure of Truth at the left, cf. nude maenad and Venus *pudica;* attrib. Pinturicchio, drawing with mythological and allegorical figures: Florence, Uffizi, 349 E, figure on right, cf. satyr with child on shoulders and arms arranged in the manner of the ithyphallic satyr, but the legs are in a

typical late Quattrocento mannered stance. Two scenes in Signorelli's frescoes (*c.* 1499–1504) in the Chapel of S. Brizio in the Cathedral at Orvieto may be free adaptations from the sarcophagus ends: the damned soul riding on the back of a demon (right end), and the fictive relief of the Lamentation of Christ (left end). Enzo Carli, *Luca Signorelli. Gli Affreschi nel Duomo di Orvieto*, Bergamo 1946, pls. 41 and 70. I am grateful to Suzy Butters for these observations. See below pp. 118, 120, and n. 38, and 121–2 for examples of Cinquecento *invenzione*.

31 The various antiquarian traditions are clearly described by E. Mandowsky and C. Mitchell, *Pirro Ligorio's Roman Antiquities*, London 1963. Hereafter, Mandowsky and Mitchell, *Ligorio*. For Dosio, see Hülsen in bibliographical note. For G. B. Cavalieri and his tradition, see T. Ashby, 'Antiquae Statuae Urbis Romae', *Papers of the British School at Rome*, ix, 5, 1920, pp. 107–58.

32 N. Dacos, *La Découverte de la Domus Aurea et la Formation des Grotesques à la Renaissance*, London and Leiden 1969, pp. 79–81. Hereafter, Dacos, *Découverte*.

33 P. Bober (see bibliographical note, p. 127), esp. pp. 3–4, 10, 27–8, 32, and 38–9. For a recent monograph on Aspertini as a painter, see Helga Kropfinger-v. Kügelgen, *Amico Aspertinis Malerisches Werk*, Dissertation, Bonn 1973.

34 H. Egger, *Codex Escurialensis. Ein Skizzenbuch aus der Werkstatt Domenico Ghirlandaios*, Vienna 1906, e.g. f. 5 v.

35 For connections between Ripanda, Peruzzi and Aspertini, see M. Petrassi and O. Guerra, *Il Colle Capitolino*, Rome, n.d., pp. 133–48 and M. V. Brugnoli, 'Baldassare Peruzzi nella chiesa di S. Maria della Pace e nella "uccelliera" di Giulio II', *Bollettino d'Arte*, ser. v, lviii, 1–2, 1973, pp. 113–22, esp. p. 121, n. 17 (with wrong reference to Bober, should be p. 47) and fig. 28. Philip Pouncey has attributed a quick wash study for this fresco to Peruzzi: Louvre, R.F.592, formerly attributed to Perino, illustrated and discussed by C. L. Frommel, *Baldassare Peruzzi als Maler und Zeichner*,

Vienna 1967–8, fig. xxxvi b and no. 52, pp. 91–93.

36 On Raphael's archaeological interests, see V. Golzio, *Raffaello nei documenti*, Vatican City 1936 (rev. ed., Gregg Reprint, Farnborough 1971), pp. 78–92; Mandowsky and Mitchell, *Ligorio*, pp. 15–19. For stucco of Bacchus and Ariadne, see N. Dacos, 'Il Trastullo di Raffaello', *Paragone Arte*, 219, 1968, fig. 6b and p. 24. I am most grateful to Madame Dacos-Crifo for sending me this photograph. Her work on the repertory of antique works of art inspiring the *Logge* is to be published. For other motifs directly from the sarcophagus which appear in the stucchi, see W. Amelung, 'Die Stuckreliefs in den Loggien Raffaels und ihre Vorbilder', in T. Hofmann, *Raffael als Architekt*, IV, pl. xlv: nude maenad and musical centaurs.

37 Dacos, *Découverte*, pp. 43–8.

38 Later used by A. Bocchi, *Symbolicarum Quaestionum de Universo Genere quas Serio Ludebat Libri V*, Bologna 1574, Bk. v, 'Virtutis et Felicitatis formula', cxxvii, with inscription on base: VIRTUTI MERITO SEDES QUADRATA DICATUR. Other engravings by Marcantonio or his school which mingle and transform motifs from the sarcophagus are described in A. Bartsch, *Le Peintre Graveur*, xiv, Leipzig 1867 (hereafter B.), xiv, 231. 305 (right end); and B. xiv. 207. 258 (nude maenad with ithyphallic satyr herm). An example of an elaboration of multiple sources is a drawing by Galeazzo Mondella, Louvre 5078, Matz, ii, p. 204, no. 13.

39 Vasari, ed. Mil., VI, p. 573.

40 Vasari, ed. Mil., VI, p. 583.

41 Sir Henry Ellis, *The Townley Galleries of Classic Sculpture in the British Museum*, ii, London 1836, p. 134, says that the ends were first published by Battista Franco in 1570, and are also illustrated by P. S. Bartoli in *Admiranda*, 1693 (see n. 55). I have not traced these engravings. The first illustrated edition of Cartari was Venice, 1571. **174** is from the Padua 1615 ed., p. 559. A woodcut of the detail of the triumphal chariot is also used in both Cartari and Conti. See J. Seznec, *The Survival of the Pagan Gods. The Mythological Tradition and its Place in Renaissance Humanism and Art*, New York 1961, pp. 219–56 on

Cartari. Hereafter, Seznec, *Survival*. The *Imagini* continued to be used in the seventeenth century: A. Blunt, *Nicolas Poussin*, New York, London 1967, p. 327.

42 Giovanni Paolo Lomazzo, *Trattato dell'arte della Pittura Scultura ed Architettura*, iii, Rome 1844, p. 272. Seznec, *Survival*, p. 232.

43 For Dosio, see Hülsen, bibliographical note, p. 127.

44 On Pighius, see Mandowsky and Mitchell, *Ligorio*, pp. 21–5.

45 J. A. Gere, *Taddeo Zuccaro. His Development Studied in his Drawings*, London 1969, pl. 23, and p. 138, no. 23; the owner is Dr Robert Landolt, Chur.

46 Gere, *Taddeo*, pl. 139, and p. 107.

47 C. d'Onofrio, *Gli Obelischi di Roma*, Rome 1965, pp. 193–4, figs. 59, 60, and 67. For comments on the Cross and inscription of the Esquiline Obelisk, see Heydenreich and Lotz, *Architecture*, p. 286.

48 G. Baglione, *Le Vite de'Pittori Scultori et Architetti*, Rome 1642 (facsimile ed. V. Mariani, Rome 1935), p. 72. For Vacca's works, see A. Riccoboni, *Roma nell'Arte*, Rome 1942, pp. 107–10, pls. 163, 167, and pl. between pp. 96–7.

49 F. Vacca, *Memorie di varie antichità trovate in diversi luoghi della Città di Roma scritte da Flaminio Vacca nell'Anno 1594*, 24 pp. in Famiamo Nardini, *Roma Antica*, 2nd ed., Rome 1704.

50 I am grateful to Professor Max Seidl for this information; his study on Nicola Pisano's antique sources, including this krater, is in the press (*Flor. Mitt.*, 1975). For an illustration *in situ*, see Hülsen, *Dosio*, pl. xxiv, no. 43, f. 17.

51 Matz, ii, no. 89.

52 Hülsen, *Dosio*, pl. xx, no. 37, f. 14 v., and p. 10. A more probable source for the new satyrs was the Icarius relief also brought by Sixtus V to the Villa Montalto (British Museum 2190, see n. 2). Eight of its original figures were similar to those on the krater in Pisa including the three satyrs. See C. M. Havelock, *Hellenistic Art*, London 1971, fig. 174; Hülsen, *Dosio*, p. 16 for a list of Renaissance drawings of it.

53 F. Perrier, *Icones et segmenta illustrium e marmore tabularum quae Romae adhuc extant a Francisco Perrier delineata*, Rome 1645 (Paris 1650), pls. 8 and 9. See E. Schleier, *Paragone Arte*, 217, 1968, pp. 42–54.

54 J. G. van Gelder, *Jan de Bisschop 1628–1671*, The Hague, 1972 (offprint from *Oud Holland*, lxxxvi, 4, 1971, pp. 201–30), pp. 1–2, n. 1; 9–10; 18–9, n. 73.

55 Pietro Santi Bartoli, *Admiranda Romanarum Antiquitatum ac Veteris Sculpturae Vestigia*, with notes by G. P. Bellori, Rome 1693, pls. 48–9. On Bartoli (1635–1700), see M. C. Mazzi, 'L'incisore perugino Pietro Sante Bartoli', *Bollettino della Deputazione di Storia Patria per l'Umbria*, lxx, 1973, pp. 21–39; for Bellori (1613–96), see K. Donahue, in *Dizionario Biografico degli Italiani*, vii, Rome 1965, pp. 781–9.

An attack on the Accademia di S Luca: Ludovico David's *L'Amore dell'Arte*

NICHOLAS TURNER

Assistant Keeper, Prints and Drawings

Missirini, writing the history of the Accademia di S Luca, the Roman Academy of painters, sculptors and architects, describes the virulent criticisms made against that institution in 1704 by the little-known painter Ludovico David.[1] Although Missirini concedes that there must have been some justification for this attack, otherwise David would not have approached Pope Clement XI (Albani), the fact that no remedial action was taken led him ultimately to dismiss these criticisms as groundless. Believing this shameful episode best forgotten he obscured the circumstances of the controversy and did not discuss its precise form. However, the identification of two manuscripts by David, one in the Biblioteca Estense, Modena and the other in the Archivio dell' Accademia di S Luca, Rome, both versions of a work entitled *L'Amore dell'Arte*, dedicated to Clement XI, permits the conclusion that it was here that David's criticisms were presented.[2] A full account of David's proposals for the reform of the Academy may now be given.

David publicized his views strenuously by circulating *L'Amore dell'Arte* in manuscript amongst his friends in an attempt to gain support for himself and to broaden his campaign against the Academy.[3] From a letter he wrote to his friend Ludovico Muratori, historian and archivist to the Duke of Modena (**209**), dated 4 April 1705, it is recorded that another was sent to Clement XI who, on reading it, probably forwarded it to the secretary of the Academy, then the painter Giuseppe Ghezzi (**210**).[4] The result was that *L'Amore dell'Arte* was read by several persons, and where their written opinions of this work have survived they will be discussed here.

L'Amore dell'Arte marks the first major confrontation in Italy between an artist and an established academy and is one of the earliest critical investigations of the institutionalization of art education. This article will therefore investigate David's

209 *Portrait of Ludovico Muratori, engraving.*

210 *Self-portrait by Giuseppe Ghezzi.*
Stockholm, Nationalmuseum.

objections to the Accademia di S Luca. It is at the beginning of the Romantic period at the end of the eighteenth century with the belief in the power of genius to transcend the limitation of rules that resentment against academic teaching was common but objections to this system of education, though rare, had been made before then. *L'Amore dell'Arte* is a critique of academic teaching, but it is not made in the name of the romantic preconception of the power of artistic inspiration to defy all boundaries. Against the background of the widespread success of artist academies in the seventeenth and early eighteenth centuries it is unexpected.[5]

The curriculum almost universally accepted and applied at this period comprised both practical and theoretical instruction: life drawing was the most important constituent of the practical course while lessons devoted to perspective, anatomy, architecture and sometimes mathematics were the basis for the teaching of theory. In *L'Amore dell'Arte* David does not offer a completely new alternative to this standard form of schooling but suggests that a number of its ingredients be emphasized; his ideas are not abolitionist as later ones were to be, but are recommendations for change within an existing structure. The plea for the thorough reform of the Accademia di S Luca is furthermore consistent with the thought of the Enlightenment which stressed the need for the efficiency of institutions, condemning their corruption. The notion of the academy as the ideal establishment for the teaching of the artist was not therefore abandoned but was only regarded as suitable for such teaching after extensive alterations to the curriculum had been made.

Ludovico David is not well known, and the facts of his biography have been frequently confused with those of his son Antonio.[6] A painter, he was born in Lugano in 1648. His artistic career started in Milan in the mid-1660s where he was taught first by Francesco del Cairo and then by Ercole Procaccini; he was later active in Venice from 1667/8 to 1685, making short visits to other cities, notably to Bologna and Parma. In 1686 he moved to Rome where he stayed until the end of his life. He did not establish a reputation there but was nonetheless awarded public commissions including: the *Adoration of the Magi* and the *Adoration of the Shepherds* (**211** and **212**), both lateral paintings, in the first chapel to the left in S Andrea al Quirinale; the *Gloria of Saints and Angels* (**213**), since destroyed, cupola fresco of the former Collegio Clementino which he described in a pamphlet published in 1695.[7] More successful as a portraitist, David was patronized by members of the Roman court including Pope Clement XI; in the third discourse of *L'Amore dell'Arte* David recounts that both he and his twenty-year-old son, Antonio, portrayed the Pope at a sitting.[8] David was much inspired by the Lombard influences of his early training and by the work of Correggio. The date of the artist's death is unknown but is probably no later than 1710.[9]

Painting was not David's sole occupation; he was also an historian of art, for which he is perhaps better known. He wrote a three-part revision of Vasari's *Vite dei pittori* called *Il disinganno delle notizie ed erudizioni dell'arti più nobile del disegno*, now lost, but which was announced in 1704 by Orlandi.[10] The existence of *L'Amore dell'Arte*, the longest work by David to have survived, is unjustifiably neglected.[11] In the introduction to the reader in the latter, a summary of the contents of *Il disinganno* is given which greatly expands that provided by Orlandi's notice.[12] How accurate *Il disinganno* would have been historically and the extent to which it would have replaced Vasari's *Vite* as an authoritative survey of the history of Italian art cannot be fully ascertained, but the insight that the summary gives into David's

211 *Ludovico David:* Adoration of the Magi.
Rome, S Andrea al Quirinale.

212 *Ludovico David:* Adoration of the Shepherds.
Rome, S Andrea al Quirinale.

methods would suggest that *Il disinganno*, though of critical interest, would not have proved to be as factually reliable as the work it was intended to replace.

Judging from his writings David was an eccentric and, according to his own testimony, he was disliked by many of his contemporaries.[13] His disagreeable and rebellious character anticipates the typical romantic temperament of the later eighteenth century. The one-man campaign that he staged against the Accademia di S Luca did not make him a hero but an enemy of its members who saw him as an innovator and a malcontent. The exclusion of his life from the compendious biographies of artists written by Niccolò Pio and Leone Pascoli would suggest that they considered his work was unremarkable and best forgotten;[14] this largely seems to have been his critical fate ever since. In the one early, but short, biography of the artist in existence

213 *Ludovico David:* Gloria of Saints and Angels,
destroyed. Formerly Rome, Collegio Clementino.

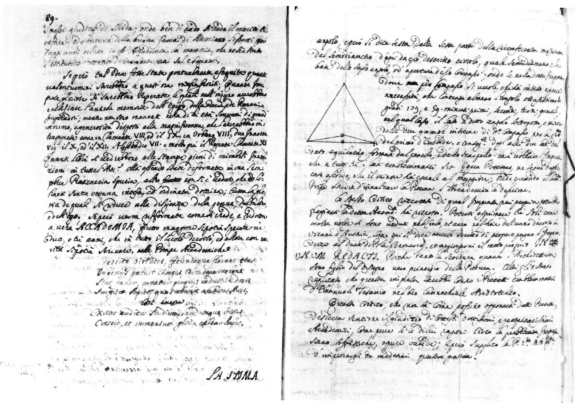

214 *Manuscript, in the hand of Ludovico David.*
Rome, Accademia di S Luca, Archivio Storico 35,
p. 89.

215 *Autograph letter, in the hand of Ludovico David.*
Bologna, Biblioteca Universitaria 1865, unpaginated.

written by the Florentine connoisseur Niccolò Gabburri it is maliciously related that
David died at an inn while travelling; the precious manuscript of *Il disinganno* which
was then at his side promptly disappeared never to be seen again.[15]

There are two manuscript versions of *L'Amore dell'Arte*.[16] The first which is not
autographed is in the Biblioteca Estense, Modena, and was formerly in the possession
of Marchese Giuseppe Campori; it is incomplete, lacks a title and does not contain
the diagrams intended for it.[17] The second, in the Archivio dell'Accademia di S
Luca, Rome, is a later redaction of the first written in David's own hand; the script
is identical with that of letters written to Orlandi which are now in the Biblioteca
Universitaria, Bologna (214, 215).[18] The Modena manuscript was discussed by Bassoli
in 1957 who, despite the lack of a title, was able to identify it as a version of *L'Amore
dell'Arte*.[19] The later complete version in the Accademia di S Luca was unknown to

him. In writing the history of the Accademia di S Luca, Missirini consulted a manuscript of *L'Amore del'Arte* which he cited as being in the possession of the antiquarian, Filippo Visconti.[20] That this was a third version is unlikely and it seems probable, though this is only conjecture, that the Visconti manuscript passed into the hands of the Accademia di S Luca.[21]

Apart from the major differences between the Modena and Rome manuscripts described above, the variants between them are of only slight textual importance. Perhaps the most interesting feature of the first version, lacking in the second, is that the paragraphs which initiate subsections of the manuscript are numbered with Roman numerals; this is in imitation of Leon Battista Alberti's treatise, *Della Pittura* where each paragraph is numbered.[22] An echo of a treatise format within the larger oratorical arrangement of the matter into discourses is deliberately archaizing and is used to make ordinary pronouncements appear axiomatic. That such statements are presented as indisputable is further shown in the language where borrowings from mathematical terminology are employed to give an argument the finality of a proof.

Both the Modena and Rome manuscripts are versions of the first part of a two-part work as the title of the Rome manuscript makes clear.[23] In a letter dated 6 February 1706 written by David to Muratori, the planned second part is referred to 'which will be entitled the moral comedy unhinged and disconcerted'.[24] *L'Amore dell'Arte* comprises a dedication to Pope Clement XI, an address to the reader and three discourses each of which analyses an aspect of the Academy's malfunction. The first, 'Origin and contributions of the Academy of St. Luke of Rome first discourse', traces the history of the Academy and describes its over dependence on life drawing as a means of educating the young artist.[25] A programme for the organization of competitions in painting, sculpture and architecture, said to have been implemented by the painter Girolamo Muziano upon the foundation of the Academy, is copied out at the end of the discourse. The second, 'The valuation that the Academy of St. Luke has made of the Divine Raphael Sanzio, founder of the Roman School and of other worthy Italian masters Discourse II', chastizes the Academy *stimatori* for the valuation at a derisory sum of an important cartoon then believed to be by Raphael, and suggests it has no interest in perpetuating the best traditions of the Roman School.[26] The third, 'Censure of the *impresa* of the putative equilateral triangle exhibited by the Accademia di S Luca in the Campidoglio on the day of 24 April 1704. Discourse III', discards the *impresa* (**216**) invented by Giuseppe Ghezzi as failing to conform to the rules that underlie their design.[27] He goes on to criticize the equal status within the Academy of painting, sculpture and architecture which the *impresa* metaphorically assumes and suggests that this should not be the case, and that architecture and sculpture should be relegated to a place below that of painting.

RELAZIONE.

RIMA ch'Io t'efponga, ò faggio amico Lettore, ciocbè di fingolare porta feco la noftra Accademia del Difegno, che in queft' Anno torna di nuovo ful Campidoglio à ricevere dalla beneficenza del Sovrano Principe *i Premj della Virtù, e da Roma, anzi dal Mondo tutto, i giufti Applaufi del Merito; fermati meco à confiderare sù la fronte del Libro i fentimenti della medefima.*

Tù vedi efpreffa in nobile fcudo la maeftofa Idèa di Sommo Monarca. *Circondalo il Serpente fimbolo dell'Eternità, fopra al cui capo lucidiffima Stella, poftavi dal coftume degl' Egizzj, fi fcorge. Nel dintorno dell'ornato fi legge incifo à lettere di Oro.* Bonis Artibus Restitutis. *Reggono la veneranda* Effigie *i Numi della Sapien-*
B   za

216 *The* impresa *of the Accademia di S Luca designed by Giuseppe Ghezzi.*

217 *Giovanni Angelo Canini:* Drawing Academy. *London, British Museum.*

Before examining David's criticism of the life class in the first discourse, a little must be said of the history of this activity. Since the late sixteenth century, with its revival by the Carracci in their academy in Bologna, life drawing was regarded as essential to the training of the artist and was rapidly incorporated into the curricula of other later academies.[28] A drawing by Giovanni Angelo Canini in the British Museum, and a painting traditionally attributed to Sebastian Bourdon in the Castle Howard collection, York (**217** and **218**), show how such classes were conducted. The model, situated at the centre of the room, holds a staff to sustain his pose as students roundabout made drawings. By the later part of the seventeenth century the life class was well established in the Accademia di S Luca; taking place every week during the summer months—it was too cold for the model during winter—a rota

218 *Sebastian Bourdon:* Drawing Academy. *From the Castle Howard collection.*

219 *Carlo Maratta:* Drawing Academy, *engraved by N. Dorigny.*

system was employed whereby six members were chosen to direct the class and to give instruction to newcomers. One member and an assistant took charge for each month of the six-month season.[29]

Skill in the representation of the human figure in different attitudes was regarded as essential to the successful painter; the humanistic notion that the ultimate function of painting, like poetry, was to instruct by the presentation of significant human action was widely accepted. Seventeenth-century writings on art therefore stress that successful history painting was often the result of an ability to portray the human figure in motion. Bellori, writing in 1672, says that Annibale Carracci, Domenichino and Poussin made painstaking studies of the human figure with the result that their compositions move the spectator by their convincing depiction of action; Caravaggio, on the other hand who made no such drawings, painted figures that did not attract attention in the same way.[30]

The utility of life drawing began to be questioned in the later seventeenth century. Bellori in his life of Carlo Maratta refers to certain painters who thought such a study to be irrelevant and who believed it was sufficient to, 'satisfy the eye and to produce a general resemblance to nature . . . from which principle', Bellori adds, 'the young abandon study and hard work'.[31] To contradict those misconceptions Maratta made a drawing of an ideal Academy for the Marchese del Carpio later engraved by Dorigny (**219**) where the study of Geometry, Optics, Colour and Design are shown as parallel and mutually complementary occupations.[32] That criticisms of life drawing were widespread is further demonstrated by Agostino Scilla in a discourse read to the Accademia di S Luca in 1688 where he condemns those who wished to 'abandon the exact finish of figures' for it was enough for them 'to be sketched in according to fashion'.[33]

David, as if inheriting the position of the stylists censured by Scilla, is the most articulate spokesman of the opponents to life drawing of this period for he rigorously attacks this central axiom of the Academy's teaching, claiming it has wrongful priority in the curriculum. At best of only limited significance, he says, life drawing can only be useful to the painter after a study of geometry. The latter is not understood to be the mere implementation of a system of human proportion but a thorough grounding in the principles of Euclid. A sense of overall pictorial unity, the result of mathematical knowledge, is therefore preferred to gratuitous detailing in the representation of the human figure:

There is no need to prove that the study of the nude and of drapery are a spurious practical imitation while every boy beginner who does not even know how to give the very first definition of geometrical elements is admitted there.[34]

Whereas every preceding writer had praised the Carracci Academy for the introduction of regular life classes as part of the training of the artist, this fact prompts
David's condemnation:

[The Carracci Academy] was the first to introduce the habit of drawing continuously from some
naked menial because the great artists who flourished there and indeed the majority of artists
since, believed that this is the principal study of the art of *disegno* and as a result this practice
has multiplied so much that there is not a place in Europe where it has not been introduced
for the instruction of pupils.[35]

In David's strictures, and particularly in his deprecatory use of the word 'facchino',
signifying labourer or menial, to denote the model, there is the suggestion that the
constant practice of life drawing besides being unnecessary was somehow repellent
to him;[36] his antipathy is, however, justified by an elevated claim that such a base
pursuit is irrelevant to a liberal art which is a gentlemanly occupation requiring
intellectual stimulus. According to David, by taking priority in the Academy's
curriculum, the life class had usurped the place of mathematics.[37]

By questioning the value of the careful study of the human figure, David
conflicts with the naturalistic tendencies prevalent in the classicist–idealist aesthetic
of the later seventeenth century and calls into doubt those elements in history painting
to which it was thought to be of value; the depiction of credible movement and expression of the figure, the product of careful observation and drawing, should be
supplanted in his view by a preference for abstract harmony and proportion. The
depiction of nature raised to its ideal by study and the copying of the works of the
ancients was no longer as necessary to the work of art whose organic unity was the
result of the inherence of an abstract geometrical scheme.[38] By stressing such a
metaphysical approach to painting, David disregards much seventeenth-century
writing on art which had preached the empirical doctrine of the careful study of
nature. Instead, and his views are indicative of the age of the Enlightenment, he is
fascinated by the logic of science and mathematics and is anxious to see a similar
system of absolute rules incorporated into a theory of painting.

Though novel in the context of the literary and antiquarian conceptions of the
imitation of nature of the early eighteenth century, David's emphasis on mathematics
as fundamental to painting harks back to the views of Renaissance writers. There is a
quality of deliberate revivalism in his recourse to these works. This is especially the
case in David's dependence on Leonardo's writings of which he made a serious study.
It is known that David had access to at least one of Leonardo's manuscripts containing scientific notes, which was then in the possession of Ghezzi, and that he made
attempts to learn of the contents of others in the Ambrosiana, Milan.[39] The digest of

Leonardo's writings, the *Trattato della Pittura* published in 1651, was of course available to him.[40]

Leonardo had insisted on the learnedness of the painter and on the necessity of his familiarity with the theoretical foundations of his art, 'study science first and then practice follows born of that science'.[41] Whilst there was particular justification for Leonardo's emphasis on the intellectual roots of painting at a time when painting had only recently been admitted to the number of the liberal arts and was still felt by many to be a craft activity devoid of mental stimulus, David's employment of the familiar dichotomy between the mechanical and intellectual aspects of painting is largely motivated by the desire to discredit life drawing in the Accademia di S Luca and later, in the third discourse, to weaken the position of architecture. There can be no doubt that David drew inspiration from Leonardo's writings where the division between intellectual and craft occupations is frequently discussed. Leonardo had described the vain efforts of those enamoured solely with practice as akin to sailors in a boat attempting to maintain their course without the aid of a rudder; David similarly accuses the members of the Accademia di S Luca of groping without direction because theory is ignored.[42] In such a position, to seek to teach others the art of painting is mere foolishness.

Leonardo's insistence on the artist's conversance with mathematics and science is offset by an empiricism, a fastidious attention to the minutiae of the sensual world. The two courses were inseparable because the artist could only understand nature by first knowing the metaphysical principles that underlay its being. The fact that David should largely ignore the need for careful observation of nature in his reading of Leonardo's writings only to accept their metaphysical intonation is significant, for it reveals a change in the aesthetic outlook of the period. This was a time when painting's internal but traditionally mechanical properties such as handling and colour were being explored, often at the expense of its naturalistic and humanistic functions, in the new rococo style.

The first discourse of *L'Amore dell'Arte* is not devoted exclusively to an assessment of the merits of the teaching of the Accademia di S Luca but is also intended to show how this Academy, by its maladministration, had actively caused harm to the arts in Rome. The Academy, David says, has dissipated the endowments of its two principal benefactors, Muziano and Zuccaro;[43] its irresponsibility in financial matters caused Pietro da Cortona, who donated his money to the Academy's church of SS Martina e Luca, to leave the administration of his estate in the hands of the deputies of the Congregazione di S Eufemia.[44] With his supplication to Clement XI particularly in mind, David goes on to show that the Academy's continuing corruption is manifest in the rigging of the results of the new competition which Clement

XI had inaugurated himself. Prizes, he says, were being given to the favourites of those artists chosen as judges.[45] Furthermore, he accuses the Academy of cheating its students: money allocated for the prizes was being squandered on unnecessary ceremonial such as the hanging of costly drapes, singing and the reading of poetry so that the prize-winning students were receiving only a third of that sum.

An account is given at the end of the discourse of the purported programme of studies and competition rules of the Accademia di S Luca instituted by Muziano at its infancy and which David cites *in extenso* as a model for its future reform, so much he says, has it strayed from the path set by its worthy founder.[46] This passage has been the source of much confusion to historians of the Academy: sections of it were quoted by Missirini who believed this was how the Academy was first organized; its authenticity was later doubted by Pevsner who, working from Missirini, did not know the original passage in *L'Amore dell' Arte*.[47] A careful reading of the discourse reveals that the account of Muziano's directives for the running of the Academy, far from having any documentary basis, was related by some 'Brescian painters' to a certain Giulio Ceruti who then reported this account to David.[48] It is difficult to resist the conclusion that it is a fabrication by David himself. Ceruti, according to David, had been prompted to make known this account after a visit to the Academy where he had discovered that Muziano's role as its founder had been wantonly suppressed.

In the second discourse David is preoccupied by the declining artistic influence of Rome which he feels is demonstrated by the growing neglect of the work of Raphael. Something must be said of the shift of artistic influence in Europe at this time before David's views can take on their full significance. By the end of the seventeenth century, Rome no longer spearheaded the major artistic developments of the period; instead, Paris which had grown in prestige with the political dominance of France under Louis XIV became a centre where experimentation with new styles in painting took place. The theoretical foundations of the rococo style that flourished in France in the eighteenth century were thus laid from 1670 onwards in discussions in the Académie Royale de Peinture, Paris.[49] The successful campaign championed by Roger de Piles to make an art based largely on the appeal of colour critically acceptable caused the older italianate conception of painting as a dependent of *disegno* seem chilly and outmoded. The sensuous appeal to the eye of the former which could be readily appreciated by all was opposed to the notion that painting was an exclusive intellectual pursuit. Rubens, the great colourist of the early seventeenth century who, of all painters according to de Piles, seemed to embody the different parts of painting most completely in his works, was the hero of the new faction and to him the great Italian masters were often unfavourably compared.[50]

It would seem natural that Italian theorists of the period might express resentment in their writings against this eclipse of their great compatriots. Surprisingly this is not the case, and many Italian commentators of the arts of the middle and late seventeenth century paid homage to the ever increasing artistic authority of France. To begin with, as is the case with Bellori's praise of the work of the painter Poussin, French painting was admired for its Roman qualities of classical purity.[51] It was, however, only a short step to the appreciation of the aesthetic of colour of more recent French painting so that by the beginning of the eighteenth century the Italian biographers Pio and Pascoli, unconfined by the critical preconceptions of their predecessors, were enthusiastic in their praise of the rococo art of their day.[52]

Against this background of the gradual accommodation of artistic ideas from outside Italy, David's plea in his second discourse for an independent Roman School of painting unfettered by external influences though deliberately isolationist, is significant in its recognition that Italy no longer dominated Europe artistically. The discourse is the first serious consideration by an Italian writer of a situation where external influences from outside Italy were proving to be as compelling as those from Italy's own artistic past. Much of the blame for this state of affairs is heaped upon the Accademia di S Luca, which he accuses of being over enamoured of the work of other national schools, particularly that of the Flemish and the work of Rubens.[53] The Academy, he argues, is under an obligation to preserve the best traditions of the Roman school as established by Raphael whose work contains all that is best in painting, but instead of acting as the custodian of the Roman school it has been tempted by the appeal of innovation, and has lost sight of the fundamental rules of painting so that the work of its members is careless and uninspired. As a result, the Roman school has lost its integrity and has been diluted in influence.

The increasing disregard for the work of Raphael shown by the Academy is symbolized by the derisory valuation by its *stimatori* of an important preparatory cartoon for the *Transfiguration* (Rome, Vatican Gallery), then believed to be an original drawing by the artist.[54] He bitterly remarks that at a time when the work of the very greatest artists of the past is underpriced, that of inferior quality by talented contemporaries is absurdly expensive. The cartoon would have been sold by the heirs of the Marchese Nerli to the English painter Charles Jervas had it not been for the timely intervention of Clement XI who, by purchasing it for himself, prevented it from leaving Rome.[55]

To coincide with the celebrations of the annual competition in 1704, Ghezzi published the *impresa* of the Accademia di S Luca. Introducing the device in a preliminary *Relazione* to the published discourse he stressed the equality between the three arts of painting, sculpture and architecture which the Academy represented and which the *impresa* was intended to symbolize:

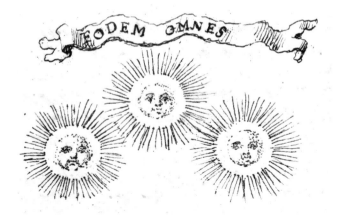

220 *Ludovico David: Design for an* impresa. *Rome, Accademia di S Luca, Archivo Storico 35, p. 227.*

I have chosen the equilateral triangle from mathematical proofs, a figure which is most symbolic of the equality and unity of our three beautiful arts of painting, sculpture and architecture . . . whence instead of the simplicity of its three perfect lines, I have substituted the principal instruments of those same three professions, namely instead of one, the brush, instead of the other the chisel and instead of the third a pair of compasses lying open, which united together form a perfect triangle.[56]

To spiritualize the device the motto 'Aequa Potestas', a phrase from the *Ars Poetica* of Horace, was added.[57] The fashioning of an *impresa*, a seemingly unimportant exercise and one to which the Academy had already devoted itself in the days of Zuccaro's presidency, aroused David's dissenting voice and the third discourse of *L'Amore dell'Arte* is devoted to a criticism of it.[58] David first made his objection to the *impresa* immediately after it had been shown at the Campidoglio in April when he approached Ghezzi with proposals for another of his own design (**220**).[59] When in July the transactions of the competition appeared in print, David was particularly incensed to find that the very *impresa* which he had recommended the Academy to reject as unworthy had been published in the *Relazione*.[60]

A dispute over the suitability of an *impresa* might at first seem a trivial event, but the importance attached to such devices in the sixteenth and seventeenth centuries must not be overlooked and arguments over their form and significance possessed wider implications than might at first be supposed.[61] An *impresa*, a badge of an individual or of an institution, was intended as a visual metaphor for a particular commitment or ideology; in the case of an institution, such an image was employed to symbolize its function and provided a point of debate to its members.

In the new *impresa* the Accademia di S Luca declared once more its purpose to represent democratically as equal dependents of *disegno* the arts of painting, sculpture and architecture. In the introduction to his lives of artists, Vasari had adopted a conciliating attitude towards the rivalry between painting and sculpture, a topic much discussed in the early sixteenth century, demonstrating that these two arts, with architecture, shared a common source of inspiration in *Disegno*; such a spirit of alliance between the three arts is implicit in the rules for the Accademia del Disegno which Vasari had drafted.[62] The doctrine that painting, sculpture and architecture were co-equal disciplines was the result of a deliberate attempt to suppress arguments as to their relative merits. Later under Zuccaro's presidency and also subsequently in its published statutes, the Accademia di S Luca accepted this policy and such competitive discussions were expressly forbidden.[63] The reasons for an alliance of this nature were obvious enough: quarrels which no doubt took place in the normal run of events would have been further aggravated had disputes occurred for the primacy within the Academy of any one of the three arts practised by members. By pronouncing the *impresa* to be invalid together with the assumptions which underlay its composition, David threatened the very rationale upon which the coherence of the Accademia di S Luca depended and revived arguments which had been largely moribund since its foundation. His plea for the recognition of the superiority of painting in the Academy was deliberately divisive. The pedantic attention to the smallest detail in his analysis may make David's views seem unimportant but as the *impresa* is seen as a symbol of the Academy's failings exteriorized to public view, they are at once more telling; the *impresa* is in David's words, 'a satire against the Academy'.[64]

The equilateral triangle, David objects, is not appropriate as an *impresa* because it is a two-dimensional figure and not the representation of a three-dimensional body normally recommended; the employment of the three instruments symbolic of the three arts represented in the Academy is likewise unsuitable in that they recall craft professions also dependent on their use such as carpentry and bricklaying; and the process of manufacture rather than inception is emphasized.[65] Neither is its internal structure credible as he illustrates (**221**): the weight of the chisel placed against the hairs of the tip of the brush would in reality cause the latter to yield, rendering unequal the angles of the triangle and altering the lengths of two of its sides.[66] To give the illusion that the chisel supports the brush, David accuses the author of the *impresa* of distorting the chisel's real form (**222** and **223**): the chisel in the *impresa* is shown with its cutting end at an oblique angle to its long axis so that it rests against and does not overlap the tip of the brush; it is not drawn correctly with the end perpendicular to the long axis. The most severe criticism is reserved for the position and form of the compasses. Lying open at the base of the triangle they are

221 *Ludovico David: Diagram from the* impresa *of the Accademia di S Luca. Rome, Accademia di S Luca, Archivo Storico 35, p. 140.*

223 *Ludovico David: Diagram of a chisel. Rome, Accademia di S Luca, Archivio Storico 35, p. 140.*

222 *Ludovico David: Diagram of a chisel. Rome, Accademia di S Luca, Archivo Storico 35, p. 141.*

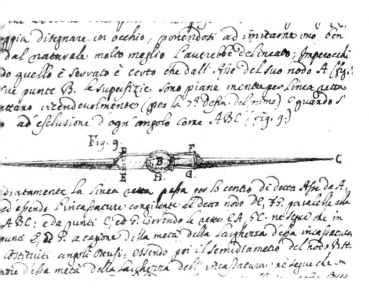

224 *Ludovico David: Diagram of compasses showing their correct design, Rome, Accademia di S Luca, Archivio Storico 35, p. 145.*

225 *Ludovico David: Diagram of compasses as represented in the* impresa *of the Accademia di S Luca, Rome, Accademia di S Luca, Archivio Storico 35, p. 146.*

subject to the misinterpretation voiced by certain architects in the Academy, namely that they represent 'the foundation, base and support of painting and sculpture'.[67] The compasses in the form that they are shown in the *impresa* would be unusable, David says, as their main axis does not extend through their centre but along the outside of their arms so that when closed the latter would not come together (**224** and **225**).

David's discussion of the *impresa* is a pretext for an assessment of the comparative status of the arts to the detriment of architecture. The arts, he says, 'are most unequal both in prerogative and merit'.[68] Because architecture does not have an imitative function, it is at the furthest remove from painting which of the three arts adumbrates this purpose the most effectively. Bearing in mind architecture's inferiority, David draws attention to the disproportionate influence that architects enjoy within the Academy and his third discourse turns into a thinly veiled attack on Carlo Fontana who had been president of the Academy from 1694–8. David bitterly condemns Fontana's incompetence in two architectural projects in Rome: the building of the *campaniletto* of the Montecitorio palace and the raising of the Antonine column, both of which had caused his employers to shoulder needless expense because of professional ineptitude.[69]

The evidence of commentators on *L'Amore dell'Arte* shows that it was the criticism of the *impresa* and not the more general objections to the running of the Academy

226 Impresa *of the Accademia di S Luca, 1768.*

which aroused the most response. Despite David's strong views, the design of the *impresa* remained unaltered and was employed to decorate the title-page and to head the preliminary *Relazioni* of the subsequently published discourses. It is only in 1763 that alterations which are in accord with David's recommendations but which were doubtless made accidentally without conscious recourse to his writings are apparent in Ghezzi's *impresa*: on the title-page of the published discourse of that year the compasses are shown with their long axis running through the centre of its arms, and two *puttini* obligingly support the chisel and the brush (**226**).[70]

L'Amore dell'Arte was written expressly to expose the impotence of a particular academy and to embarrass its most senior members. The extent to which David achieved his aim to reform the Accademia di S Luca cannot be properly gauged, but it seems unlikely that his protests had any substantial effect despite his boastful claims to the contrary in his letters to Muratori.[71] The dispute is not mentioned in the Academy minutes and a reorganization of the curriculum did not occur at this time.[72] That Clement XI intervened personally to halt the controversy is likely although there is no evidence to show that this was the case; an assiduous patron of the Academy, he had the interests of that institution at heart and it is possible that at his initiative the whole affair was brought to a close.[73]

Stages in the dispute are described by David in letters to Muratori. In one dated 4 April 1706, David reports that Clement XI on reading the manuscript had asked the Academy to justify the design of its *impresa* and to defend itself from attack:

My book [*L'Amore dell'Arte*] dedicated to the Pope has had a very good effect both on my own private interests, giving me hope of some advantage and favour to my sons, and on those of the public, in the reform of the Accademia di S. Luca that is now expected. His Holiness after reading my book carefully and giving it to many experts to examine, has approached the secretary of that body to ask about those things that it has exhibited in public that have caused my criticism. He (the secretary) has excused himself by saying that those things were approved by famous *letterati* who would defend them from my objections if they could only have the book in their hands, and so he has asked if he may borrow it.[74]

In a subsequent letter David states his readiness to defend *L'Amore dell'Arte* against any reply that the Academy might prepare and if necessary to write a sequel to it, 'because I did not empty the sack in that book and am equipped for the second part'.[75] Far from being crushed by the conflict he had created, David enjoyed it and writes with pride to Muratori of its progress; his triumphs over Ghezzi whom he succeeded in placing in a most unenviable position with the Pope are recorded with great glee.

The first defence of the Academy's position is a brief *Apologia* written by Giuseppe Terzi in 1704.[76] It is a reply, not to *L'Amore dell'Arte*, but to a *Censura* of the *impresa* which was submitted to the Academy for its consideration sometime after 24 April 1704.[77] The *Censura* is now lost, but in it David must have first set out his objections to the employment by the Academy of an equilateral triangle as an emblem to the union of the three arts and discussed the merits of another *impresa* of his own invention showing three suns. Terzi's *Apologia* copied out by David in the third discourse of the Rome version of *L'Amore dell'Arte* is divided into two parts: the first is a discussion of David's plan to dismiss architecture from the Academy curriculum and is a defence of this subject against allegations that it is unscientific and therefore unworthy to be ranked among the liberal arts; the second is a commendation of the Academy's *impresa* and therefore a rejection of David's alternative design.[78]

Terzi did not manage to silence David with his arguments. Indeed his *Apologia* was superseded by the writing of *L'Amore dell'Arte* whose third discourse, an enlargement of the original *Censura*, incorporates the Apologia and rebuts its principal points in two carefully worded replies.[79] What had begun merely as a criticism of the *impresa* was now turned into a far more comprehensive attack on the Academy's very capability as a centre of instruction for the arts, so that a statement not only justifying the design of the *impresa* but also defending the Academy's teaching function was now called for in default of which a second attack in the form of a sequel to the first part of *L'Amore dell'Arte* was promised.

Such a reply was not forthcoming and the next step in David's campaign was taken in 1705 with the publication of the broadsheet *Duo Problemmata*.[80] Appealing for the open discussion of the two points presented, David challenges the Academy to publish a reply to *L'Amore dell'Arte* and so to vindicate the study of architecture within its walls. The broadsheet, far from being a pirated work, was issued by the Tipografia della Camera Apostolica which was used by the Vatican for official publications. This would imply that David enjoyed some support from Clement XI who was, according to David's letter to Muratori, desirous that the Academy should answer its accuser.[81]

In the same year, possibly as a result of official coercion, an exhaustive defence of the Academy's *impresa* appeared in print: written by Bartolommeo Nappini it is entitled, *Parere del Signor canonico Bartolommeo Nappini in forma di lettera al Signor Giuseppe Ghezzi* and forms an appendix to the discourse of 1705.[82] It is probably to this essay that he refers when he tells Muratori that the Academy's defence of itself had not met with official expectations: 'these academicians are very confused because of the poor response to their publications and it is now known that the Pope has told them that if they don't know how to reply it would be best if they kept silent'.[83] Despite these derogatory remarks, Nappini's essay is entirely reasonable in tone. At the outset he emphasizes the impossibility of composing an *impresa* which conforms to all the rules laid down by every author who has written on this art, and he praises the Academy's *impresa* as satisfying most of those requirements. It is only half way through his essay which he says is devoted to an appreciation of the mathematical and poetic invention of the design that he turns his attention to the criticisms of 'some person'. These have caused him 'to add a few things, not because it is necessary to confute these criticisms, but so that the perfection of the said *impresa* will emerge more strongly'.[84] David is nowhere honoured by being mentioned by name but is referred to throughout the letter as 'some person', 'somebody' or 'the critic'.

Nappini underrates the importance of David's objections, making them appear trivial and insignificant. Taking the claim that the triangle is not a 'perfect figure' as Ghezzi had stated it to be in his *Relazione* but is 'the most imperfect' of all two-dimensional figures, Nappini retorts that a general quality—that triangles are imperfect—has been adduced from a particular observation made earlier by Galileo— that the triangle is the least perfect figure that can be described within a circle.[85] Another criticism that David had made and which Nappini dismisses is that the image of an *impresa* must represent a three-dimensional body (Corpo) and that a triangle, being a two-dimensional figure (Figura), cannot be regarded as such. Nappini's answer is that the critic has misapprehended the principles of designing an *impresa* and has interpreted too literally the definition of the components of such an image given by Paolo Giovio, *Dialogo dell'Imprese* as that which possesses a body (Corpo) and a soul (Anima).[86] These, Nappini says, are metaphorical expressions for figure and motto of which an *impresa* in reality consists. It is therefore incorrect to say that a two-dimensional figure is inadmissible as an *impresa*. Nappini compromises the force of his last argument by observing that the Academy's *impresa* is in fact a single body formed of three separate bodies—the three instruments.

David is accused of giving careless references: the passage from Emanuele Tesauro's, *Il Cannocchiale Aristotelico* cited in the third discourse of *L'Amore dell'Arte* in which mechanical instruments are said to be inappropriate to *imprese* cannot be found in thesis 6 where it is said to appear.[87] To show that there is authority for the use of such objects in emblems, Nappini quotes a passage from Giovanni Ferro where they are actually recommended.[88] David's elaborate demonstration that a chisel resting on the point of a brush in the configuration presented by the Academy's *impresa* would cause the hairs of the brush to yield, so distorting the equality of the triangle is dismissed as mere pedantry.[89]

No further defence of the Academy's position followed Nappini's *Parere* and it would seem that after 1705 the controversy had largely ceased; the second part of *L'Amore dell'Arte* which was being written in 1707 was probably never finished. The dying embers of the conflict were momentarily fanned into flame in 1710 when Concetto Concetti, introducing a collection of poems in praise of a painting of the *Pentecost* which Ghezzi had executed for the church of S Antonio dei Portoghesi, Rome, took the opportunity to praise the design of the Academy's *impresa*, for which Ghezzi was responsible, as an appropriate symbol of that institution.[90]

David did not intend to publish *L'Amore dell'Arte* but simply wished it to be circulated among friends:

It is not my intention to publish this bagatelle [written] in so short a time . . . but merely to show it to some friends who might be adversely informed about me.[91]

In this way he extended his campaign against the Academy beyond Rome in an attempt to muster opinion in his favour from a wider circle of experts and friends. The manuscript was sent to Muratori in 1707; it was dispatched together with certain of the Academy's publications in a package which was intercepted by the Customs at Bologna, but there is no reason to doubt that the manuscript did reach its eventual destination.[92] It was then forwarded to Orlandi in 1708 and to the Florentine painter Antonio Franchi (**227**) in 1709; the critical comments of the last two recipients have survived. The transcription by Orlandi of certain passages from the manuscript he received show that the Modena version with the numbered paragraphs was circulated.

The detailed notes taken down by Orlandi after a careful reading of *L'Amore dell'Arte* have survived in a volume containing discourses read to the Accademia di S Luca.[93] David had already informed Orlandi by letter of the developments in his dispute with the Academy. In a heading on the first page of the notes Orlandi relates how in 1708, after preaching at a Lent service in the church of the Carmine at Brescia, he was handed the manuscript by a Sig.re Dottore Boni.[94] Orlandi read the manuscript carefully and the notes he took are divided broadly into two parts: the first consists of several extracts from the beginning of the manuscript; the second, entitled 'Replies to the present information by Fr. Pellegrino Orlandi Carmelite, dilettante of Painting', is devoted to a commentary on the manuscript.[95]

It is the second part of Orlandi's notes which is of relevance here. Orlandi is careful not to involve himself too deeply in David's dispute with the Academy, but on the particular issue of the propriety of the *impresa* he supports David:

227 *Engraving after a self-portrait of Franchi, Florence, Uffizi.*

As to the section of the book on the *impresa* of the Academy, I do not think that the Author is wrong since the body of the *impresa* must correspond with the motto and the motto with the *impresa*.[96]

He is unhappy to see three-dimensional instruments replacing the sides of a two-dimensional figure and adds of the *impresa*, 'I didn't like it either when I first saw it'.[97]

Orlandi was principally interested in the summary of *Il disinganno* which David had provided in the address to the reader in *L'Amore dell'Arte*. He is sceptical of David's revisionist opinions and is reluctant to accept the new interpretation of the development of the history of art which is offered, supporting the historical scheme outlined by Vasari:

Vasari . . . spoke as an historian and of his fellows who were his contemporaries or lived only a little time before him, thus it was easy for him to have facts which are certainly more precise than those which the Author pretends to have who lives two hundred years later.[98]

That the Florentine painter Franchi also received and read *L'Amore dell'Arte* is clear from a letter dated 13 July 1709 which was published by Bartolozzi in his biography of the artist and who wrongly believed it to have been directed to the Flemish painter David Koninck.[99] In the letter Franchi thanks David for sending the manuscript and from his statements it is clear that he is referring to *L'Amore dell'Arte*. He also asks for permission to incorporate sections of the manuscript into his own treatise on painting which he was in the process of writing:

I have copied out many of those erudite statements relevant to my bauble (for this is what I call my treatise on picturesque theory) and if you would favour me with the authority [to use them] you will be doing me a great favour.[100]

The treatise entitled, *La Teorica della Pittura* was published posthumously in 1739.[101] A careful reading of it shows a dependence on David's manuscript; this is particularly evident in the short list of Italian artist academies given in the second chapter which corresponds in all essentials to that given earlier in the first discourse of *L'Amore dell'Arte*.[102] The central theme of Franchi's treatise is similar to that of *L'Amore dell'Arte* in that a study of theory as well as practical skill goes into the make-up of the great painter. Significantly, as David had viewed it, theory is thought to consist of a knowledge of mathematical theorems and science.

   L'Amore dell'Arte is a puzzling document, but its novelty in Italian art literature of the period cannot be doubted. David's dissenting attitude stems only in part from that undercurrent of criticism of the artistic establishment which was apparent by the middle of the seventeenth century and which was expressed by such artists as Pietro Testa and Salvator Rosa but there is no precedent within this tradition for a written attack of such length against a recognized artists' academy. The vitriolic tone of David's objections and the prolixity with which he sets out his views give character and identity to his work and if David's literary skills are unremarkable—at the outset of *L'Amore dell'Arte* he renounces any attempt to cultivate a high-flown style of writing—his sense of the satirical and his ironical alignment with the most outrageous opinions produce a mitigating humour. By taking the critical commonplace that great art was produced by the adherence to rules and that slovenliness was a result of their neglect, and applying it to the Accademia di S Luca, he is able to show that by failing to maintain standards this academy was damaging the quality of the arts and particularly that of painting. It is the freedom to question the accepted assumptions behind art education which is at the core of David's root-and-branch approach, and it is this enquiring attitude that anticipates Romantic thinking on the subject less than a century later.

Photographic Credits. Biblioteca Universitaria, Bologna: 215; Accademia di S Luca, Rome: 214, 220, 221, 222, 223, 224, 225; Gabinetto Fotografico Nazionale, Rome: 213; Nationalmuseum, Stockholm: 210; Castle Howard Collection, Yorkshire: 218.

NOTES

1 M. Missirini, *Memorie per servire alla Storia della Romana Accademia di S. Luca*, Rome 1823, pp. 154-5.

2 Modena, Biblioteca Estense, Raccolta Campori Cod. 1071-γ. H. 1. 38, described by L. Lodi and R. Vandini, *Catalogo dei manoscritti posseduti dal Marchese Giuseppe Campori*, iv and v, Modena 1844, p. 402 and identified as a version of *L'Amore dell'Arte* by F. Bassoli, 'Un pittore svizzero pioniere degli studi vinciani: Ludovico Antonio David', *Raccolta Vinciana*, xvi, 1954, p. 280; Rome, Archivio Storico dell'Accademia di S Luca, Vol. 35. The unpublished manuscript in the Arch. Stor. dell'Acc. di S. L., 22 × 16 cms., contains 133 leaves, 125 of which are numbered on both sides in the sequence 1-19 and 1-229. Bound in its original red morocco binding, it bears in gilt on the front cover the Albani arms and on the spine the inscription: *DAVID L'AMOR D'ARTE*.

3 See p. 179 below.

4 G. Campori, *Lettere artistiche inedite*, Modena 1866, p. 540. David's correspondence with Muratori is discussed by Bassoli, pp. 264 ff.

5 For reactions to artist's academies during the Romantic period, see N. Pevsner, *Academies of art past and present*, Cambridge 1940, pp. 190 ff.

6 For David's biography see: N. Pelicelli, *Thieme-Becker*, viii, 1913, s.v. David, with previous bibliography; U. Donati, *Artisti Ticinesi a Roma*, Bellinzona 1942, pp. 607-14; F. Bassoli, pp. 260-314; N. Ivanoff, 'Lodovico David da Lugano e la sua Accademia Veneziana', *Emporium*, cxxvi, 1957, pp. 248-53.

7 David's paintings in S. Andrea al Quirinale are cited by F. Haskell, *Patrons and Painters*, London 1963, p. 88; the account of his fresco in the former Collegio Clementino is L. Davide, *Dichiarazione della Pittura della Cappella del Collegio Clementino*, Rome 1695, of which a copy is to be found in Rome, Biblioteca Vaticana, Cicognara IV. M. 37 int. 5.

8 Arch. Stor. 35: pp. 156-7.

9 A letter to Muratori written in Correggio, dated 6 July 1709, Campori p. 549, is the last document to my knowledge which testifies that David was living. Bassoli, 1957, p. 261 states that he died in 1628 but gives no evidence to support this claim.

10 P. Orlandi, *Abecedario pittorico*, Bologna 1704, pp. 258 and 393.

11 It is not cited by Schlosser, *La letteratura artistica*, Florence and Vienna 1956, who, on pp. 467 and 475, discusses *Il disinganno*.

12 Bibl. Est. Camp. 1071: fols. 1-13; Arch. Stor. 35: pp. 1-19.

13 Bibl. Est. Camp. 1071: fol. 7; Arch. Stor. 35: p. 9: '. . . hò bensi incontrato continue persecuzioni dagl'emoli . . .'.

14 N. Pio, *Vite de' pittori, scultori ed architetti in compendio*, 1724, Rome, Biblioteca Vaticana, Cod. Capponi 257; L. Pascoli, *Vite de' pittori, scultori ed architetti moderni*, Rome 1730-6.

15 Florence, Biblioteca Nazionale, Cod. Pal. E. B. 9. 5, N. Gabburri *Vite di artisti*, iii, p. 1697.

16 See note 2 above.

17 Bibl. Est. Camp. 1071 ends at fol. 154 of Arch. Stor. 35.

18 Bologna, Biblioteca Universitaria, Cod. 1865, unpaginated collection of letters to P. Orlandi; the correspondence between David and Orlandi was first cited by L. Frati, 'Lettere autobiografiche di pittori al P. Pellegrino Orlandi', *Rivista d'Arte*, 1907, pp. 63-76.

19 Bassoli, p. 280.

20 Missirini, p. 18.

21 In a letter to Muratori, Campori p. 545, David says that he hopes to make three versions of what must be the second part of *L'Amore dell'Arte* which was then being copied in Venice, but it is far from clear how many versions of the first part were made.

22 L. B. Alberti, *On painting and on sculpture*, ed. C. Grayson, London 1972.

23 Arch. Stor. 35, title-page: *L'Amore dell'Arte, Ritratto ne gli Utili, e Danni che la Pretesa Accademia del Disegno di San Luca di*

Roma ha recato alla Pittura, Scultura, ed Architettura, ed a i principali virtuosi d'Italia (Prima Parte in tre discorsi divisa . . .).

24 Campori, p. 544: '. . . che sarà intitolata la comedia morale sgangherata o sconcertata . . .'.

25 Bibl. Est. Camp. 1071: fols. 14–73; Arch. Stor. 35: pp. 1–89: 'Origine, e Frutti Dell' Accademia di S. Luca di Roma Discorso Primo.'

26 Bibl. Est. Camp. 1071: fols. 74–104; Arch. Stor. 35: pp. 90–131: 'La Stima che L'Accademia di San Luca hà fatto del Divino Rafaello Sanctio Fundatore della Squola Romana, e degl'altri insigni Professori d'Italia Discorso II.'

27 Bibl. Est. Camp. 1071: fols. 105–20; Arch. Stor. 35: pp. 132–229: 'Censura. Sopra l'Impresa del creduto Triangolo Equilatero esposta dall' Accademia di S. Luca in Campidoglio il dì 24 Aprile 1704. Discorso III'.

28 For a recent discussion of the Carracci academy see D. Posner, *Annibale Carracci*, i, London and New York 1971, pp. 62–5.

29 Though life drawing was regularized in the Academy before 1670, lists of the six academicians and their assistants who were to pose the model only appear from 1670 onwards. That appearing in Arch. Stor., 44, fol. 57 (25 April 1670) is the first of such rotas to be given.

30 G. P. Bellori, *Vite de pittori*, Rome 1672, pp. 64, 212–13, 307, 437–8.

31 Bellori, *Vite*, 3rd ed., Pisa 1821, p. 190: '. . . Basta rassomigliare il naturale, basta contentar l'occhio . . . i giovani . . . volentieri abboriscono gli studj e le fatiche . . .'.

32 Dorigny's print after Maratta's drawing of an academy is discussed by O. Kutschera-Woborsky, 'Ein Kunsttheoretisches Thesenblatt Carlo Marattas und seine ästhetischen Anschauungen', *Mitteilungen der Gesellschaft für vervielfältigende Kunst*, 2–3, 1919, pp. 9–28 and by M. Winner, 'Gemalte Kunsttheorie', *Berliner Jahrbuch*, iv, 1962, pp. 159–60.

33 Rome, Biblioteca Casanatense, Cod. 1482: A. Scilla, 'Discorso per l'Accademia del disegno in Roma in occasione del concorso dell'anno 1688' fol. 190: '. . . Abbandonate . . . il finire con esatezza le parti delle vostre figure . . . bastara toccarle di gusto . . .'.

34 Bibl. Est. Camp. 1071: fol. 27; Arch. Stor. 35: pp. 22–3: '. . . Lo studio dell'*ignudo, e delle pieghe de panni* non è bisogno di provare, che sieno una pratica immitazione spuria, mentre à quello s'admette ogni principiante ragazzo, che non sappia dar conto ne meno della prima deffinizione delli elementi geometrici . . .'.

35 Bibl. Est. Camp. 1071: fols. 29–30; Arch. Stor. 35: p. 26: '. . . la prima ad introdurvi l'usanza di disegnare del continuo il Facchino nudo, onde per li gran virtuosi che in essa sono fioriti ha creduto, e crede il maggior numero delli artefici, che questo sia lo studio principale dell'arti del disegno e perciò tanto sono multiplicate le fachinerdi, che non è luogo in Europa . . . ove non sia introdotta per esercizio de loro discepoli . . .'.

36 Using the word 'facchini' to signify painted figures, Dolce reports a disapproving opinion of Michelangelo's depiction of 'menials' which were compared unfavourably to Raphael's noble types: '. . . Nè dirò come già disse un bello ingegno, che Michelangelo ha dipinto i facchini e Raffaello i gentiluomini . . .'. See, M. W. Roskill, *Dolce's 'Aretino' and Venetian Art Theory*, New York 1968, p. 172.

37 Bibl. Est. Camp. 1071: fols. 26–7; Arch. Stor. 35: pp. 21–3.

38 H. Osborne, *Aesthetics and art theory: an historical introduction*, London 1968, pp. 61–4.

39 Bassoli, pp. 273–86 and 295–6.

40 Leonardo da Vinci, *Trattato della Pittura*, ed. R. Du Fresne, Paris 1651.

41 Leonardo da Vinci, p. 2, vii; '. . . Studia prima la scienza, e poi seguita la pratica nata da essa scienza . . .'.

42 J. P. Richter, *The Literary Works of Leonardo da Vinci*, 2nd ed., London, New York, Toronto 1939, p. 119. Bibl. Est. Camp. 1071: fols. 25–6 and 37; Arch. Stor. 35: pp. 19–20 and 37.

43 Bibl. Est. Camp. 1071: fols. 14–16; Arch. Stor. 35: pp. 1–5.

44 Bibl. Est. Camp. 1071: fols. 17–18; Arch. Stor. 35: pp. 5–7.

45 Bibl. Est. Camp. 1071: fol. 39; Arch. Stor. 35: pp. 39.

46 Bibl. Est. Camp. 1071: fols. 66–73; Arch. Stor. 35: pp. 81–9.

47 N. Pevsner, pp. 58–9.

48 Bibl. Est. Camp. 1071: fol. 66; Arch. Stor. 35: p. 81: '... In altra guiza intendeva Muziano d'incamminarla [the Accademia di S Luca] per quanto molti anni sono mi fù raccontato da vecchij professori di bon gusto...'.

49 See, B. Teyssèdre, *Roger de Piles et les Débats sur le Coloris*, Paris 1957, pp. 151 ff.

50 See, B. Teyssèdre, *L'Histoire de l'Art vue du Grand Siècle*, Paris 1964, pp. 133–6 and 216–25.

51 Bellori, 1672, p. 436: '... le Gratie arrisero verso la Francia la quale ... si rese ... illustre nella fama del pennello, contrastando con l'Italia il nome, e la lode di Nicolò Pussino, di cui l'una fù madre felice, l'altra maestra, e patria feconda ...'.

52 See note 14 above.

53 Bibl. Est. Camp. 1071: fols. 95–7; Arch. Stor. 35: pp. 119–21.

54 J.-D. Passavant, *Raphael d'Urbin*, ii, 2nd ed., Paris 1860, pp. 295–6. It is possible that the cartoon to which David refers is that now at Badminton, a very weak copy of the lower section of the *Transfiguration*. I would like to thank Professor John Shearman for providing me with this information.

55 Bibl. Est. Camp. 1071: fol. 80; Arch. Stor. 35: p. 99.

56 Accademia di S. Luca, *Le Buone Arti*, Rome 1704, pp. 11–12: '... Hò eletto delle Matematiche dimostrazioni il Triangolo equilatero, corpo il più simbolico all 'uguaglianza, & unità delle nostre trè belle Arti, Pittura, Scultura, & Architettura ... onde in luogo della semplicità delle sue trè perfette linee, hò posto li principali stromenti delle medesime trè Professioni, cioè in vece dell'Una il Penello, in vece dell'Altra lo Scalpello, ed in vece della Terza il Compasso ...'.

57 *Ars Poetica*, 10.

58 See, R. Alberti, *Origine et Progresso dell' Accademia del Dissegno* in F. Zuccaro, *Scritti d'Arte*, ed. D. Heikamp, Florence 1961, pp. 39–46. Various badges and *imprese* employed by the Academy are discussed by G. Ceccarelli, 'Emblemi e privilegi dell'Accademia di S. Luca', *La Reale Insigne Accademia di S. Luca nella inaugurazione della sua nuova sede*, Rome 1934, pp. 109–13.

59 Bibl. Est. Camp. 1071: fols. 9–10; Arch. Stor. 35: pp. 12–14.

60 See letters to Orlandi, Bologna, Biblioteca Universitaria, Cod. 1865: in one dated 11 June 1704 he doubts if, 'quella [the *impresa*] del triangolo uscirà in istampa, come si dice', because of the criticisms made against it; but in another, dated 23 July he announces with surprise that the *impresa* had been published in *Le Buone Arti*.

61 For a recent discussion of the significance of *imprese*, with bibliography, see E. H. Gombrich, *Symbolic Images*, London 1972, pp. 160–8.

62 Vasari, *Le Vite*, ed. G. Milanesi, i, Florence 1878–85, pp. 215–244; the statutes for the Accademia del Disegno are published by Pevsner, pp. 296–304.

63 R. Alberti, p. 25: '... Si prohibisce parimente, che non si debba trattare nell' Accademia di preminenza di Pittura, Scultura, & Architettura, che essendo ciascuna figlia di un'medesimo Padre cotanto nobile, come è il Dissegno ...'; Accademia di S Luca, *Ordini Dell'Accademia de Pittori et Scultori di Roma*, Rome 1609, p. 33: '... che non si possa ammetter, ne ricever per Accademico alcuno, che havesse scritto, ò fatto scrivere contra li professori dell' Accademia, ò insolentato con parole alcun Officiale in essa Accademia ...'.

64 Bibl. Est. Camp. 1071: fol. 109; Arch. Stor. 35: p. 138.

65 Bibl. Est. Camp. 1071: fols. 108–9; Arch. Stor. 35: pp. 137–9.

66 Bibl. Est. Camp. 1071: fols. 109–10; Arch. Stor. 35: pp. 139–40.

67 Bibl. Est. Camp. 1071: fol. 112; Arch. Stor. 35: p. 143: '... il fundamento, base, e sostegno della pittura, e della Scultura ...'.

68 Bibl. Est. Camp. 1071: fol. 120; Arch. Stor. 35: p. 153: '... sono di prerogative inequalissime, e di merito ...'.

69 For the building of the *campaniletto*, see E. Coudenhove-Erthal, *Carlo Fontana und die Architektur des Römisches spätbarocks*, Vienna 1930, p. 78.

70 Accademia di S Luca, *In Lode delle Belle Arti Orazione e componimenti poetici*, Rome 1768.

71 Campori, pp. 542–3.

72 See Arch. Stor. 46a for the years 1700–17.

73 In 1708 Clement XI intervened on behalf of Benedyckt Renard against the Academy. Renard, gaining an audience with the Pope, claimed that he had only been given the second prize in the architecture competition of that year and felt he deserved the first: Arch. Stor. 46a, fols. 95–6.

74 Campori p. 540: '. . . il mio libro umiliato al papa ha fatto bonissimo effetto sì per quello riguarda i miei privati interessi facendomi sperare qualche vantaggio a favore de' miei figliuoli, come per i publici nella riforma che si attende dell'Accademia, dicendosi che S.S. dopo d'averlo letto attentamente e fatto esaminare da molti dotti abbia fatto una repassata al Segretario della stessa per le cose in publico esposte, che m'hanno dato motivo di censurarla, e che questo si sia scusato d' essergli quelle state approvate da famosi letterati i quali le difenderebbono dalle mie censure se avessero in mano il libro, onde abbia supplicato la S.S. d'imprestarglielo . . .'.

75 Campori, p. 540: '. . . perchè non avendo in esso libro votato il sacco, già mi trovo apparecchiato per la seconda parte'.

76 I have, as yet, been unable to discover further information about Giuseppe Terzi whom David describes as a 'Sicilian mathematician'.

77 Bibl. Est. Camp. 1071: fol. 11; Arch. Stor. 35: p. 16.

78 Arch. Stor. 35: pp. 186–90 and 209–14.

79 Arch. Stor. 35: pp. 190–208 and 215–29.

80 *Illustrissimo, & Excellentissimo Principi, Coeterisque Divi Lucae Academicis Artium Graphidis . . . duo Problemmata*, Rome 1705. Rome, Biblioteca Corsiniana, 29. A. 21. int. 11 is the only copy I know of this previously unrecorded broadsheet.

81 For the Tipografia della Camera Apostolica, see the exhibition catalogue: Biblioteca Vaticana, *Tipografie Romane promosse dalla Santa Sede*, Rome 1972, pp. 15–18.

82 Accademia di S Luca, *Il premio tra gli applausi*, Rome 1705, pp. 61–79. I have been unable to discover further information on Nappini.

83 Campori, p. 543: '. . . questi Accademici si ritrovano molto confusi per lo scarso applauso di loro stampe e per essersi penetrato che il Papa gli abbia detto che quando in altro modo non sapevano far rispondere, era meglio tacere . . .'.

84 *Il premio*, p. 71: '. . . vi sia stato Taluno . . . che . . . mi farò lecito d'aggiungere alcune cose, non perche sia necessario il confutar le dette opposizioni, ma acciò maggiormente apparisca la perfezzione di detta Impresa . . .'.

85 *Il premio*, pp. 71–2.

86 *Il premio*, p. 72; Giovanni Ferro, *Teatro d'Imprese*, Venice 1623, pp. 165–82.

87 *Il premio*, p. 73; E. Tesauro, *Cannocchiale Aristotelico*, ed. Turin 1670, pp. 642–3.

88 *Il premio*, p. 73; Giovanni Ferro, p. 69.

89 *Il premio*, pp. 74–5.

90 Concetto Concetti, *Poesie di diversi Autori per lo nobilissimo Quadro della Venuta dello Spirito Santo del Signor Gioseppe Ghezzi*, Rome 1710, p. ii.

91 Bibl. Est. Camp. 1071: fol. 13; Arch. Stor. 35; p. 18: '. . . non essendo poi mia intenzione di stampare questa bagatella in poco tempo . . . partorita; mà solamente di mostrarla a qualche amico, che fosse sinistramente informato . . .'.

92 Campori, pp. 543–7.

93 Orlandi's manuscript addition is in a volume entitled, *Le scienze illustrate dalle Belle Arti nel Campidoglio*, Rome 1708. This was among a group of other volumes containing discourses read to the Academy formerly in Orlandi's possession sold at Sotheby's, 11 December 1950 (lot 53). The set of discourses and Orlandi's manuscript addition are now in the collection of Denis Mahon.

94 *Le Scienze illustrate*, Mahon Collection, unpaginated MS addition: 'Dall'Ecc.mo Sig.r Dottore Boni fu presentato à me Fr. Pellegrino Antonio Orlandi Carmelitano, mentre predicavo

la quaresima dell' anno 1708 nella Chiesa del Carmine di Brescia, un Libro manoscritto, tanto da me sospirato, per averlo ennunziato nel mio Abecedario Pittorico in Lodovico David à fol. 258 e fol. 394 quale avendo letto, ne rilevai il seguente frontespizio, e notizie appartenenti alla Pittura, ed alle Accademie Romane come seguono'. It is clear from this statement that Orlandi believed *L'Amore dell'Arte* to be *Il disinganno* which, as he says, he announced in *L'Abecedario pittorico*.

95 *Le Scienze illustrate*, Mahon Collection, unpaginated MS addition: 'Risposte alla presente informazione fatte da Fr. Pellegrino Antonio Orlandi Carmelitano, dilettante di Pittura'.

96 *Le Scienze illustrate*, Mahon Collection, unpaginated MS addition: '. . . Circa poi il seguito del libro sopra l'impresa dell' Accademia de' Pittori di Roma, penso che l'Autore non abbia torto, stantecchè il corpo dell'impresa deve quadrare il moto ed il moto l'impresa . . .'.

97 *Le Scienze illustrate*, Mahon Collection, unpaginated MS addition: '. . . ne pure à me piacque quando la vidi . . .'.

98 *Le Scienze illustrate*, Mahon Collection, unpaginated MS addition: '. . . Vasari . . . hà parlato da istorico, e di soggetti suoi contemporanei, o di anteriorità à lui poco lontani, onde gli era facile l'avere notizie piu sicure; di quelle, che pretenda l'Autore quale vive circa 200 anni dopo di loro . . .'.

99 S. Bartolozzi, *Vita di Antonio Franchi Lucchese Pittor Fiorentino*, Florence 1753, p. xxi. The text of the letter is given on pp. xxi–xxiii; Bartolozzi copied the letter from the unpublished life of Franchi written by F. S. Baldinucci. See Florence, Biblioteca Nazionale, Cod. Pal. 565, i, fols. 32–3.

100 Bartolozzi, p. xxi: '. . . Ho copiato molte di quelle erudizioni attenenti al mio trastullo (così chiamo il mio trattato della Teorica Pittoresca) e se ella mi potrà favorire della autorita . . . mi farà un gran favore . . .'.

101 A. Franchi, *La Teorica della Pittura ovvero Trattato delle Materie più necessarie per apprendere con fondamento quest'arte*, Lucca 1739.

102 Franchi p. 48–9. Bibl. Est. Camp. 1071: fols. 28–30; Arch. Stor 35: pp. 23–6.

Blake and the antique[1]

ANDREW WILTON

Assistant Keeper, Prints and Drawings

All the inventions and thoughts of the Ancients, whether conveyed to us in statues, bas-reliefs, intaglios, cameos, or coins, are to be sought after and carefully studied; the genius that hovers over these venerable relics may be called the father of modern art.

When Sir Joshua Reynolds voiced this idea, in his Presidential Discourse to the Royal Academy in 1774,[2] he expressed the opinion of the majority of his contemporaries. But Blake's annotations to the Discourses make it clear that he at least was opposed, and quite violently opposed, to the President and his views. 'This Man', he wrote, 'was Hired to Depress Art';[3] and it comes as no surprise that he should have held a view contrary to Reynolds: 'We do not want either Greek or Roman Models if we are but just & true to our own Imaginations'.[4] He certainly never conformed to the fashion, which Reynolds implicitly approves in his remarks quoted, of travelling to Italy where the most renowned masterpieces of ancient art, as well as of the Renaissance and Baroque periods, were to be found. He never so much as left the shores of England. Apart from three experimental years, in his forties, which he spent under the patronage of the poet William Hayley at Felpham near Bognor,[5] he seems hardly to have left London, where he was born in 1757, and the countryside that surrounded it from Dulwich to Hampstead. His drawings and paintings, indeed, do not appear to be concerned with the subject-matter that wider travels would have provided: they are evidently the products of Blake's own imagination, and, as he said: to 'the Man of Imagination, Nature is Imagination itself . . . To Me This World is all One continued Vision of Fancy or Imagination'.[6] His contemporaries agreed that his preoccupations were very personal; his friend Fuseli, a decidedly imaginative artist, commented that 'Fancy is the end, and not a means in his designs'. He did not employ it 'to give novelty and decoration to regular conceptions; but the whole of his aim is to produce singular shapes and odd combinations'.[7]

There was, then, little apparently in common between Blake's visions and the well-regulated, Classically based art of his time. Yet Blake was trained as an engraver, and consequently came into intimate working contact with the whole range of artistic activity in England; and, since he never achieved a success that would have enabled him to abandon such work, he continued to engrave plates after other designers for much of his life. What is more, he formed close and long-lasting connections with some of the artists most representative of current fashion; in particular with Fuseli and Flaxman.

Blake first met these two men in about 1780, that is to say, when he was a young man in his early twenties. He had occasion many times in his life to express his admiration for the work of Fuseli, which he called 'supereminent',[8] exhorting contemporaries to realize its merits; and Fuseli, in spite of the criticisms that I have already quoted, was alive to Blake's powers. When the two men met in the Royal Academy, much later in their careers, Fuseli, seeing Blake engaged in drawing from a cast, exclaimed, 'We ought to come and learn of you, not you of us!'[9] Flaxman especially proved a constant source of support and encouragement to Blake until his death, a year before Blake's, in 1826. Their relations suffered a period of coolness, but this was comparatively brief,[10] and in general their references to each other are cordial. 'You, O Dear Flaxman,' Blake wrote in 1800, 'are a Sublime Archangel, My Friend & Companion from Eternity.'[11] At that period, Flaxman even exerted some influence over Blake's attitude to his own work: 'Flaxman is the theme of my emulation in this of industry, as well as in other virtues and merits.' Most significant for us, Blake recognized the specifically Greek origin of Flaxman's inspiration: 'Happy son of the immortal Phidias, his lot is truly glorious, and mine no less happy in his friendship.'[12]

This quotation shows not only that Blake admired Flaxman; but that he admired Phidias as well. In fact, Greek art figured as prominently in his view of civilization as it did for any of his contemporaries: 'Milton, Shakspeare, Michael Angelo, Rafael, the finest specimens of Ancient Sculpture and Painting and Architecture, Gothic, Grecian, Hindoo, and Egyptian, are the extent of the human mind'.[13] All these sources can be seen to have played their part in forming Blake's visual language (as well as his philosophy),[14] but it is with the 'Grecian' that we are concerned primarily, and it was the Grecian that Blake saw, at least during part of his life, as the most universally beneficent influence upon modern culture. In 1800 he wrote to a friend, George Cumberland, rejoicing in 'the immense flood of Grecian light & glory which is coming on Europe';[15] and when he wished to commend his own city, it was to Greece that he referred for a comparison: he observed that 'from a City of meer Necessaries or at least a commerce of the lowest order of luxuries' it had become 'a City of Elegance in some degree ... its once stupid inhabitants' had entered 'into an Emulation of Grecian manners. There are now, I believe, as many Booksellers as there are Butchers ...'.[16]

London was, at any rate, a centre rich in collections of Classical art, and throughout the period of Blake's lifetime these were becoming ever more accessible to the public. Original works of Greek art, as opposed to the Roman copies which had hitherto passed as Greek, were beginning to find their way to England. Private galleries were opened to students and artists, and the British Museum acquired Sir William Hamilton's collection of Greek pottery and other antiquities in 1772, following this early in the 1800s with the Elgin and Towneley marbles. Casts of the most famous classical sculptures were also accessible: the Duke of Richmond's Gallery was used by artists during most of the second half of the eighteenth century, and included the Apollo Belvedere, the Medici Venus, the Capitoline Flora, and the Group of Wrestlers;[17] the Royal Academy's collection was yet more comprehensive, boasting even a cast of the Laocoön group.[18] As a boy of ten, Blake entered Henry Pars's drawing school in the Strand, where drawing from casts was an important part of the curriculum.[19] In 1779, when his seven years' apprenticeship to the engraver James Basire[20] came to an end, Blake became a student at the Academy;[21] he therefore underwent for a time all the classically-orientated disciplines of the institution. There was regular and extensive copying from the antique, and, we are told, he 'drew with great care all or certainly nearly all the noble antique figures in various views'.[22] It may be added that Flaxman's father was the proprietor of a shop making and selling plaster casts, in Covent Garden, and Blake would doubtless have known it and profited from the information provided by its wares.[23]

Basire's workshop was responsible for the engraving of plates illustrating many of the lavish volumes which gave expression and publicity to the expanding interest in the ancient past. In the year before Blake came to him, 1771, Basire had engraved an important neo-classical picture, Benjamin West's *Pylades and Orestes*, and during his apprenticeship Blake was engaged on such work as plates for Jacob Bryant's *Analysis of Ancient Mythology*, a book that seems to have played an important part in the formation of his views on ancient history,[24] and Gough's *Sepulchral Monuments*, published in 1786, which dealt with medieval sculpture in England and provided a strong practical impetus for Blake's lifelong interest in Gothic Art. Later, in 1792, he made four plates for the third volume of Stuart's *Antiquities of Athens*,[25] much of the work for which had been under Basire's supervision. His plates were from drawings made in about 1765 by William Pars of the frieze of the Athenian temple known as

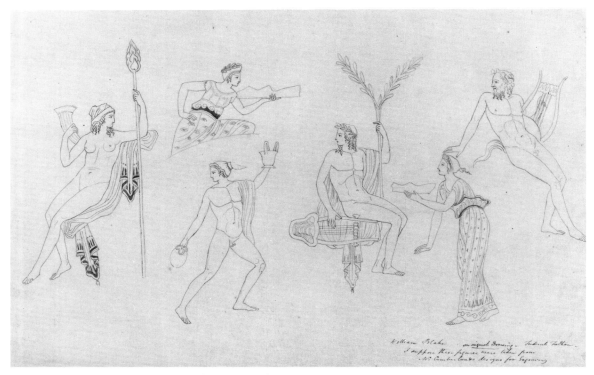

228 *William Blake: drawings after figures from d'Hancarville's* Hamilton Cabinet *(1867.10.12.202). Pen and ink over pencil.*

the 'Theseum';[26] in a letter to Willey Reveley, the editor of this third volume, he declared himself 'glad to embrace the offer of engraving such beautiful things'.[27] Although the Elgin Marbles did not arrive in England until after 1800, the numerous fine plates in the *Antiquities of Athens* must have given him a vivid idea of the quality of Greek art in the Periclean period, even if he was not, any more than most of his contemporaries, fully able to assess its importance. Many other such books publishing the treasures of the ancient world were available to Blake, of course. No full record remains of his own library of books and prints, although some of the works he knew are referred to in his writings, and we have several examples of his youthful exercises in copying prints, either from the collection which he began to make when still a child, or from plates borrowed from others (see **228** and note 29 below). For a general picture of the kind of library he would have been familiar with, we may take the hints afforded by records of Flaxman's collection.[28] This contained, among many similar works, Perrier's *Iconae et Segmentae Illustrium et Marmore Tabularum* of 1645; Montfaucon's comprehensive *Antiquité Expliquée* of 1722, translated into English at the same date; the 1766 edition of *Antiquities* in Sir William Hamilton's collection, a superb presentation by d'Hancarville of the Greek pottery then thought to be Etruscan;[29] the *Antichità di Ercolano*, whose eight volumes appeared between 1755 and 1792; Eckhel's *Antique Gems*; Winckelmann's *Monumenti Antichi Inediti*, and so on. Among the prints which Christie's sold from Flaxman's collection in 1828[30] occur engravings of the Antonine Column and the Obelisk of Caracalla; miscellaneous prints from the antique, of Greek vases, of bronzes in the collection of Richard Payne Knight; of mausoleums, friezes, tessellated pavements, Roman coins.

Such material was of course central to the outlook and practice of a 'son of Phidias' like Flaxman; but it was also the stuff of all art appreciation. Fuseli, temperamentally opposed to Flaxman in every way, clearly affirmed, in his *Lectures on Paintings*, and elsewhere, the universal belief that 'beauty' was 'the result of the standard set by the great masters of our art, the ancients, and confirmed by the submissive verdict of modern imitation'.[31] He himself, submissively, when in Rome or Naples, made sketches from classical reliefs and from designs in Hamilton's collection of Greek vases.[32] James Barry, an artist whom Blake enormously admired—even to the extent of planning a large-scale poem on him[33]—points just as firmly to this irresistible source of inspiration: 'that unaffected air of the ancients, which alone constitutes true taste'.[34] As a young man, Barry was even set to copying in oil the gouache drawings that Stuart had made of the Greek monuments for his *Antiquities of Athens*, so that he underwent an early experience not unlike Blake's.[35] His passion for antiquity was decidedly more emphatic than that which he entertained for the Italians: 'The parts of the art in which Michael Angelo and Raphael excelled are almost annihilated by the superiority of the antiques.'[36] And Fuseli too could say: 'Michael Angelo filled part of the Capella Sistina with imitations and sometimes transcriptions of the Torso' (i.e. the Torso Belvedere)—'will any one', he challenged, 'stand forth and say that he reached it?'[37]

The work of these three men, Fuseli, Flaxman and Barry, is referred to by Blake in terms of the highest praise: he was ready to accept that a worthwhile art could be founded on the standards established by the ancients, and at the same time was, to some extent at least, reliant on his contemporaries for his view of those standards. He absorbed classical influences through them, and when such influences appear in his work they do so modified, very often, in accordance with their practice. 'My figures', he stated in a letter of 1799, '. . . are those of Michael Angelo, Rafael & the Antique, & of the best living Models.'[38]

In practice, those 'living models' turned as much to the Italians as they did to antiquity: many of their ideas are derived directly from Michelangelo, especially the Sistine Chapel Ceiling and Last Judgment; and from Raphael, especially the

Vatican Stanze, and the Loggie which are now recognized as the work of Raphael's assistants, Perino del Vaga, Giulio Romano, and G. F. Penni.[39] These Renaissance painters employed an idiom more dramatic in character than that of the greatest works of antiquity, using the muscular contortion of the body to express a wider range of feeling than is common in Greek art; and Fuseli in particular borrowed extensively from Italian and Flemish followers of Michelangelo and Raphael. The electric vitality which is so important a feature of his art is present in Blake's use of the human form, too. It was inherent in the romantic classicism of the late eighteenth century but largely absent from Greek art, which was remarkable rather for its grace and restraint than for its dynamism, as Winckelmann had pointed out: 'All the remains of ancient art', he argued, prove 'that Grace alone places them above the reach of modern skill'.[40] Barry, who, like Fuseli, often sought to depict the extremes of human passion and sometimes strained the body to its limits in order to do so, also claimed 'my objects of study . . . are purity of design, beauty, elegance, and sublimity of expression'.[41] Even Fuseli (who had translated Winckelmann in 1765) talks of 'the "little more or less," imperceptible to vulgar eyes, which constitutes GRACE'.[42] This quality of classic restraint, no less than that of romantic frenzy, can be seen as a recurring, consciously cultivated element in Blake's visual language.

Although he claimed that everything he drew was executed direct from his 'imagination'—from the heaven-sent visions which were so much more real to him than the material world—in the actual physical process of transcribing what he imagined, Blake inevitably incorporated into his work something of this enthusiasm for Greek art, and for the work of those of his contemporaries who had turned to it most receptively. His earlier essays, indeed, reflect the popular classicizing style of the period which, imitating the reliefs on Roman sarcophagi and Greek tombstones, made such free use of hieratic gestures and frieze compositions. His engraving of *Edward and Elenor*,[43] after a lost painting from his own hand, shows a medieval subject, but is a fully-fledged classical composition in the manner of Gavin Hamilton or Benjamin West.

Two early series of drawings, the illustrations to his poem *Tyriel*, of the late 1780s, and the three scenes from the *Story of Joseph*, shown at the Royal Academy in 1785, have equally strong ties with the current style. In the *Tyriel* drawings the bareness of composition and stiffness of gesture suggest the influence of West and, perhaps, Flaxman, though their date makes it likely that Blake is here responding rather to the same stimuli that acted on Flaxman: and the monochrome colouring and frieze-like arrangement of figures with broad spaces between them contribute to an impression that a study of Hamilton's vases lies behind the designs.

One, showing *Har and Heva bathing*,[44] echoes a motif from a picture on which

229 *George Cumberland: drawing after a classical group in the Borghese Gallery (1866.2.10.688). Pen and ink and wash.*

Barry was working at about the same time: his *Jupiter and Juno on Mount Ida*.⁴⁵ The two heads pressed into such close proximity have the appearance of being a modern, or at any rate a mannerist device; but Barry may have had in mind a classical group such as one in the Borghese Gallery copied by Cumberland (**229**). Blake may well have been thinking of Cumberland's drawing when he made his version of *Satan with Adam and Eve* in 1808; though, of course, the effect achieved by both Barry and Blake here is essentially a two-dimensional one and changes its character altogether when translated into three dimensions.

Barry's influence seems to be strong in the *Joseph*⁴⁶ series, with its crowded groups of classical heads, partaking of the luxuriance of curling hair and the nobility of profile which is particularly prominent in the portraits to be found on antique gems. The seated figure of Joseph immediately calls to mind the seated figures on Greek funerary slabs, which became a standard type throughout the ancient world, recurring on the Parthenon, on vases, in late Roman reliefs, and elsewhere. A more personal variant, tinged with the mood of one of Fuseli's pensive characters, appears on a page of the series illustrating Young's *Night Thoughts*.⁴⁷ (Pl. III, p. 289). The raised arm is

230 *William Blake:
Detail of a fan design
showing* The Origin
of Painting (*1874.
12.12.147v*).
Watercolour.

characteristic of the pose: it recurs in the many figures related to the reclining
Ariadne, or *Cleopatra*, of which a version is incorporated into the design of the Portland
Vase; Blake actually engraved the vase for Erasmus Darwin's *Botanical Garden*, published
in 1791.[48]

Another little drawing, *The Origin of Painting*,[49] perhaps of the early 1780s (**230**),
already has the austere poses, more akin to Romney's romantic figure-subjects than to
West or Barry, which were later to appear in simplified, grander form in many of
Blake's scenes of death—the frontispiece to the *Songs of Experience* is an early specimen
of his mature use of this idea. The oval format of the drawing suggests that of an
engraved gem, a form of antique art much prized by Blake; in 1804 he had two
'correct & enlarged copies from antique Gems' over his chimney piece, and hung a
medallion of Romney between them, considering it 'worthy' of them.[50]

In the little vignette of *The Origin of Painting* Blake employs sharp, sweet colours
very similar to those favoured by the sentimental decorators of the time—Cipriani,
Angelica Kauffmann, Biagio Rebecca—who all looked back to the Rococo, with its
sugary pastel colours, but were also conscious of the more robust harmonies of the
newly-popular antique Roman wall-painting. Blake's design, with its garland,
putto and fairy, also suggests a semi-Rococo, semi-Classic source. The cherub holding

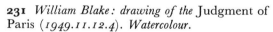

231 *William Blake: drawing of the* Judgment of Paris (*1949.11.12.4*). *Watercolour.*

232 *Detail of an illustration from d'Hancarville's* Hamilton Cabinet *1, pl. 130, showing the figure of a stooping woman on one of the Hamilton vases. Colour-printed engraving.*

a torch on the left is closely based on a classical prototype; a similar one appeared in one of the plates of Montfaucon's *Antiquity Explained*.[51]

The subject of this drawing was a favourite of the time.[52] It is, however, extremely rarely that Blake treats of a classical theme. His sources, when not entirely from his imagination, were modern authors, from Dante and Chaucer on, and especially Milton; of ancient texts he used simply the Bible. But there is a scene of *Philoctetes and Neoptolemus on Lemnos*,[53] illustrating Sophocles' play *Philoctetes* and dated 1812. The subject had been treated by Barry.[54] Blake makes hardly any visual allusion to the ancient world: the principal figure is almost nude, and the others clad in imaginary armour. A more elaborate composition making use of a classical subject is the *Judgment of Paris*[55] (**231**) which again, apart from the stylization of its arrangement on the sheet, is not strongly classical in feeling, although the strange pose of Paris does occur in a figure on one of the vases in Sir William Hamilton's collection, published by d'Hancarville[56] (**232**). The three goddesses are *not*, as one might expect, disposed in the attitudes of the three Graces, but their restrained, stylized postures are perhaps

233 *Detail of an illustration from Stuart's* Antiquities of Athens, *1, chapter IV, pl. 23, showing a figure of the 'fallen warrior' type on the frieze of the Choragic monument of Lysicrates. Engraving.*

closer to Winckelmann's idea of Greek decorum than such a direct quotation might have brought them. Blake actually did make use of that model in a more unlikely context: the plate of *Europe supported by Africa and America* which he engraved for a book on the *Negroes of Surinam* by Captain John Gabriel Stedman, published in 1796.[57] This subject, displaying as it does an approach to the female nude very different from Blake's usual one, was probably executed under the instructions, and from a sketch, of Stedman, who took credit for the design of the illustrations to his book. The overt classical allusion is also rather unlike Blake, who generally invests his borrowings with more of his own personality. One of Blake's earliest and most original works seems to have an equally immediate source in the antique: the print of *Albion* (known as *Glad Day*) first engraved in 1780, and reissued in colour fifteen years later, is based with remarkably little modification on a figure published in the *Antichità di Ercolano*.[58] The stance, with arms outstretched and one leg at an angle, has been compared with that of 'Vitruvian Man' in illustrations of the theory of human proportion by Leonardo and Scamozzi; but the mood of Blake's print is much closer to that of the Roman bronze of a faun, and indeed, the mathematical aspect of the Vitruvian approach was not one which would have appealed to Blake. This *Albion* might be interpreted as his highly personal Apollo, its completely open nakedness,

234 *William Blake: drawing of the* Stoning of Achan (*Tate Gallery*). *Watercolour.*

and allusion to the sun in the glory which streams out from the figure, inviting comparison with Classical representations of that god, or of Hermes, who sometimes appears in prints standing before the radiance of sunrise.[59] The type with which Blake's generation was most familiar was the Apollo Belvedere, which Blake himself actually used as the basis for an Apollo statue appearing in one of his illustrations to Milton's *Ode on the Morning of Christ's Nativity*: 'Apollo from his shrine / Can no more divine, / With hollow shriek the steep of Delphos leaving'.[60] Similarly, the type of the winged *Victory*, such as the one in the right hand of Phidias' *Olympian Zeus*, becomes for Blake *Satan in his Original Glory*,[61] holding orb and sceptre, with wings outspread and cloak fluttering symmetrically out on either side of him.[62]

The catalogue of associations, from the most obvious to the most tenuous, could be extended indefinitely. Blake, like the ancients, was content to use stock attitudes over and over again in different contexts, and they vary enormously in mood and detail from one to another; the outstretched *Albion*, for example, is re-used in one of the plates of *Jerusalem*;[63] and the 'fallen warrior' type which appears frequently in classical battle-scenes is taken over by Blake for his *Resurrection*[64] and many other subjects; it even appears, twisted sideways, as *Satan departing from the presence of the Lord*, in plate 5 of the *Job* engravings. One of the most striking representations of the type in antiquity is that occurring in the frieze of the Choragic monument of Lysicrates at Athens, published by Stuart in vol. I of his *Antiquities of Athens*, 1762, and engraved by James Basire and others (**233**).[65] While the pose is ubiquitous in classical reliefs and Blake's use of it is equally free and varied, this particular example may have recommended itself to him especially since it was so finely engraved. The pose of Achan in the drawing of *The Stoning of Achan* now in the Tate Gallery[66] seems to be a contorted, dramaticized variant on it (**234**). Another of Stuart's plates of the frieze contained a figure even more Blakean in feeling,[67] with a head expressing horror in a way that closely parallels the engraving of *Buoso Donati attacked by a Serpent* in the Dante series made at the end of Blake's life (**235, 236**). The image of a naked figure in conjunction with a snake is one that Blake frequently returns to: his *Eve Tempted* is a characteristic example. The preliminary pencil drawing for this (**237**), now in the Victoria and Albert Museum, shows the snake coiling round the stiff upright figure of Eve in a design which is strongly reminiscent of the image of Isis entwined by a snake as published by Montfaucon.[68] (**238**) The illustrations in works like these, with which Blake must have been very familiar, became wholly absorbed into his visual unconscious and seem to exercise an indirect influence over numerous designs, made at different periods of his life.

But Blake did not only borrow from Classical models simply by adopting standard poses. He could also take over the idea behind a Greek original and express it in his

235 *Detail of an illustration from Stuart's* Antiquities of Athens, *1, chapter IV, pl. 18, showing a figure from the frieze of the Choragic monument of Lysicrates. Engraving.*

236 *William Blake:* Buoso Donati attacked by a Serpent *(1855.4.14.466). Engraving.*

237 *William Blake: drawing of* Eve Tempted
(*Victoria and Albert Museum*). *Pencil.*

238 *Detail of an illustration from Montfaucon's* Antiquity
Explained, *Supplement vol. 11, p. 215, pl. 46,
showing the figure of Isis entwined by a snake. Engraving.*

own, totally new language. When he did this in the case of his imaginative re-creation of the great Laocoön group, he clothed the figures, naked in the original, in long Biblical robes.[69] Blake referred specifically to the absence of drapery in the Laocoön: the ancients 'often deviated from the Habits to preserve the Manners, as in the instance of Laocoön, who, though a priest, is represented naked'.[70] Reynolds had made this point in 1776, in his seventh Discourse. Blake believed with Fuseli that 'Subordination is the character of drapery';[71] and indeed in this he concurred with Reynolds whose teaching was that 'the historical Painter . . . does [not] debase his conceptions with minute attention to the discrimination of Drapery'; Blake comments: 'Drapery is formed alone by the Shape of the Naked'[72]—meaning that it always implies and augments the expression of the figure beneath it. The antique dispenses with drapery when, as in the case of the Laocoön, strong emotion is to be expressed and the whole body needs to be enlisted to do so; or when, as with the Apollo, it is concerned with the ideal. As Barry said, 'The Grecian artists and all the great moderns, who have judiciously followed their heroic example instead of idly and meanly wasting their attention upon imitating the work of the taylor or mantua-maker, employed their whole care and solicitude upon those beauties . . . which always discover themselves in the natural motions and gestures of the naked figure'.[73] *Glad Day* perfectly demonstrates Blake's agreement with this; but he recognized the value of drapery, using it very much as the Greeks did, to suggest movement, and to emphasize form by following and extending the lines of the figure. The close-fitting, transparent veils which are hardly distinguishable from the flesh of many of his figures derive more closely from classical precedent than from any other, and the lines of many of his windblown robes fall into rounded curls similar to those of Bacchic revellers in classical reliefs. His engraving of *Mirth*,[74] illustrating Milton's *Allegro*, is an apt embodiment of part of Fuseli's aphorism that 'The forms of virtue are erect, the forms of pleasure undulate: Minerva's drapery descends in long uninterrupted lines; a thousand amorous curves embrace the limbs of Flora'.[75] *Mirth*, frontal and symmetrical, again recalls the Phidian *Victory*, and many Classical presentations of the Dance.[76]

If the work of his early career betrays extensive serious study of the antique, both in the original and in its multifarious modern adaptations, Blake's work for Hayley at Felpham, between 1800 and 1803, brought him, briefly, even closer to the Classics than he had previously been. Hayley had been introduced to Blake by Flaxman, whom he greatly admired, and whom he 'assisted' in designing the austere tomb of William Cowper for Dereham Church in Norfolk.[77] With him, Blake began to learn the classical languages: he wrote to his brother James in 1803: 'I go on Merrily with my Greek & Latin; am very sorry that I did not begin to learn languages early in life as I find it very Easy; . . . I read Greek as fluently as an Oxford scholar & the Testament is my chief master . . . .'[78]

Among many projects arranged by Hayley to provide Blake with employment was an unusual one for the decoration of the octagonal library of Hayley's house: a series of portrait designs executed in tempera on canvas, featuring the heads of eighteen

239 *William Blake:* Demosthenes (*Manchester City Art Gallery*). *Tempera.*

To face Page 126

ΠΟΣΕΙΔΩΝΙ

T. H. invenit.

W. Blake sc.

The DEATH of DEMOSTHENES.

*He views this Outrage with indignant Eyes,
And at the Base of Neptunes Statue dies.*

Epistle 5. Verse 61.

Publishd June 14. 1800 by Cadell & Davis Strand

240 *William Blake: illustration of* The Death of Demosthenes *from Hayley's* Essay on Sculpture, *facing page 126. Engraving.*

writers including Homer and Demosthenes.[79] The heads are conceived as trompe-l'oeil bas-reliefs in circular medallions, following the classical practice of using medals, coins and gems as surfaces for portraiture; though it is interesting to note how Blake's preoccupation with line militates against the success of their effect. The wreath of laurel which surrounds the head of Homer is a characteristic Roman motif; even the musical instrument hanging upon a palm tree can be found in Montfaucon—though there the example given shows a drum rather than a lyre.[80] The panel of Demosthenes follows the same pattern, but here Blake incorporates into the background a scene of the *Death of Demosthenes* from an idea supplied by Hayley's son Thomas (**239**). For Hayley's *Essay on Sculpture*, a didactic poem inspired by Flaxman and published in 1800, Blake engraved another version of the *Death of Demosthenes* subject which shows clearly that Thomas's invention was very closely modelled on Flaxman (**240**).[81] The design aspires after that simplicity which Flaxman said 'The Ancients . . . considered . . . as a characteristic of perfection',[82] and it makes use of the simple, pure outline popularized by Flaxman in his illustrations to Homer and Aeschylus, which he called 'a series of compositions on the principles of the Ancients',[83] engraved in Italy by Piroli and at that date enjoying enormous popularity throughout Europe.

Some of Piroli's plates of the *Iliad* designs were accidentally lost, and Blake undertook to repeat them for the 1805 edition. In 1817 Flaxman's designs for Hesiod appeared, all of them engraved by Blake. Whereas Piroli's line is incisive, variable in width, and flowing, Blake's response to the Flaxman drawings seems almost timid, the lines stippled in rather than engraved. The same applies to the illustrations of sculpture—including the Apollo Belvedere, Venus de' Medici and Laocoön—which he made for Flaxman's article on Sculpture in Abraham Rees's *Cyclopedia* at about the same time. (For these, we are told, Blake returned to the Royal Academy to make drawings from the casts there.[84])

This kind of fine outline was associated very closely with Greek art, and the popularity of Flaxman's *Homer* both illustrated and increased the feeling that only by such a delicate and refined means of drawing could the spirit of the Antique be caught. The theory was given full expression in George Cumberland's *Thoughts on Outline Sculpture, and the System that Guided the Ancient Artists in composing their Figures and Groupes* published in 1796, with a selection of 24 of the author's designs 'of Classical Subjects invented on the Principles recommended in the Essay'. Cumberland employed Blake to engrave some of these plates, although he did most of them himself. Blake was a good friend, in fact, who greatly admired Cumberland and his work. In 1799, he declared that 'the purpose for which alone I live . . . is, in conjunction with such men as my friend Cumberland, to renew the lost Art of the Greeks'.[85] It was

Cumberland, almost more than Flaxman, who seemed to be bringing the true spirit of antiquity to the modern world. Blake adjured him, 'Do not throw aside for any long time the honour intended you by Nature to revive the Greek workmanship.' He added, 'I study your outlines as usual, just as if they were antiques.'[86] Cumberland produced a large number of outlines, in pen and black ink on a reddish background, in imitation of Greek red or black figure pottery;[87] only a small proportion was published and Blake may well be referring here to original specimens given or lent him by Cumberland. Some of the figures are from classical sources, often characterized as expressing different types of action: gentle action, violent action, enthusiastic action, heroic action, or heavy motion, composed grave motion, celestial or gliding motion. Others are improvised by Cumberland, sometimes from Renaissance designs; for example, one group of figures, which seems Greek enough, is carefully classicized from different sources in the Baptistery gates at Florence by Ghiberti. All these drawings, and even more markedly the engravings from them, exemplify the theory of Outline—'the inestimable value of chaste outline' being 'the best rudiment of Art'.[88] It is the hallmark of that simplicity to which I have already referred, contrasting with 'the tyrants of the trade, with their fierce contrasts, good lights, and double burnished ornaments'.[89] This attack on academic teaching was, of course, echoed by Blake; but in his annotations to the *Discourses* he frequently has occasion to fall into uncharacteristic agreement with Reynolds on the subject of outline. Where the President says 'A firm and determined outline is one of the characteristics of the great style in painting', Blake writes 'A noble sentence!'[90] and on the rule that students should 'contend who shall have the purest and most correct outline' Blake comments 'Excellent!'[91]

Although much has been written on the subject,[92] some explanation is perhaps required for the strong association in the minds of Blake and his contemporaries between Greek art and outline. Fuseli, in his lectures on painting, referred to 'The Tale of the Corinthian Maid, who traced the shade of her departing lover by the secret lamp' as a poetically, if not historically, accurate account of the origin of Greek painting which, he said, was characterized by 'that *linear method* . . . which seems to have continued as the basis of execution, even when the instrument [i.e. the stylus] for which it was chiefly adapted, had long been laid aside.'[93] But 'Outline' was more than a mere technical accident: it comprehended the very nature of classical art, which at that time meant principally sculpture. Cumberland argues that it is above all in sculpture that outline is important: 'A statue is *all* outline' he says.[94] 'A fine simple Outline may possess grace, action, expression, character, and proportion. A fine statue is only better, as it contains all these qualities when varied in a thousand ways; . . . there are statues in the world which, if turned round on a pivot before a lamp, would produce, on a wall, some hundreds of fine Outlines.'[95] Here he echoes Winckelmann who had, indeed, already pointed to 'Precision of contours, that characteristic distinction of the Ancients'.[96] Winckelmann observes that 'The middle parts of a full face are the outlines of its profile, and so on. Consequently, there is no such a thing as middle parts to be met with by the designer'. He goes on, applying the idea to painting rather than sculpture: 'The idea of a painter, well skilled in the contours of the outlines, but ignorant of their contents, is an absurd one.'[97]

Since the outline embodied the very essence of art, it must accurately conform to very specific rules. Cumberland disapproved of Piroli's interpretation of Flaxman's designs: he describes the engravings of the *Iliad* and *Odyssey* as '*Outline thick and thin alternately*, like the flourishes of a penman', which give a 'very unmathematical idea of form in general'.[98] The line which Cumberland wished to see was 'That . . . which has been so often recommended, I mean *pure*, *flowing*, and *fine*'. 'A flowing outline', he continues, 'gives motion'; he would tolerate 'even . . . incorrect outlines, when their direction is just'.[99] He stipulates, however, that outline 'To be distinct, must have colour; and, if it have colour it represents a wire that surrounds the designs'.[100] Blake's thought chimes in with this view, although he expresses it in a way that makes it an altogether more convincing theory of art; 'The great and golden rule of art, as well as of life, is this: That the more distinct, sharp, and wirey the bounding line, the more perfect the work of art . . . Protogenes and Apelles knew each other by this line', he adds, linking the concept once more firmly to that of the antique.[101] He seems to suggest here, that outline represents more than simply the form of an object, although he often refers to outline as 'form': 'What kind of Intellects', he asks, 'must he have who sees only the Colours of things & not the Forms of Things.'[102]

His training as an engraver provided an additional and very basic reason for Blake's attachment to line as the key to art. The incised, and incisive, line is the medium through which the engraver must express everything he wishes to convey; precision of line is a matter of second nature to him. Blake's *Canterbury Pilgrims*, for instance, was engraved[103] 'in a correct and finished Line manner of Engraving, similar to those original Copper Plates of Albert Durer, Lucas, Hisben [i.e. Holbein], Aldegrave and the old original Engravers, . . . whose method, alone, can delineate Character as it is in this Picture, where all the Lineaments are distinct'.[104] He referred back to the Renaissance as the source of the greatest modern art; as we have seen he frequently coupled the Antique with Michelangelo, Raphael and Durer, and we find that outline is, for Blake, a vital feature of both classical and modern art. He contrasted the *disegno* of the Florentine and Roman masters, the linear clarity of the northern engravers, with what he called the 'blotting and blurring' art of Rubens, Rembrandt, Correggio and the Venetians.[105] He abhorred 'that infernal machine called Chiaro Oscuro':[106] the submerging of outline in shadow or the definition of form by colour alone were anathema to Blake. 'Broken Colours & Broken Lines & Broken Masses are Equally Subversive of the Sublime.'[107] He quotes with approval an observation of Reynolds to William Gilpin: 'Uniformity of Colour & a long continuation of lines produces Grandeur.'[108] This axiom sums up succinctly much of the character and purpose of the revival of Greek ideas in painting, and might be used to describe many of Blake's most successful essays in the sublime. Blake's own summary of his views is equally succinct: 'he who draws best must be the best Artist'.[109]

Line, then, had a central philosophical significance for him. 'Every Line', he said, 'is the Line of Beauty.'[110] Line was the testimony of a clear, vivid imagination. He inveighs against Reynolds with particular vehemence when 'generalization' is the subject of discussion, although he often, in pursuance of his idealized themes, practised exactly the kind of generalization which Reynolds advocated. He remarks that 'All Forms are Perfect in the Poet's Mind, but these are not Abstracted nor Compounded from Nature, but are from Imagination'.[111] Although he relied heavily on standard forms, types of character and gesture which, as I have suggested, were used repeatedly in different compositions throughout his life, he found the vague unspecific grandeur admired by theorists like Burke—and, he thought, by Reynolds—a contradiction in terms. 'Grandeur of Ideas is founded on Precision of Ideas.'[112] He speaks of 'that greatest of all blessings, a strong imagination, a clear idea, and a determinate vision of things in his own mind'.[113]

This law governing the expression of the imagination applied, for Blake, equally to ancient and modern art. It was not merely by accident that the great Italians of the Renaissance worked in a manner comparable to that of the Greeks. Blake's contemporaries traced the line of art directly from those Greeks who, imported by the Romans, supplied the Republic and the Empire with sculptures and paintings, through the period of the introduction of Christianity and the transportation of the culture to Byzantium, to early Christian art in Italy and then via Duccio and Giotto to the Renaissance: 'Seven or eight Greek Christian compositions', Flaxman says in one of his lectures, were 'standards to the Italian painters, from which they scarcely ventured to deviate for ages, viz., The Creation of Adam and of Eve, the Nativity, the Transfiguration, the Crucifixion, the Resurrection, the Glorification, with some others, which amply prove that the sacred flame remained in Greece which kindled light and life in the modern arts of Western Europe'.[114]

In Blake's own practice we have no difficulty in recognizing the importance of line as defined by Cumberland. His pencil studies, it is true, do not have it—they usually seem to be rapid attempts to seize in their passage the main features of his fleeting visions. But the finished drawings are frequently worked up with the pen, coloured in such a way as not to obscure the pen lines, and demonstrate palpably Blake's faith in the line to express both details of character and broad ideas of mood and atmosphere. His compositions often depend on overall linear movements of great clarity and breadth—typical of the dramatic approach to design which prevailed at the time. Flaxman's outline drawings are models of the regular, sensitive line that Cumberland required, and their sculptural compactness is a quality to be found in many of Blake's designs; but Blake's freer, flowing movements have more in common with the bold pen sketches of Romney, whom he praised as 'Sublime',[115] and the nervous pen drawings of Fuseli. In this context, Blake's frequently expressed admiration for John Hamilton Mortimer[116] takes a natural place. Of all the English artists of the generation preceding Blake's, Mortimer excelled in the use of line: his pure, fluent pen drawing translated perfectly into etching, which he employed (like Barry) as a ready means of publishing his ideas. His subject-matter, too, was of a fanciful and imaginative kind which might have indicated to Blake a kindred spirit. Perhaps Blake had Mortimer's *Nebuchadnezzar* in mind when he drew his own version of the subject.[117]

The large colour prints, of which *Nebuchadnezzar* is an example, although initially etched by Blake's special process, were heavily overlaid with colour both before printing and afterwards by hand, and it has to be admitted that it is colour, not line, which is the principal agent of expression here. In the works that he executed in tempera, or, as he called it, 'fresco', he claimed that 'Clearness and precision have been the chief objects . . . Clear colours unmudded by oil, and firm and determinate lineaments unbroken by shadows.'[118] Time has rather obscured this intention, but the conception is always dependent on flowing, twisting line which evokes muscular structure, movement and mass as well as creating Blake's personal rhythm of expressive posture and gesture. Blake asserted that 'He who makes a design must know the Effect & Colouring Proper to be put to that design';[119] but he felt that a satisfactory drawing was better left unspoilt by colouring. His 'frescoes', however, were really 'watercolour'—that is, painted with water as the vehicle—and, he said, 'properly Miniature, or Enamel Painting; every thing in Fresco is as high finished as Miniature or Enamel, although in Works larger than Life'.[120] 'Colouring', he wrote, 'does not depend on where the Colours are put, but on where the lights and darks are put, and all depends on Form or Outline, on where that is put; where that is wrong, the Colouring never can be right.'[121]

The frescoes that Blake executed of *Pitt* and *Nelson*[122] are quite explicitly public works, designed to do for England what Raphael had done for Italy; Blake justified them by reference to such illustrious precedents. Painting, in his view, 'is more adapted to solemn ornament than Marble can be, as it is capable of being Placed on any heighth & indeed would make a Noble finish Placed above the Great Public

Monuments in Westminster, St Pauls, & other Cathedrals . . . Monuments to the dead, Painted by Historical & Poetical Artists, like Barry & Mortimer (I forbear to name living Artists tho' equally worthy), I say, Monuments so Painted must make England What Italy is, an Envied Storehouse of Intellectual Riches.'[123] It is interesting to note that among the memoranda relating to his remarks on his paintings, he again invokes the example of the Ancients: 'That Painted as well as Sculptured Monuments were common among the Ancients is evident from the words of the Savants who compared Those Sepulchures Painted on the outside with others only of stone.'[124] And when talking of fresco he mentions Apelles and Protogenes along with Raphael and Michelangelo.[125]

In their lectures on painting, Fuseli and Barry laid great stress on the lessons of the great Greek painters, although their works had not survived, drawing long examples from the descriptions of Pausanias and other historians. Reynolds had set the precedent for this in his eighth Discourse, going in some detail into a problem posed by Timanthes' *Sacrifice of Iphigenia* as described by Pliny. Barry actually chose subjects recorded by Pliny as having been executed by Greek masters—e.g. *Medea Meditating revenge against Jason*, by Timomachus.[126] These detailed reconstructions of ancient paintings are, however, primarily concerned with the depiction of emotion: Reynolds reiterated the standard Classical idea that 'the expression of the Passions' is 'the most essential part of our art',[127] and since such a heavy emphasis was placed upon this function of painting it is understandable that he and his contemporaries tolerated the lack of perspective and the elementary composition that marked the pictures in which the figures appeared. Blake attached little importance to these faults; he observed, 'The Ancients were chiefly attentive to Complicated & Minute Discrimination of Character; it is the whole of Art'.[128] Fuseli, speaking of the paintings of Polygnotus at Delphi which, of course, he knew only from descriptions, admitted that 'what is now called composition was totally wanting in them as a whole . . . it appears as plain that they had no perspective'.[129] There was no attempt, apparently, to subordinate some figures to others; they were arranged across the picture space in rows or, in fact, as they would appear on vases and friezes. One design which Blake hoped would appeal to the general public, the *Canterbury Pilgrims*, is planned strictly as a frieze, the figures spread in a solemn procession regularly across the picture-space; but more often, his 'public' works are very evidently dependent for their compositional structure upon the tradition that found its fullest expression at the Italian Renaissance, making strong use of symmetry and centrality. He could, on occasion, take a whole compositional type, and restate it in terms of one of his own subjects—*Satan Rousing the Rebel Angels*,[130] (**241**) for instance, illustrating Milton, makes use of the standard plan of a *Transfiguration* or a *Resurrection*. But even when his

241 *William Blake: drawing of* Satan rousing the Rebel Angels (*Victoria and Albert Museum*). *Watercolour.*

242 *William Blake: drawing of* The Descent of the Soul *(1894.6.12.15). Watercolour.*

243 The Apotheosis of Homer. *Relief carving by Archelaos of Priene, Greek, second century BC (No. 2191).*

debt to Raphael and Michelangelo is most obvious, we feel a tendency of his designs to break up into sections or compartments; his idea of the *Last Judgment*, which exists in several different forms[131] and owes much to that in the Sistine Chapel, is developed in numerous almost independent areas which are sometimes even isolated from each other by a firm formal barrier—rocks, flames, clouds; a clear example of this process is the *Descent of the Soul*,[132] (**242**) an idea elaborated in connection with his series of illustrations to Blair's poem *The Grave*, on which he was working in 1806. Here the 'cross-section' of an underground system of caves and passages provides the perfect framework for a series of separate scenes. This is not the sophisticated practice of the High Renaissance, although it certainly has affinities with earlier Italian wall-decorations, precisely the kind of primitive religious art which Flaxman thought to have derived directly from ancient Greek practice. We may take this hint and trace the formula to Classical sources, such as a Greek relief, in London in Blake's day, of the *Apotheosis of Homer*,[133] (**243**) which has just such a layout as Blake's, including even the motif of the enclosed 'room'; and some of the individual figures provide parallels with his.

Blake himself says that he used compositions from Antiquity as the bases of his own, and again in the context of 'public' works. The *Pitt* and *Nelson* were both, he explained, 'compositions of a mythological cast, similar to those Apotheoses of Persian, Hindoo and Egyptian Antiquity, which are still preserved on rude monuments, being copies from some stupendous originals now lost or perhaps buried till some happier age'.[134]

This brings us to an important aspect of Blake's attitude to ancient art. He looked upon Greek art, no less than Hindoo, Persian and Egyptian art, as second-hand. 'No man can believe that either Homer's Mythology, or Ovid's, were the production of Greece or of Latium; neither will any one believe, that the Greek statues, as they are called, were the invention of Greek Artists; perhaps the Torso is the only original work remaining; all the rest are evidently copies, though fine ones, from greater works of the Asiatic Patriarchs'.[135] He based this judgment, interestingly, upon the evidence of the majority of the classical sculptures admired at the time, which are indeed copies, mostly Roman, of earlier originals; like most of his contemporaries he knew little of Periclean Greek art, outside the publications of Stuart, and, when the Elgin collection eventually reached England, underestimated it, along with Payne Knight and many other connoisseurs. We are told that 'he thought with Fuseli and Flaxman that the Elgin Theseus, however full of the antique savour, could not, as ideal form, rank with the very finest relics of antiquity'.[136] What distinguishes his view from that of others, however, is his idiosyncratic opinion that the masterpieces of Classical art were derived from an even more ancient Jewish culture, and his claim to have been 'taken in vision into the ancient republics, monarchies, and patriarchates of Asia', and to have seen 'those wonderful originals called in the Sacred Scriptures the Cherubim, which were sculptured and painted on walls of Temples, Towers, Cities, Palaces, and erected in the highly cultivated states of Egypt, Moab, Edom, Aram, among the Rivers of Paradise, being originals from which the Greeks and Hetrurians copied Hercules Farnese, Venus of Medicis, Apollo Belvidere, and all the grand works of ancient art. They were executed in a very superior style to those justly admired copies, being with their accompaniments terrific and grand in the highest degree . . . some of them one hundred feet in height; some were painted as pictures, and some carved as basso relievos, and some as groupes of statues, all containing mythological and recondite meaning, where more is meant than meets the eye.'[137] 'What we call Antique Gems', he says elsewhere, 'are the Gems of Aaron's Breast Plate.'[138] On an engraving of the Laocoön which he made in about 1820 Blake inscribed this description: 'Jah, his two Sons, Satan & Adam, as they were copied from the Cherubim of Solomon's Temple, by three Rhodians, & applied to Natural Fact or History of Ilium.'[139] As I have mentioned, Blake's own drawing of the Laocoön subject actually shows the priestly robes which would be appropriate to his view of Jehovah. It was monuments comparable to these primordial marvels that Blake wished to see erected in England, and which the *Pitt* and the *Nelson* sought to emulate 'on a smaller scale'.

It emerges from these passages that, in Blake's view, the Greeks did not, after all, possess that Imagination which was for him the centre of all creative activity. He went so far as to say in one place, 'The Greek Muses are daughters of Mnemosyne, or Memory, and not of Inspiration or Imagination'; and 'Imagination', he declared, 'has nothing to do with Memory'.[140] He was not unusual in holding this opinion; indeed, it had been outlined by Jacob Bryant in the very *Analysis of Ancient Mythology* that Blake had helped to illustrate under Basire. And yet we frequently find in his writing that it was precisely because they demonstrated the power of imagination in its highest degree that Blake admired the ancients. 'Greek statues are all of them representations of spiritual existences, of Gods immortal, to the mortal perishing organ of sight' he pronounces in the same work, the Descriptive Catalogue to his 1809 exhibition, which contains the outline of his theory of the art of the Patriarchs.[141] Again, 'The Ancients did not mean to Impose when they affirm'd their belief in Vision & Revelation';[142] and he asks, 'What is it sets Homer, Virgil & Milton in so high a rank of Art? Why is the Bible more Entertaining & Instructive than any other book? Is it not because they are addressed to the Imagination, which is Spiritual Sensation but mediately to the Understanding or Reason? Such is True Painting, and such was alone valued by the Greeks & the best modern Artists.'[143]

This inconsistency became more strongly marked towards the end of his life. As early as 1804, in his poem *Milton*, Blake affirmed, as I have already quoted, that 'We do not want either Greek or Roman Models if we are but just & true to our own Imaginations, those Worlds of Eternity in which we shall live for ever in Jesus our Lord'. *Milton* was the first of the prophetic books to appear after his three years with Hayley, and seems, in part, to embody a violent reaction against the intense studies of classical art in which Hayley had encouraged him. It attacks 'The Stolen and Perverted Writings of Homer & Ovid, of Plato & Cicero, which all Men ought to contemn', as opposed to the 'Sublime of the Bible'; and makes a thrust at the whole basis of the ancient cultures, 'the silly Greek & Latin slaves of the Sword'.[144] These views appear again in an engraved plate of about 1820, *On Homer's Poetry & On Virgil*.[145] Here Blake expands his ideas on the subject with alarming completeness: 'Sacred Truth has pronounced that Greece & Rome, as Babylon & Egypt, so far from being parents of Arts and Sciences as they pretend, were destroyers of all Art'. The fact which rendered void all that the Ancients achieved was, in Blake's eyes, their 'slavery to the Sword': 'Rome & Greece swept Art into their maw & destroy'd it; a Warlike State can never produce Art. It will Rob & Plunder & accumulate into one place, & Translate & Copy & Buy & Sell & Criticise, but not Make'. This is reminiscent of some verses in a notebook kept by Blake some years earlier, about 1808–11:

> 'Twas the Greeks' love of war
> Turn'd Love into a Boy,
> And Woman into a Statue of Stone—
> And away fled every Joy.[146]

In the annotations to Thornton's translation of the Lord's Prayer, which he made in the year of his death, Blake's antagonism is at its most uncompromising: 'The Greek & Roman Classics is the Antichrist'.[147]

Greece and Rome were civilizations of the mind and the reason, but not of the soul and the imagination. 'The Gods of Greece & Egypt were Mathematical Diagrams'[148]—Blake's hackles rose at the idea of mathematics, and in this he had always been at odds with men like Flaxman, who could refer with enthusiasm to 'Pamphilus, the learned Macedonian painter, who denied that anyone could succeed in the study of painting, without arithmetic and geometry'.[149] Blake had in fact arrived at a polarized view of art, in which 'Grecian is Mathematic Form: Gothic is Living Form'.[150] Indeed, his whole interpretation of history conformed to this polarization: 'it is the Classics, & not Goths nor Monks, that Desolate Europe with Wars.'[151]

This is all very different from the 'flood of Grecian light & glory' which Blake celebrated in 1800; but if his philosophy was modified in the course of his life, the visual lessons which he imbibed from his youthful study of classical art remained inherent in his style as an artist. And confident as he was of his own achievement, he was content to remain in friendly rivalry with the ancients: 'He knows that what he does is not inferior to the grandest Antiques. Superior they cannot be, for human power cannot go beyond either what he does, or what they have done; it is the gift of God, it is inspiration and vision. He had resolved to emulate those precious remains of antiquity . . . his ideas of strength and beauty have not been greatly different.'[152] Reynolds himself would have recognized here a model pupil: to emulate, but not to copy, was Blake's aim: he followed the spirit rather than the letter of Greek art. As he was so fond of quoting, 'The letter killeth, the Spirit giveth Life'.

Photographic Credits. Tate Gallery, London: 234; Victoria and Albert Museum, London: 237, 241; City Art Gallery, Manchester: 239.

NOTES

1 First given as a lecture at the Victoria and Albert Museum in November 1972. The subject-matter of this article is merely an expanded footnote to a section of the study 'Blake's Pictorial Imagination' by Anthony Blunt, *Journal of the Warburg and Courtauld Institutes*, vol. VI (1943), pp. 190–212, much of which was incorporated into *The Art of William Blake*, Columbia, 1959. The author acknowledges a heavy debt to both these works.

2 Sir Joshua Reynolds, *Discourses* ed. Roger Fry, 1905. Sixth Discourse, p. 163.

3 Blake, *Complete Writings*, ed. Sir Geoffrey Keynes, Oxford 1966 (paperback edn.) p. 445. Blake seems to have made his annotations to the Discourses between about 1798 and 1809. (See David V. Erdman, *The Poetry and Prose of William Blake*, 1965, pp. 801–2, and David Bindman, 'The Dating of Blake's Marginalia to Reynolds', *Burlington Magazine*, CVIII, 1966, p. 522.)

4 Blake, *Writings*, p. 480.

5 From 1800 to 1803. See Morchard Bishop, *Blake's Hayley*, 1951.

6 Blake, *Writings*, p. 793.

7 Joseph Farington, *Diary*, 24 June 1796.

8 Blake, *Writings*, p. 864.

9 Alexander Gilchrist, *Life of William Blake*, 2nd edn. 1880, I, p. 297. See also the pencil drawing of *Laocoön*, inscribed by Frederick Tatham with another version of the anecdote: 'Fuseli came in & said "Why Mr. Blake you a student you might teach us" ' (Keynes, *Blake's Pencil Drawings*, 2nd Series, 1956, No. 30).

10 It lasted from about 1809 to 1812.

11 Blake, *Writings*, p. 802.

12 Blake, *Writings*, p. 807.

13 Blake, *Writings*, p. 579.

14 See Kathleen Rayne, 'Blake's Debt to Antiquity', *Sewanee Review*, LXXI, No. 3, pp. 352–450, for a survey of the artist's interest in the philosophy of the ancient world.

15 Blake, *Writings*, p. 797.

16 Blake, *Writings*, p. 798.

17 See 'A List of Figures in the Duke of Richmond's Gallery', published by Edward Edwards in his *Anecdotes of Painters*, 1809, p. xviii.

18 See Joseph Barretti, *A Guide through the Royal Academy*, 1781.

19 Gilchrist, *Life*, I, p. 9.

20 See Gilchrist, *Life*, I, pp. 13–21.

21 See Sidney C. Hutchison, 'The Royal Academy Schools, 1768–1830' in the *Walpole Society*, XXXVIII, p. 144.

22 Gilchrist, *Life*, I, p. 30.

23 Gilchrist, *Life*, I, pp. 33–4.

24 The book was published in 1774–6. See Ruthven Todd, 'William Blake and the Mythologists' in *Tracks in the Snow*, 1946, pp. 31 etc.

25 Published in 1795 under the editorship of Willey Reveley.

26 Pars's drawings are now in the British Museum Department of Greek and Roman Antiquities.

27 Blake, *Writings*, p. 790.

28 See the Catalogue of the Sale of Flaxman's Library, Christie, 12 June 1828 (Lugt 11777).

29 D'Hancarville was a nom de plume of P. F. Hugues. The book, *Collection of Etruscan, Greek, and Roman Antiquities from the Cabinet of the Honble Wm Hamilton*, appeared in four volumes, 1766–7. Two sheets of outlines copied by Blake from d'Hancarville are in the British Museum Print Room (1867.10.12.202).

30 Christie, 1 July 1828 (Lugt 11800).

31 John Knowles, *Life and Writings of Henry Fuseli Esq.*, M.A., R.A., 1831, vol. II, pt. I, Lecture 1, p. 22.

32 For example the *Girl led by a Bacchante* in the Kunsthaus, Zürich (Hürlimann collection) repr. Paul Ganz, *The Drawings of Henry Fuseli*, 1949, pl. 11.

33 Among Blake's drafts for poems are fourteen lines of satirical verse with the note: 'to come in Barry, a Poem' (*Writings*, p. 553). See also the remarks on Barry among Blake's annotations to Reynolds, pp. 445–6, and p. 451: 'Barry Painted a Picture for Burke, equal to Rafael or Mich. Ang. or any of the Italians'.

34 *The Works of James Barry, Esq.*, 1809. I, p. 15.

35 Barry, I, p. 23.

36 Barry, I, p. 208.

37 Knowles, *Fuseli*, II, pt. 2, Lecture 6, p. 317.

38 Blake, *Writings*, p. 793.

39 See Blunt, *Blake's Pictorial Imagination*, p. 201.

40 Winckelmann, *Reflections on the Painting and Sculpture of the Greeks*, trans. H. Fuseli, 1765, p. 274.

41 Barry, *Works*, vol. I, p. 141.

42 Knowles, *Fuseli*, vol. II, pt. 2, lecture 6, p. 311.

43 Geoffrey Keynes, *Engravings by William Blake: The Separate Plates*, 1956, No. VI, pl. 11.

44 Of *c.* 1785–9. See David Bindman, *Catalogue of the Blake Collection in the Fitzwilliam Museum*, 1970, No. 3, pl. 5.

45 In the City Art Galleries, Sheffield, repr. Exhibition Catalogue, *Romantic Art in Britain*, Detroit and Philadelphia, 1968 (63).

46 Bindman, *Fitzwilliam Catalogue*, No. 1, A, B, C, pls. 1, 2, 3.

47 British Museum, 1929.7.13.141. Night 7, page 7 (f. 279).

48 Repr. Keynes, *Blake Studies*, 1949, pl. 21. The *Cleopatra* figure was published by Montfaucon, V, supplement, p. 490, pl. 104.

49 British Museum, 1874.12.12.147. See Andrew Wilton, 'A Fan Design by Blake', in *Blake Newsletter*, vol. 7, No. 3, pp. 60–3, repr.

50 Blake, *Writings*, p. 836. See also his reference to 'our admired Sublime Romney', p. 849. Blake's relationship to Romney is discussed by Robert Rosenblum, 'Toward the Tabula Rasa' in *Transformations in late Eighteenth-century Art*, 1967, pp. 156–7.

51 I, supplement, p. 22, pl. 4.

52 See Robert Rosenblum, 'The Origin of Painting: a Problem in the Iconography of Romantic Classicism', *Art Bulletin*, 1957, vol. XXXIX, pp. 279—90.

53 In the Fogg Art Museum, Harvard.

54 In a painting in the Pinacoteca Nazionale, Bologna; repr. *The Age of Neo-Classicism*, London, 1972, pl. 31.

55 British Museum, 1949.11.12.4. The drawing is dated 1811, or possibly 1817.

56 D'Hancarville, *Hamilton Cabinet*, vol. 1,

pl. 130 Blake may equally well have seen the drawing by George Cumberland of a stooping woman, from a classical ivory (?), BM 1866.2.10.588 (see note 87 below).

57 Stedman's Journal contains several passing references to Blake. See *The Journal of John Gabriel Stedman*, ed. Stanbury Thompson, 1962, index, p. 418.

58 Vol. VI, p. 147. The resemblance was pointed out by Blunt, *The Art of William Blake*, 1959, p. 34. See also Blunt, 'Blake's "Glad Day" ', *Journal of the Warburg and Courtauld Institutes*, vol. II, pp. 65–8 where the figure is shown to derive from one in Scamozzi, *Idea dell'Architettura universale* of 1615.

59 Compare also the figure of Mercury in Perrier, *Iconae et Segmentae. . . .*, pl. 43.

60 In the Huntington Library, San Marino. See C. H. Collins Baker, *Catalogue of William Blake's drawings in the Huntington Library*, 1938, No. IV, repr. pl. 15.

61 In the Tate Gallery, No. 5892.

62 See note 76 below.

63 f. 76.

64 British Museum, 1856.7.12.208. Dated 1806.

65 Chap. IV pl. 18; a very similar pose occurs in the volume to which Blake himself contributed plates, III, chap. 1, pl. XV.

66 No. 5195.

67 I, Chap. IV, pl. 23.

68 II, supplement, p. 215, pl. 46. See also Jupiter Sol Serapis, p. 211, pl. 45.

69 In the collection of Sir Geoffrey Keynes. Repr. Keynes, *Blake's Pencil Drawings*, 1956, No. 31.

70 Blake, *Writings*, p. 583. Blake's extension of this idea was to treat clothing as a symbol of materialism, as for instance in *Milton*, Book the Second, f. 41: 'To cast off Bacon, Locke & Newton from Albion's covering, To take off his filthy garments & clothe him with Imagination' (lines 5–6), and 'the Sexual Garments, the Abomination of Desolation, Hiding the Human Lineaments as with an Ark & Curtains . . .' (lines 25–26), *Writings*, p. 533.

71 Knowles, *Fuseli*, vol. III, pt. 1, 'Aphorisms', p. 135, no. 195.

72 Blake, *Writings*, p. 462.

73 Barry, *Works*, vol. I, Lecture III 'On Design', p. 418. See the comments on the nakedness of Albion by Anthony Blunt in 'Blake's "Glad Day" ' (see note 58).

74 Keynes, *Separate Plates*, No. XIX, pl. 25. The drawing is in the Pierpont Morgan Library, one of a series illustrating Milton's *Allegro*.

75 Knowles, *Fuseli*, vol. III, pt. 1, 'Aphorisms', p. 135, no. 194.

76 Compare, e.g., the figure of Victory on the West Front of the Parthenon, engraved in Stuart, *Antiquities of Athens*, II, 1787, chap. 1, pl. III. A figure similar to Mirth appeared in Thomas Hope, *Costume of the Ancients*, 1809, pl. 148.

77 Blake engraved a drawing of the tomb in position at Dereham for the frontispiece of Hayley's *Life of Cowper*, vol. III, 1804.

78 Blake, *Writings*, p. 821.

79 Now in the City Art Gallery, Manchester. See E. Croft-Murray, *Decorative Painting in England*, vol. II, 1970, pp. 171–2, pls. 143–8.

80 The laurel wreath occurs in *Antiquity Explained*, V., p. 68, pl. 24; the drum on the tree in III, supplement, p. 361, pl. 79.

81 Hayley, *Essay on Sculpture*, opp. p. 126.

82 Flaxman, *Lectures on Sculpture*, 1829, Lecture vi: *Composition*, p. 175.

83 See G. E. Bentley, jr., *The Early Engravings of Flaxman's Classical Designs*, New York Public Library, 1964.

84 See note 9 above.

85 Blake, *Writings*, p. 792.

86 Blake, *Writings*, p. 795.

87 An album containing many of Cumberland's outline drawings is in the British Museum, 1866.2.10.560–792. Cumberland's friendship with Blake is recounted in Mona Wilson, *The Life of William Blake*, 1932, pp. 84 ff. For a discussion of Cumberland's drawings in relation to Blake and the Neo-Classicists, see Robert Rosenblum, 'Toward the Tabula Rasa', pp. 166 ff.

88 Cumberland, *Thoughts on Outline*, p. 1.

89 Cumberland, p. 5.

90 Blake, *Writings*, p. 461.

91 Blake, *Writings*, p. 454.

92 See Rosenblum, 'Tabula Rasa'.

93 Knowles, *Fuseli*, vol. II, pt. 1, Lecture I, on *Ancient Art*, p. 25.

94 Cumberland, p. 9.

95 Cumberland, p. 33.

96 Winckelmann, p. 22 n.

97 Winckelmann, pp. 174–5.

98 Cumberland, p. 6.

99 Cumberland, p. 28.

100 Cumberland, p. 15.

101 Blake, *Writings*, p. 585.

102 Blake, *Writings*, p. 597.

103 In 1809. Keynes, *Separate Engravings*. No. XVII, pls. 27–33.

104 Blake, *Writings*, p. 586.

105 Blake, *Writings*, pp. 562, 563–64 and elsewhere.

106 Blake, *Writings*, p. 582.

107 Blake, *Writings*, p. 464.

108 Blake, *Writings*, p. 814. The quotation is from William Gilpin, *Three Essays on Picturesque Beauty*, 1792, p. 35.

109 Blake, *Writings*, p. 602.

110 Blake, *Writings*, p. 603. The reference is to the aesthetic theory propounded by Hogarth in *The Analysis of Beauty*, 1753, where 'a serpentine line' or S-shape is the source of 'infinite variety' (Preface, p. 42, etc.) Blake's rejection of this preference sums up the change in taste between the Rococo and Neo-Classical periods. See also Robert Rosenblum, 'Tabula Rasa', where the late eighteenth century concern with outline is placed in its context of aesthetic revaluation.

111 Blake, *Writings*, p. 459.

112 Blake, *Writings*, p. 457. An answer to Reynolds's advocacy of grandeur in art, *Discourse* III.

113 Blake, *Writings*, p. 439.

114 Flaxman, *Lectures*, 1829, V. *Composition*, pp. 168–9.

115 Blake, *Writings*, p. 849.

116 See for example, *Writings*, p. 445 and the quotation on p. 208 below.

117 The Mortimer drawing is in the British Museum, O o·5–16, L.B. 20; Blake's colour print of 1795 is in the Tate Gallery, No. 5059. See Blunt, *The Art of William Blake*, p. 19.

118 Blake, *Writings*, p. 564.

119 Blake, *Writings*, p. 603.

120 Blake, *Writings*, p. 561.

121 Blake, *Writings*, p. 563–4.

122 Both in the Tate Gallery, Nos. 1110, 3006; both works can be dated about 1808. Blake's catalogue entries describing them are reprinted in *Writings*, pp. 564–6.

123 Blake, *Writings*, p. 601.

124 Blake, *Writings*, p. 603.

125 Blake, *Writings*, p. 560.

126 See Barry's Sale Catalogue, Christie, 10 April 1807, Lugt No. 7215. Lot No. 116 was a picture listed as 'Medea meditating Revenge against Jason by the murder of his Children; a subject painted by Timomachus, and considered one of the finest productions of Grecian Art, mentioned in Pliny's History'.

127 Reynolds, *Discourses*, p. 202.

128 Blake, *Writings*, p. 466.

129 Knowles, *Fuseli*, vol. II, pt. 1, Lecture 1; *Ancient Art*, p. 31.

130 In the Victoria and Albert Museum, No. 697.

131 One is in the Rosenwald Collection, Washington, repr. Keynes, *Blake's Pencil Drawings*, Second Series, No. 27; another at Petworth; a third appears as one of the plates to Blair's *The Grave*. A similar method of building up the composition is to be found in the *Meditation among the Tombs* (Tate Gallery, No. 2231).

132 British Museum, 1894.6.12.15.

133 British Museum, Department of Greek and Roman Antiquities, No. 2191. The relief, by Archelaos of Priene, had been published by Montfaucon, *Antiquity Explained*, V, p. III, pl. 33. It was brought from the Colonna Palace to London in 1805 and acquired by the British Museum in 1819.

134 Blake, *Writings*, p. 565.

135 Blake, *Writings*, p. 565.

136 Gilchrist, vol. I, p. 345.

137 Blake, *Writings*, pp. 565, 566.

138 Blake, *Writings*, p. 777.

139 Keynes, *Separate Engravings*, No. XX, pl. 37.

140 Blake, *Writings*, pp. 565–6; 783.

141 Blake, *Writings*, p. 576.

142 Blake, *Writings*, p. 473.

143 Blake, *Writings*, p. 794.

144 Blake, *Writings*, p. 480.
145 Blake, *Writings*, p. 778.
146 Blake, *Writings*, p. 552.
147 Blake, *Writings*, p. 786.
148 Blake, *Writings*, p. 776.

149 Flaxman, *Lectures*, 1829, No. VI, *Composition*, p. 185.
150 Blake, *Writings*, p. 778.
151 Blake, *Writings*, p. 778.
152 Blake, *Writings*, p. 579.

Notes on selected acquisitions
in 1974

COINS AND MEDALS

The Water Newton hoard of gold solidi

The thirty gold coins comprising this hoard were found at Water Newton near Peterborough in 1974. Together with some fragments of folded silver plate, they had been concealed in a bronze bowl which was itself placed inside a pottery bowl with a lid.

The hoard consists of gold solidi of Constantine I (AD 307–37), Constantine II (AD 337–40), ten of Constantius II (AD 337–61) and eighteen of Constans (AD 337–50). Hoards of Roman gold coins have only rarely been found in Britain; the three such previous hoards securely documented are all in the British Museum—those from Bredgar 1957 of the time of Claudius I, Corbridge 1911 of the time of Antoninus Pius and Corbridge 1908 of Valentinian I to Magnus Maximus. The Water Newton find is thus without parallel in Britain. Many of the solidi included were new to the British Museum collection and there are examples of unusual types with a wreath border. The mints represented by the coins in the hoard are: Treviri, Aquileia (**245**), Siscia, Thessalonica (**246**), Constantinople (**244**) and Nicomedia.

The hoard has additional interest as being the unique example of the treasuring of gold coins with other precious metal objects, the folded fragments of silver plate. Partial parallels for this are the Coleraine and Traprain Law treasures, though these are of later date, and closest to the present find is the rich treasure found at Kaiseraugst in Switzerland in 1962 containing a large number of silver objects

244 *Gold solidus of Constantius II (AD 337–61)*
from the Water Newton hoard (obverse and reverse).
    245 *Gold solidus of Constans (AD 337–50)*
from the Water Newton Hoard (obverse and reverse).

246 *Gold solidus of Constans (AD 337–50)*
from the Water Newton Hoard (obverse and reverse).

together with silver medallions and coins. As the latest coins in the hoard date to the joint reign of Constantius II and Constans, and are in such fine condition that they cannot have been long in circulation, the treasure must have been put together by about AD 350 and its deposit may perhaps be related to the troubled conditions of AD 350–70.

                                                 R. A. G. CARSON
Deputy Keeper, Coins and Medals

Islamic Silver Dirhams from Iran

This important group of coins, comprising 582 Islamic silver dirhams of the ninth to tenth century AD, forms an entire hoard which, it is understood, was discovered in the vicinity of Isfahan, Iran, in 1972. It is the first sizeable hoard of the period from the central lands of the Caliphate to become available for study. The coins represent a

247 *An Islamic silver dirham of Aḥmad ibn Muḥammad of the Ṣaffārid dynasty from the Isfahan hoard. Minted at Sijistān in AD 933 with the name of al-Ḥusain ibn Bilāl as governor (obverse and reverse).*

total of 33 different mints ranging from Egypt to Transoxiana and are of the following dynasties: 1 Umayyad, 303 Abbāsids, 254 Sāmānids, 16 Ṣaffārids and 8 Būyids. The hoard provides valuable evidence for the currency of western Iran and contrasts with the typical distribution found in the Viking age hoards from northern Europe in which vast numbers of Islamic coins occur. The Isfahan hoard is also important for its bearing on the question of mint output and representation, as well as for die-study. Furthermore, it affords valuable material for metallurgical analysis, with some results that already seem promising: some specimens have been subjected to atomic absorption spectrometry and those from the Afghanistan mints found to contain silver of a distinctive type.

N. LOWICK
Assistant Keeper, Coins and Medals

EGYPTIAN ANTIQUITIES
A rare commemorative scarab of Amenophis III

In the early years of his reign, the Egyptian king Amenophis III (*c.* 1417–1379 BC) instituted five issues of large scarabs commemorating events, four of which particularly reflected his own achievements: his marriage to Tiye, a wild-bull hunt, a series of successful lion hunts, the excavation of a lake for Queen Tiye. The fifth scarab celebrated the arrival in Egypt of Gilukhepa, daughter of the king of Mitanni, with 317 female attendants, her marriage to Amenophis representing a political act of considerable importance. Of the five known examples of the Gilukhepa scarab[1] the most complete was at one time in the possession of a Mme Hoffmann in Cairo, but had not been seen since 1880 when Émile Brugsch made a squeeze and copy of its text. From measurements and significant textual variants it is possible to identify as the Hoffmann example the Gilukhepa scarab acquired by the Museum at Sotheby's

248 *A rare commemorative scarab of Amenophis III. (Department of Egyptian Antiquities no. 68507)*

in April 1974. It is made of steatite and shows no signs of ever having been glazed (no. 68507; **248**). The Museum now possesses fine examples of all five of these commemorative issues.

1 See C. Blankenberg-van Delden, *The Large Commemorative Scarabs of Amenhotep III*, Leiden 1969, pp. 129–33, 160–3.

A Late Predynastic flint knife

A major acquisition by the Department of Egyptian Antiquities during 1974 was a Late Predynastic flint knife (no. 68512; **249**). At one time in the collections of the Pitt-Rivers Museum at Farnham, Dorset, it was acquired in 1891 at Sheikh Hamada, in Upper Egypt, by the Revd. Greville Chester.

249 *A late Predynastic flint knife with ivory handle. (Department of Egyptian Antiquities no. 68512)*

The flint blade itself is finely worked, one face being ground smooth, and the other flaked to produce a rippled effect. The lower edge is finely serrated, the knife in consequence being an exceptionally effective cutting tool. A slight up-turn at the tip enhances the elegance of the blade's shape, and undoubtedly improves its efficiency. At the handle end the blade has been trimmed, rather roughly, into a tang which is cemented into a socket in the ivory handle. It is not impossible that the blade was originally made for use without a handle, and was subsequently adapted in antiquity to receive one.

When Flinders Petrie first described this knife, he associated it on stylistic grounds with material found by him at Naqada. In this assumption he was correct, although he believed initially that his Naqada material was to be dated to later than the Old Kingdom. Subsequent discoveries showed that a date before the First Dynasty (*c.* 3100 BC) was to be preferred, and ivories of the kind exemplified by the handle of this knife are now considered to be among the finest products of this Predynastic Period. The side of the handle corresponding with the smooth side of the blade is carved with seven rows of animals and other creatures, marching in file in the direction of the blade. Six rows of similar representations decorate the other side, which was also originally fitted with a knob to facilitate holding. The carving of the figures, at miniature scale, is precise and wholly naturalistic, exhibiting an advanced feeling for the organization of space, and a fine control in the use of simple tools. In spite of its early date there is nothing primitive about this handle; in conception, style, and execution it contains much of what was to become characteristic of Egyptian art in the convention established in the Early Dynastic Period.

A sphinx of Sesostris III

The fine-grained brown quartzite stone used to carve the headless sphinx acquired by the Department of Egyptian Antiquities in 1974 (no. 1849; **250**) provides an especially suitable medium for the representation of the sleek, tawny lion whose body incorporates the divine strength of the royal sphinx. The head, wearing the characteristic *nemes*-head-dress (the two lappets of which are partly preserved), would have shown the strong features of king Sesostris III of the Twelfth Dynasty (*c.* 1878–1843 BC). This identification is confirmed by the bold inscription carved on the lion's chest, which describes the king as 'the good god', and gives his *prenomen* Khakaure.

250 *Sphinx of Sesostris III. (Department of Egyptian Antiquities no. 1849)*

The presentation of the animal form, while lacking the acute observation of anatomical detail characteristic of the best tradition of Egyptian animal sculpture, is yet in its summary treatment of the mass distinguished by a sensitive restraint which skilfully suggests the immanent power of the beast. A secondary inscription, roughly carved on the right upper fore-leg, considerably enhances the interest of the piece. It reads: '[The good god] Apophis, beloved of Wadjet, lady of Imet. The overseer of treasurers Wedjehu, justified'. The text indicates that the sphinx belongs to a group of Middle Kingdom monuments usurped during the period of the Hyksos domination, and moved from their original situations to embellish the Hyksos cities of the Delta. It is not impossible that this piece was originally set up in the city of Memphis, and was subsequently moved to Nabesha (Imet) in the Eastern Delta, where Petrie found other usurped monuments of the Middle Kingdom in 1886. The official Wedjehu, who served under the Hyksos king Apophis (*c.* 1608–1567 BC), is otherwise unknown.

A painted linen shroud

Among the most interesting funerary objects which have survived from Egypt from Late Antiquity are those which combine, in their sepulchral purposes and iconographic elements, details which may be derived from both the Egyptian and the Greek traditions. The best-known of these objects are the mummy portraits, now commonly removed from their mummies and exhibited as panel paintings.

These portraits in themselves demonstrate little of the Egyptian influence which infected normal Greek burial practices in the alien surroundings of Egypt. Nevertheless, the attachment of Greeks to certain aspects of the Egyptian funerary cults is readily to be observed in the forms and decoration of the coffins they used, and particularly in the shrouds which enveloped their mummies. These linen wrappings are frequently painted in tempera with full-length portraits of the deceased and occasionally with native Egyptian divine representations. The example recently acquired by the Museum (no. 68509; Plate IV, p. 290) is particularly fine, and, in its most important part, very well preserved.

The subject is a young woman with closely cropped hair, holding in one hand a cup and in the other a bouquet. She is shown wearing a long rose-coloured tunic, trimmed with white at neck and wrists, and decorated with two vertical bands of black (*clavi*). Over the tunic is draped the loose *pallium* which is of the same colour as the tunic. Traces of gold leaf indicate the rich jewellery with which the figure was decked: bracelets on both wrists, rings on the third finger of the right hand and on the little finger of the left, and a necklace of spherical beads around the neck. A few painted traces also suggest earrings, but their form is unclear and no gold is visible.

In every respect the painting of this central figure indicates the hand of an unusually talented artist. The confidence of the draughtsmanship, the skill with which the folds of the garment are indicated, the relaxed and convincing painting of the hands, and, in particular, the sensitive execution of the head, proclaim, in the context of fourth-century Egypt, a painter of uncommon ability, one to whom the term 'master' may justly be given.

A round-topped surround, painted to simulate a jewel-studded wooden frame, encloses the figure, and between the figure and frame, painted by a less competent hand, are representations drawn from the ancient Egyptian funerary repertory. To right and left of the head are winged figures of Isis and Nephthys; opposite the left hand, the ibis-headed Thoth, beneath whom squats a knife-holding demon; in the panel below, a ram, drawn from the zodiac signs sometimes found on coffins of the early centuries AD from Egypt. Other figures remain unidentified.

The combination in this painted shroud of the Greek and Egyptian traditions greatly enhances its interest and importance. It is surprising to find that the latter tradition retained so much force in Greek burials as late as the fourth century AD. The use of the Egyptian figures is not wholly without significance, but it would be difficult to determine to what extent it should be explained by belief, superstitious tradition, or decoration. Yet, in their simple, rather gauche, presentation, they provide surprisingly not a distraction, but a foil to the charm and elegance of the central figure.

T. G. H. JAMES
Keeper, Egyptian Antiquities

ETHNOGRAPHY (THE MUSEUM OF MANKIND)

A basalt memorial figure of a Nigerian chief

This figure (**251**) belongs to a group of nearly three hundred carved monoliths found on the sites of villages, mostly now deserted, in the region immediately north of Ikom on the middle Cross River in south-eastern Nigeria, an area of less than four hundred square miles inhabited by six small Ekoi-speaking tribes. Their existence was first reported in 1905 and they were thoroughly surveyed and recorded by the Nigerian Antiquities Department in 1961–2. The example acquired by the Museum was, however, collected in the 1930s.

The monoliths are known as *akwanshi*, literally 'dead person in the ground', or *alaptal*, 'long stones'. They were carved from naturally-occurring basalt or limestone boulders, varying in length from twelve inches to over six feet, by sculptors

251 *A basalt memorial figure of a Nigerian chief.*
(Department of Ethnography 1974.Af18.1)

252 *Porphyry head of a Tetrarch, possibly Constantius I*
(AD 293–306). (Department of Greek and Roman
Antiquities 1974.12–13.1)

apparently using both iron and stone tools, and each tribe has a recognizably different range of styles. Traditions relating to the figures are vague. However, they probably commemorate deceased chiefs and sometimes other important ancestors, and it seems likely that they were carved during a period of three hundred years up to 1900. Within that period there is, so far, little evidence for the precise dating of individual monoliths.

J.W. PICTON
Deputy Keeper, Museum of Mankind

GREEK AND ROMAN ANTIQUITIES
Porphyry head of a Tetrarch

This imposing head of a Tetrarch (**252**) has recently been acquired by the Department of Greek and Roman Antiquities (Reg. No. 1974.12–13.1). No more is known of its history than that it was formerly in a private collection in Switzerland. The total height, including the fragment of neck, is 43 cms, which gives a scale about one and a half times life size. The head is turned a little to its left and the whole expression of the face is concentrated in the huge, wide-open eyes, whose penetrating gaze is further emphasized by the arching eyebrows and furrowed forehead. The nose has a pronounced curve. The close-cut hair and beard are schematically rendered by parallel rows of short incised lines. Nose, eyes, lips and ears have suffered some damage, but it hardly impairs the force of the sculpture.

The head, which bears a marked resemblance to the coin-portraits of Constantius I (AD 293–306) (e.g. *RIC*, Vol. VI, p. 665, Alexandria No. 31a; *BMC Greek Coins, Alexandria*, p. 333, no. 2602), belongs to a small group of Tetrarchic portraits carved in porphyry and may be compared in particular with a bust from Athribis now in the Cairo Museum (Delbrück, *Antike Porphyrwerke*, pls. 38, 39) and a lost head from Antioch (Brinkerhoff, *A Collection of Sculpture in Antioch*, figs. 22, 23). Hieratic stylization, the antithesis of classical portraiture, characterizes all these porphyry portraits; but the present head is distinguished from the others by its intense and moving spirituality. Where it was carved, one can only guess; but it is perhaps significant that the coins that come closest to it are those from the mint of Alexandria in Egypt.

D.E.L. HAYNES
Keeper, Greek and Roman Antiquities

MEDIEVAL AND LATER ANTIQUITIES

Ivory and miniature: a matter of comparison

253 Baptism of Christ, *walrus ivory. Anglo-Saxon, last quarter of tenth century. (Department of Medieval and Later Antiquities 1974.10–2.1)*

The recent purchase of an ivory relief of *The Baptism of Christ* (**253**) adds to the Museum's collection one of a mere handful of surviving examples which can be securely connected with the so-called 'Winchester School' of the late tenth century.[1] However, the stylistic analogies between the John the Baptist of this ivory and certain figures in the *Benedictional of St Ethelwold*, on which this identification rests,[2] raise the question of the validity of such comparisons between works in different media.

Ever since the first serious studies of this group of ivories by Goldschmidt and Longhurst their identification has been based on the assumption that the nearer in style an ivory was to a manuscript, the closer it was in date and place of origin. At first sight this approach seems inevitable. The manuscripts have survived in far greater numbers than the ivories, they are usually in much better condition and, because of their documentary content, can often be pinpointed in time and space. Ivories are few, usually worn by much handling, broken and fragmentary, and, unlike the manuscripts, they rarely have a known history any earlier than the middle of the nineteenth century. Hence their completely dependent position in modern art history.

Can a case be made for claiming a different role for ivory carvings in the tenth century? If so, how would this modify the above formula for identifying them? A re-examination of the Museum's new acquisition in relation to manuscripts and other ivories of the period suggests some possible answers.

Of all the manuscripts produced in England under the impetus of the reform movement of Saints Dunstan, Ethelwold and Oswald, without doubt the greatest, and one of the earliest to exhibit the full flowering of its distinctive style, is the *Benedictional of St Ethelwold*, completed between 971 and 984.[3] Characteristic of its twenty-eight full-page miniatures are the heavy frames, either rectangular or arched, made up of panels of richly coloured acanthus ornament surrounded by wide gold borders. Capitals and bases of similar ornament link these panels in the arched frames, and acanthus rosettes mask the corners of the rectangular frames, or punctuate the middle of each side. Here and there, however, the panels are simply butted together, gold border to gold border.

Occupying these frames, and frequently overlapping them, are compositions of figures dressed in costumes of the same rich colouring as the acanthus, and with faces, hands and feet in pale tints of body colour. Here and there gold is used to accent haloes, attributes and architectural details. Both acanthus and drapery are strongly modelled in light and dark, giving the effect of low relief in a homogeneous material, and of separately carved pieces assembled rather casually.

Although there seems to be general agreement in tracing at least some aspects of this extraordinary style to Carolingian sources, convincing comparisons are hard to find in manuscript illustrations. Rather, it is among the ivory carvings, and particularly those of the Metz School, that we must look for the closest parallels. A key work, as Homburger pointed out, is the casket in the Brunswick Museum,[4] which shares three figure subjects with the *Benedictional: The Annunciation, The Nativity* and *The Baptism*. Here, as in the manuscript, the scenes are enclosed in acanthus frames which the figures sometimes overlap, suggesting a similar additive process of composition. However, a significant difference is that the border ornament is continuous, not broken into panels, nor interrupted by rosettes (**254** and **257**).

How are we to explain the transformation of the restrained acanthus borders of the Brunswick casket into the exuberant page-frames of the *Benedictional*? Possibly Anglo-Saxon ivories, in the form of book-covers, provided the link. On the scale of the casket, as on that of smaller book-covers, elephant ivory was available to the Carolingian carver in large enough pieces to include the acanthus frame. To judge by the surviving fragments, the Anglo-Saxon carver of the late tenth century had to make do with walrus tusk, which provides much smaller pieces of ivory. Thus, in order to make a cover for a manuscript the size of the *Benedictional*, for instance, not only would he have to separate the centre panel from its frame, as in the larger Carolingian examples,[5] but he would have to fit together at least two pieces for each

254 Nativity, *ivory casket. Carolingian, ninth or tenth century. Brunswick, Herzog Anton Ulrich Museum.*

255 Nativity, *walrus ivory. Anglo-Saxon, mid-tenth century. Liverpool, Merseyside County Museums.*

256 Second Coming, Benedictional of St Ethelwold. *Anglo-Saxon, 971–84. London, British Library.*

257 Nativity, Benedictional of St Ethelwold. *Anglo-Saxon, 971–84. London, British Library.*

side, and perhaps several pieces for the centre panel as well. The resulting composition attached to a wooden backing, might well look like the illustrations in the *Benedictional*, if we accept the rosettes as further attachments in ivory, as their uniformity in colouring and modelling with the rest of the frame would seem to indicate.[6]

Given this piecemeal construction, it is not surprising that no complete ivory book-covers in this style survive, and that only fragments such as the *Nativity* at Liverpool, the *Baptism* in the British Museum, the *Christ on the Cross* in the Victoria and Albert Museum, and the *Virgin* and *St John* at Saint-Omer, remain to testify that they ever existed. But even within this tiny group it is possible to trace a changing relationship between ivories and manuscript illustration in the second half of the tenth century.

Closest in composition to the Brunswick casket, but even more sculptural in style, is the *Nativity* (**255**). Not only are such non-plastic elements as haloes omitted, but the heads of both humans and animals are carved almost completely in the round, and the soft drapery is pulled tightly over the figures to emphasize their modelling.[7] The bed, for all its inconsistencies of construction, projects boldly from the panel, casting a deep shadow on the ox and ass. This three-dimensional effect was no doubt heightened by the original paint, traces of which are still visible in the drapery folds.

In contrast, the corresponding miniature in the *Benedictional* (**257**) looks two-dimensional, even though it follows the same composition. The posts and sides of the diagonally placed bed are now flat strips, and the sharply highlighted folds of the Virgin's blanket create a dazzling arabesque which conceals the form beneath. Only in the drapery on the near side of the bed do the festoons of sagging loops and gathered M-folds resemble those of the ivory.

These comparisons place the Liverpool *Nativity* closer to the Carolingian ivories than to the *Benedictional of St Ethelwold*, and indicate that in this case at least the stylistic initiative rested with the medium of ivory-carving. It therefore seems to represent an early stage in the development of the 'Winchester School'. However, the linear pattern of the M-folds on the bed, and the suggestion of calligraphic flourishes in the mounds of earth in the foreground are a reminder that the influence was not entirely one way.

Closer in style to the *Benedictional*, though different iconographically from the corresponding miniature, is the *Baptism of Christ* (**253**). As on the Brunswick casket, John the Baptist wears an ankle-length gown, rather than the camel's-hair kilt of the miniature, and carries a scroll in his left hand. But, unlike both, the British Museum ivory shows Christ as a beardless boy, half immersed in the overlapping waves of the river, his right hand behind his back and his left on his chest. If the angels, the dove of the Holy Spirit or *Jordan* were ever part of this composition, no

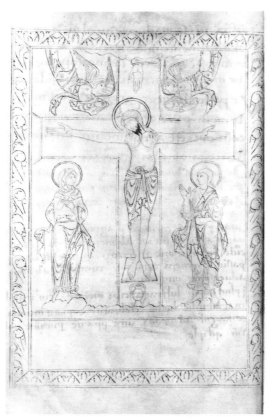

258 Crucifixion, Sherborne Pontifical.
*Anglo-Saxon, 992–5. Paris, Bibliothèque
Nationale.*

259 Christ on the Cross, *walrus ivory.*
*Anglo-Saxon, late tenth century. London,
Victoria and Albert Museum.*

trace of them has survived. The panel has been crudely trimmed around the figures, leaving an awkward piece of background between the haloes and two curious struts between John the Baptist and Christ's right shoulder and elbow. Both the Baptist's right foot and Christ's left forearm and elbow are missing, and no trace of original paint remains.

As in the *Nativity* panel the three-dimensional forms are emphasized. The heads are carved in full relief, the Baptist's arm emerges from a hollow sleeve, and his right foot was vulnerable precisely because it was free-standing. Again, tightly gathered folds encircle his waist, swing over his left thigh and under his right knee, and sag beneath his stomach, defining the form in space. These aspects of the carving, as well as the hunched-up pose of the head and shoulders can still be traced to Carolingian models.[8] However, the drapery formula for the lower half of the figure closely resembles that of the Christ in *The Second Coming* on fol. 9b of the *Benedictional* (**256**), and a number of linear embellishments also appear, which are typical of the whole manuscript. These include the pairs of short concentric arcs under the knee-cap and on the shoulder and abdomen. In the miniatures these have the function of creating highlights, and are sometimes associated with lighter spots of colour, but in the ivory carving they become a mannerism, particularly on the chest and shoulders of the young Christ. Even more typical of the manuscript style is the restless pattern of linked M-folds on the hem of the Baptist's tunic, which gives life and movement to the miniatures, but counteracts the otherwise monumental character of the ivory.

As in the case of the Liverpool *Nativity*, the style of this relief lies somewhere between that of the Carolingian ivories and that of the *Benedictional*, but in this case it comes closer to the latter, suggesting a growing influence of manuscript illustration.

A third stage in the relationship of ivory to manuscript is suggested by the *Christ on the Cross* (**259**), which probably once formed the focus of a *Crucifixion* on a book-cover. Here again the head is developed in three dimensions, but is anchored to the flat surface of the chest by the interwoven locks of hair. The drapery of the loin-cloth comes close to a drawing of *The Crucifixion* in the *Sherborne Pontifical* in Paris, dating from 992–5 (**258**).[9] In both an inverted 'V' of cloth is pulled up through a loop at the waist, and opens out into two zigzags of flattened M-folds.[10] Sagging loops mark the thigh at regular intervals. The broad band of zigzag folds between straight borders which forms a belt on the loin-cloth appears also on the figures of the Virgin and St John of the drawing.

Here the overlap of one fold on another is indicated with the minimum of projection, creating a shallow relief in which the linear pattern parallels and supports the actual modelling.

The final stage is represented by the *Virgin* and *St John* at Saint-Omer (**261**), which evidently completed a composition such as the one to which the above figure belonged. Both of these are carved almost in the round, but the holes pierced through the haloes and the mounds on which they stand show that they were once fastened to a flat background.

In spite of the thickness of the figures the handling of the drapery is almost entirely linear, consisting of deeply cut grooves which make dark accents on the light surface of the ivory, instead of defining the folds of the cloth or the shape of the human form beneath it. In this respect these two ivories resemble another Anglo-Saxon drawing, the *Philosophia* in a Boethius manuscript at Cambridge, dating from *c.* 1000 (**260**).[11] As Wormald points out, it is difficult to construct a human figure beneath the drapery

260 Philosophia, *Boethius manuscript.*
Anglo-Saxon, c. 1000. Cambridge,
Trinity College.

261 Virgin, *and* St John, *walrus ivory.*
Anglo-Saxon, c. 1000. Saint-Omer,
Archaeological Museum.

of this supernatural figure. In fact, in spite of the lines of vermilion wash next to the pulled-out M-folds, there is very little suggestion of three-dimensional form. As in this drawing, the faces of the Virgin and St John present broad unmodulated surfaces on which the crowded features seem to float, and St John's arms lack any articulation or organic connection with his body. The effect, then, is of a pen-drawing on a smooth cylindrical surface, rather than of a piece of sculpture.

If the above examples can be accepted as representative, and the foregoing comparisons justified, some general conclusions may be drawn about the role of

Anglo-Saxon ivories in the second half of the tenth century. First of all, since the most fully sculptural ivories appear at the beginning of the series, not the end, and since they are closer to the Carolingian models than are the manuscript illustrations, it seems reasonable to assume that they initially contributed to the formation of the plastic style of the *Benedictional of St Ethelwold*. Secondly, as the style develops, manuscript illustration gains the ascendency, and imposes a progressively more linear manner on ivory carving. Thirdly, the picture which emerges is not of a single line of development, but of two converging styles, one for the ivories and the other for the manuscripts, each influencing the other to a greater or smaller degree. Hence the original formula of 'the closer the style, the closer the date' must be modified accordingly when comparisons are made between the two media.

On this basis the *Baptism of Christ* in the British Museum should probably be regarded as contemporary with the *Benedictional* since, although some aspects of its style still reflect the sculptural tradition of Carolingian ivories, its drapery formula and linear mannerisms are already those of the mature 'Winchester School.'

Photographic Credits. Herzog Anton Ulrich Museum, Brunswick: 254; Master and Fellows of Trinity College, Cambridge: 260; Merseyside County Museums, Liverpool: 255; British Library Board, London: 256, 257; Victoria and Albert Museum, London: 259; Bibliothèque Nationale, Paris: 258; Musées de Saint-Omer: 261.

W. S. A. DALE
Professor of Art History, University of Western Ontario

1 1974, 10–2,1. H. 9 cms, Ex coll.: Stanislas Baron; Martin-Le Roy; J. J. Marquet de Vasselot. Refs.: R. Koechlin, *Catalogue raisonné de la collection Martin-Le Roy, II, Ivoires et sculptures*, Paris 1906, no. 17, pl. ix; W. F. Volbach, *Mittelalterliche Elfenbeinarbeiten*, Leipzig 1922, pl. 45b; H. P. Mitchell, 'Flotsam of Later Anglo-Saxon Art—III', *Burlington Magazine*, xlii, 1923, p. 303; M. H. Longhurst, *English Ivories*, London 1926, pp. 17, 79, pl. 21, no. xvii; A Goldschmidt, *Die Elfenbeinskulpturen*, IV, Berlin 1926, no. 18, pl. vi; J. Ferrandis, *Marfiles y azabaches españoles*, Barcelona 1928, p. 182, pl. lxv, 2; L. Grodecki, *Ivoires français*, Larousse, Paris 1947, p. 59; D. T. Rice, *English Art 871–1100*, Oxford History of English Art, II, Oxford, 1952, p. 168, pl. 35a; J. Beckwith,

Ivory Carvings in Early Medieval England, London 1972, pp. 34, 120, fig. 35.

2 E.g., the *Doubting Thomas* on fol. 56b (Mitchell), or the Christ of *The Ascension* on fol. 64b (Beckwith).

3 British Museum, Add. MS 49598. O. Homburger, *Die Anfänge der Malschule von Winchester im X. Jahrhundert*, Leipzig 1912; F. Wormald, *The Benedictional of St Ethelwold*, London 1959.

4 A. Goldschmidt, *Die Elfenbeinskulpturen*, I, Berlin 1914, no. 96, pls. xliv, xlv.

5 Goldschmidt, I, pls. vii, viii, xxix, xxxvii.

6 For the rosettes see the reverse of the *Christ in Majesty* in the Metropolitan Museum (Beckwith, fig. 63). The exaggerated highlights may have been suggested by the appearance of

polychromed ivory from which the paint has begun to wear (see O. Beigbeder, *Ivory*, London 1965, fig. 56). A later state may be represented by the *Crucifixion* in Harley MS 2904, where the last vestiges of colour linger in the drapery folds (F. Wormald, *English Drawings of the Tenth and Eleventh Centuries*, London 1953, front., pls. 8, 9).

7 The pose and drapery of the Virgin closely resemble those on ivories of the Ada Group (Goldschmidt, I, pls. xiii, 24, 26; xiv, 27a).

8 E.g., the Nathan on the cover of the *Psalter of Charles the Bald* (Goldschmidt, I, pl. xxix, 40a).

9 Paris, Bibliothèque Nationale, fonds lat. 943, fol. 4b.

10 For a similar knot, see the *Crucifixion* on a Metz ivory in the Victoria and Albert Museum (Goldschmidt, I, pl. xxxvi, 85).

11 Cambridge, Trinity College, MS o. 3. 7., fol. 1 (Wormald, *English Drawings*, pp. 27, 63).

A face-on-front jug from Worcester

The modelling of human faces is a characteristic decoration of medieval pottery jugs of the late thirteenth and early fourteenth centuries. A green-glazed jug decorated with a face on the front (**262**) was found near Worcester Cathedral about twenty years ago and has recently been purchased by the Museum. Standing 15¾ ins. (40 cms.) high, it is of red ware and shaped so that the shoulder and neck of the pot represent the shoulder and neck of a person, perhaps a woman. The jug has a strap handle decorated by slashing. There is no spout and the front part of the rim is raised. Most of the handle and part of the rim is restored.

The face looks to the front. All the features of the face, eyes, chin, nose and mouth are formed of pieces of clay applied to the body of the pot and moulded into the surface. The eyes are decorated with a ring and dot in the centre and the end of the nose has been squeezed. The hair is represented by a strip of clay above the top of the handle. This is decorated with pierced holes and short incised lines which probably

262 *A green-glazed face-on-front jug. English, possibly early fourteenth century. (Department of Medieval and Later Antiquities 1974.10–1.1)*

represent braiding. The arms are formed of applied strips and are bent at the elbow so that the gloved hands are pressed against the body at shoulder level.

Jugs decorated with faces on the front usually occur in England in London and in the southern counties from Kent to Wiltshire. They were made at several kilns—Rye (Sussex), Bentley (Hampshire), and Laverstock (Wiltshire). However, the shape, fabric, and handle are dissimilar to the south-eastern jugs and suggest a more westerly origin. The closest parallel to the Worcester jug is a jug found in the well at Bristol Castle.[1] This is of red ware and has a cylindrical form with a face on the front of the rim. Probably made in the Bristol district in the first half of the fourteenth century, it is decorated on the lower part by vertical applied strips not arranged in any figural form. The most northerly example of a face-on-front jug is from Nottingham, where one was found at the Moot Hall in the same group of pottery in which the Knight jug was found.[2]

The usual style of decoration on jugs in the Midlands is to use applied strips of clay to make human figures on the body of the pot. Notable examples of the type occur both at Coventry and Cardiff (though probably made at Bristol).[3] The manner of the representation of the arms recalls this style of decoration and the manner in which the arms are raised at the elbow also recalls the Coventry examples. The precise dating of the jug is difficult, but face-on-front jugs are generally assigned to the late thirteenth or fourteenth century. It may well be that the jug from Worcester dates from later in the fourteenth century. The treatment of the hair needs further research, but it may well represent one of the later forms of nebulé head-dress, such as that on the brass of Dame Margarete de Cobham (1395) at Cobham in Kent.[4]

In Europe face-on-front jugs occur in Denmark, Holland, Belgium and northern France[5] and Dr G. C. Dunning has suggested that jugs from Rouen may have provided models for some of the southern English jugs.[6] In England the different types of facial and figural decoration have regional characteristics. Faces on the side are common in eastern England; faces on the rim in the south-west, and jugs decorated with figures on the body are particularly common in the Midlands. The significance of the Worcester jug is that it shows that this type of jug occurs farther north-west than had hitherto been suspected and that there may have been a production centre in the West country.

JOHN CHERRY
Assistant Keeper, Medieval and Later Antiquities

1 K. J. Barton, 'A group of medieval jugs from Bristol Castle Well', *Transactions of the Bristol and Gloucestershire Archaeological Society*, 78, 1959, fig. 2, no. 7.

2 G. C. Dunning, 'Pottery from the Moot Hall at Nottingham', *Annual Report of the Peverel Archaeological Group*, 1955, opposite p. 26, no. 8.

3 G. C. Dunning and G. Webster, 'A medieval pottery kiln at Audlem, Cheshire', *Medieval Archaeology*, 4, 1961, fig. 46 and pl. XXIII.

4 H. Druitt, *A manual of costume as illustrated by monumental brasses*, London 1906, p. 251.

5 The European distribution of anthropo-morphic decoration has been studied by K. J. Barton, 'Anthropomorphic decoration on medieval jugs', *Res Mediaevales*, 1968, pp. 43–52.

6 G. C. Dunning, 'A sherd of Face Jug', in 'Excavations at Hangleton', *Sussex Archaeological Collections*, C1, 1963, pp. 132–5.

ORIENTAL ANTIQUITIES

The Garner Collection of lacquer

The gift of their collection of Chinese and associated lacquer by Sir Harry and Lady Garner is one of the most munificent ever made to the nation in the field of oriental art. Even when divided with the Victoria and Albert Museum, the Department of Oriental Antiquities received no less than 87 pieces covering the period from the Yüan Dynasty (AD 1280–1368) to the nineteenth century AD. The collection had been formed with scholarship and taste not only to show the history of one of the most important aspects of the Chinese genius in the decorative arts but also to ensure that each main period and technique was represented by a group of pieces of outstanding aesthetic merit. At one stroke the Garners have converted the Museum's holdings of a few fine things into a rich and comprehensive collection. It is here intended to draw attention to one series remarkable even in the Garner Collection: the carved red lacquer of the fourteenth and fifteenth centuries AD.

Lacquer, like porcelain and silk, is a Chinese invention. From incisions made in the bark of the lacquer tree (*Rhus verniciflua*) a resinous substance exudes which, strained and heated to remove excess moisture, is ready for use. Applied directly to a whole range of materials it forms an exceptionally water-resistant and durable skin and was early used to proof military equipment and the objects of every day. In the making of a quality vessel, however, the craftsman usually worked up from a wooden base or carcass primed with layers of fabric soaked in lacquer. On this priming several coats of liquid lacquer were brushed, each being carefully polished after it had set. Lacquer readily accepts colour-agents and may be stained black, yellow, green, brown, aubergine and varying tones of red. The smooth lustrous surface, itself both preservative and beautiful, makes an admirable ground for polychrome painting in liquid lacquer and for inlaid designs of other materials, gold and silver foil and mother of pearl. In these surface forms of decoration, sometimes combined to enrich the plain lacquer ground, the Chinese had achieved, especially in painting, complete mastery before the Han Dynasty (206 BC–AD 220), while in the T'ang Dynasty (AD 618–906) their handling of inlays displays an extraordinary richness and virtuosity. Under the Sung Dynasty (AD 960–1279), however, taste veered, as in the porcelain of the period, towards monochrome undecorated lacquer with emphasis on simple beauty of form.

It was not until the brief period of foreign domination under the Yüan Dynasty that the Chinese began to use lacquer, not merely as a plastic ground for inlay or as a liquid medium for painting but built up to the necessary thickness to allow it to be deeply carved like ivory or any other hard material. To construct lacquer in this way required extraordinary care and patience. On the priming were applied seven or eight coats of yellow lacquer followed by more than a hundred coats of rich cinnabar red. The latter were interrupted, about a quarter the way up, by a narrow band of black lacquer which probably indicated to the carver that he was approaching the yellow layer. Since each coat had to set hard and be polished, it took more than a year before the piece could be handed to the carver. This intricate technique, found by experience to be necessary for solidity, was not immediately mastered. A famous book for connoisseurs, the *Ko Ku Yao Lun* (*Essential Criteria of Antiquities*), first published in AD 1387 during the reign of Hung-wu (AD 1368–98), the first emperor of the native Ming Dynasty, commends the vigour of the carving in contemporary work but observes that the red layer was apt to break away from the yellow ground. Both points are well made by a fine fourteenth century AD dish decorated with two peacocks in flight against a background of moutan paeonies (**263**).

263 *Red lacquer dish. Fourteenth century AD. D. 32.6 cms. 1974.2-26.14*

264 *Red lacquer dish. First half of fifteenth century AD.*
D. 34.8 cms. 1974.2–26.20

265 *Detail from 264.*

By the early fifteenth century AD carved lacquer made for the imperial household was perfect in construction. In its decoration three types of cartoons were used: landscapes with figures, floral, and animal designs. Of the first type one of the most impressive pieces to have survived is an eight-lobed dish (**264** and **265**). The background to the central landscape, with its lake-side garden pavilion dominated by a noble pine, is carved, just above the yellow layer, with those meticulously cut but discreet diapers which represent, as in all landscape pieces, land, water and air. The border, which contains the flowers of the four seasons—moutan paeony (spring), pomegranate (summer), chrysanthemum (autumn) and camellia (winter)—has a plain ground cut down to the yellow layer. A similar border is carved on the back of the dish. The early Ming artists' handling of floral designs is illustrated by an oval dish (**266**) with a paeony-spray enclosed within a border of the four flowers and a rare vase (**267**) with the four flowers around the body, the neck an elegant simulation of a bamboo stem. One of the finest representatives of the style in the second half of the 15th century AD is a round box (**268**) with Buddhist lions circling a brocade ball, whose flying tassels they seize in their jaws: a tautly composed cartoon found on a

266 *Red lacquer dish carved to yellow ground.*
First half of fifteenth century AD. L. 19.6;
W. 15.5 cms. 1974.2–26.16

267 *Red lacquer vase carved to yellow ground.*
First half of fifteenth century AD. H. 11 cms.
1974.2–26.17

268 *Red lacquer box carved to yellow ground.*
Second half of fifteenth century AD. D. 13.2 cms.
1974.2–26.18

269 *Red lacquer panel carved to yellow ground. Second half of fifteenth century AD. H. 44.2; W. 36.1 cms. 1974.2–26.19*

270 *Red lacquer tiered box carved to yellow ground. Late fifteenth century AD H.14; W.12.5 cms 1974.2-26. 21.*

similar box in the National Palace Museum, Taiwan. A splendidly conceived animal design on a larger scale is provided by a rectangular panel (**269**) which once formed the side of a cabinet. Here in a central cartouche two dragons within a paeony-scroll pursue a flaming jewel, all on a background of carefully cut land diaper. In the corners are alternate male and female phoenixes on a ground of the four flowers. Datable to the end of the century is a handsome tiered box of four sections (**270**) with a landscape on the lid and the four flowers on the sides.

It is probable that the great period of carved red lacquer, China's most original contribution to the art, was over by AD 1500. There is, however, a small group of four pieces, which stands apart from the so-called imperial lacquer and seems seems to have been made in an atelier independent of official taste and supervision. Fortunately one of the pieces, a dish in the collection of Mrs John D. Riddell, is dated AD 1489. In the imperial pieces, though the needle was occasionally used for the finest detail, the main carving was done with deep, bold strokes of the knife, thus

271 *Red lacquer box carved to yellow-brown ground. About A.D. 1500 H. 13; D. 27 cms. 1974.2–26.22*

272 *Detail from 271.*

achieving a sculptural effect. In the small group the needle is more generally employed together with small chisels with differently shaped cutting edges: the result is that the carving is shallower, neater and more graphic in intention. This pictorial quality is further emphasized by the treatment of the background. In the imperial pieces the general effect is monochrome, even when the unobtrusive yellow ground is used to 'lift' the relief of the floral and animal carving. Now, in the landscape cartoons, the ground colour, which usually occupies the field of the water and air diapers, becomes an integral part of the design. One is aware of the composition as in red and yellow or, in one instance, black and red. On two pieces, a third layer, dark green, is introduced for the water diaper, foreshadowing the polychrome lacquer of many layers which became so popular in the sixteenth century AD. Of the four pieces, the box from the Garner Collection (**271** and **272**) is pre-eminent in quality. It is in two colours only. The central lobed panel of the lid shows a group of horsemen approaching an inn. The upper layer is in a warm brown, while the field of the water and air diapers is cut down so close to the yellow layer as to appear buff. The central panel is bordered, as in the base of the box, by eight scenes in the same technique, each described by a poem.

DOUGLAS BARRETT
Keeper, Oriental Antiquities

CATALOGUE

1974.2–26.1
Brown lacquer dish, in the form of a mallow-flower with seven overlapping petals. D. 17.7 cms.
China: Sung or Yüan dynasty (AD 960–1279, 1280–1368).
Chinese and Associated Lacquer from the Garner Collection, 1973, *Catalogue* No. 1.

1974.2–26.2
Black lacquer square dish, with sloping sides. L. 14.5; W. 14.3 cms.
China: Sung or Yüan dynasty (AD 960–1279, 1280–1368).
Cat. No. 5.

1974.2–26.3
Black lacquer box in the form of an eight-petalled mallow-flower, with an inner tray of silver. H. 3.2; D. 9 cms.
China: Yüan dynasty (AD 1280–1368)
Cat. No. 6.

1974.2–26.4
Red lacquered dish on a deep foot, with lobed edge of nine points; the base with black lacquer. H. 5; D. 26.3 cms.
China: Yüan dynasty (AD 1280–1368) or later.
S. E. Lee and Wai-kam-ho, *Chinese Art under the Mongols: the Yüan Dynasty (AD 1279–1368)*. Cleveland 1968, No. 282.
Cat. No. 8

1974.2–26.5
Carved lacquer cup, with layers of black and red lacquer carved to a buff ground; silver lining. H. 4.2; D 6.4 cms.
China: Yüan or early Ming dynasty: fourteenth to fifteenth centuries AD.
Cat. No. 10.

1974.2–26.6 (1, 2)
Pair of carved lacquer stem-cups, carved in layers of red and black lacquer to a buff ground; silvered metal lining. H. 7.2; D. 8.2 and 8.3 cms.
China: Ming dynasty; sixteenth century AD.
Cat. No. 13.

1974.2–26.7
Carved lacquer stem-cup, carved in layers of red and black lacquer to a buff ground; silvered metal lining. H. 8.3; D. 8.3 cms.
China: Ming dynasty: sixteenth century AD.
Cat. No. 14.

1974.2–26.8
Carved lacquer rectangular box with a hinged cover; carved in layers of red and black lacquer to a buff ground. H. 7.2; L. 36; D. 19.5 cms.
China: Ming dynasty: sixteenth century AD.
Cat. No. 16.

1974.2–26.9
Marbled lacquer six-lobed box; base and interior brownish-red. H. 7.7; D. 15.5 cms.
China: Ming dynasty: fifteenth to sixteenth centuries AD.
Cat. No. 20.

1974.2–26.10
Guri lacquer cylindrical box deeply carved with scrolling. D. 11.3 cms.
Japan: Eighteenth or nineteenth century AD.
Cat. No. 23.

1974.2–26.11
Guri lacquer inro with four cases, deeply carved with scrolls. Signed: Chōkan.
L. 7.3 cms.
Japan: Eighteenth or nineteenth century AD.
Cat. No. 24.

1974.2–26.12
Lacquer netsuke of double gourd shape deeply carved with scrolls in guri style, with
metal attachments. L. 4.5 cms.
Japan: Eighteenth or nineteenth century AD.
Cat. No. 26.

1974.2–26.13
Black lacquer dish, carved to a reddish-buff ground with ducks in flight on a back-
ground of lotus. Mark attributing piece to Yang Mao. D. 30 cms.
China: Yüan dynasty: fourteenth century AD.
Cat. No. 28.

1974.2–26.14 (**263**)
Red lacquer dish carved to a reddish-buff ground with peacocks on a paeony ground.
D. 32.6 cms.
China: Yüan dynasty: fourteenth century AD.
Cat. No. 30. (See separate article 'The Garner Collection of Lacquer'.)

1974.2–26.15
Red lacquer cylindrical box, carved to a yellow ground with flower scrolls. Two
fragments of lid remaining. D. 22.2 cms.
China: Ming dynasty: early fifteenth century AD.
Cat. No. 33.

1974.2–26.16 (**266**)
Red lacquer oval foliated dish, carved to a yellow ground with flowers. L. 19.6;
W. 15.5 cms.
China: Ming dynasty: early fifteenth century AD.
Cat. No. 36. (See separate article 'The Garner Collection of Lacquer'.)

1974.2–26.17 (**267**)
Red lacquer vase with ringed neck, the body carved to a yellow ground with flowers.
H. 11 cms.
China: Ming dynasty: early fifteenth century AD.
Cat. No. 37. (See separate article 'The Garner Collection of Lacquer'.)

1974.2–26.18 (**268**)
Red lacquer round box and cover carved to a yellow ground. D. 13.2 cms.
China: Ming dynasty: fifteenth century AD.
Cat. No. 38. (See separate article 'The Garner Collection of Lacquer'.)

1974.2.26.19 (**269**)
Red lacquer rectangular panel, from a cabinet, carved to a yellow ground with 5-clawed dragons. H. 44.2; W. 36.1 cms.
China: Ming dynasty: fifteenth century AD.
Cat. No. 41. (See separate article 'The Garner Collection of Lacquer'.)

1974.2–26.20 (**264**)
Red lacquer dish of eight lobes, carved with figures in a garden landscape and floral borders. D. 34.8 cms.
China: Ming dynasty: fifteenth century AD.
Cat. No. 44. (See separate article 'The Garner Collection of Lacquer'.)

1974.2–26.21 (**270**)
Red lacquer square tiered box, carved to a yellow ground with figures on top and flowers on the sides. Mark, 'Made by Chang Ch'eng'. H. 14; W. 12.5 cms.
China: Ming dynasty: late fifteenth century AD.
Cat. No. 48. (See separate article 'The Garner Collection of Lacquer'.)

1974.2–26.22 (**271, 272**)
Red lacquer round box, carved to a yellow-brown ground with scenes and poems. H. 13; D. 27 cms.
China: Ming dynasty: late fifteenth to early sixteenth century AD.
Cat. No. 49. (See separate article 'The Garner Collection of Lacquer'.)

1974.2–26.23
Red lacquer cylindrical box carved with sprays on a diaper ground. Interior black. D. 7.6 cms.
China: Ming dynasty: sixteenth century AD.
Cat. No. 51.

1974.2–26.24
Red lacquer cylindrical box carved with birds on a diaper ground. Interior black. H. 3.8; D. 7.9 cms.
China: Ming dynasty: sixteenth century AD.
Cat. No. 52.

1974.2–26.25
Black lacquer cylindrical box carved to a red ground with flowers. Interior brown.
H. 3.8; D. 7.4 cms.
China: Ming dynasty: sixteenth century AD.
Cat. No. 57.

1974.2–26.26
Red lacquer rectangular box, fitted with an inner tray and carved with figures and
birds. Interior black. H. 7.2; L. 13.5; W. 10.5 cms.
China: Ming dynasty: late sixteenth century AD.
Cat. No. 58.

1974.2–26.27
Red lacquer stem-cup. Interior and base black. H. 10.2; D. 11.8 cms.
China: Ming dynasty: second half of sixteenth century AD.
Cat. No. 62.

1974.2–26.28
Red lacquer tazza, carved with birds and flowering branches. H. 6; D. 12.7 cms.
China: Ming dynasty: late sixteenth century AD.
Cat. No. 64.

1974.2–26.29
Red lacquer round box carved with flowers. Interior black. D. 5.3 cms.
China: Ming dynasty: late sixteenth century AD.
Cat. No. 65.

1974.2–26.30
Red lacquer round box carved with prunus on diaper ground. H. 4; D. 5.7 cms.
China: Ming dynasty: late sixteenth century AD.
Cat. No. 66.

1974.2–26.31
Red lacquer round box, carved to a green and buff ground with phoenix and paeonies.
Interior brown. H. 7.9; D. 17.6 cms.
China: Ming dynasty: sixteenth century AD.
Cat. No. 67.

1974.2–26.32
Red, dark green and buff lacquer round box, carved with a large character and dragon borders. H. 9.8; D. 19.6 cms.
China: Ming dynasty: Chia-ching reign (AD 1522–66).
Cat. No. 70.

1974.2–26.33
Multi-coloured lacquer cylindrical box with sloping sides. Carved with dragons and flowering branches. H. 11; D. 26.2 cms.
China: Ming dynasty: Chia-ching reign (AD 1522–66).
Cat. No. 72.

1974.2–26.34
Multi-coloured lacquer dish carved with dragon, phoenix and pearl, and birds on flowering branches. D. 22.4 cms.
China: Ming dynasty: date corresponding to AD 1592.
Cat. No. 74.

1974.2–26.35
Red lacquer box of eight lobes carved to a yellow ground with scenes, animals and flowers. H. 24; D. 27 cms.
China: Ming dynasty: early seventeenth century AD.
Cat. No. 75.

1974.2–26.36
Red lacquer cylindrical brush-pot carved with figures in a garden. H. 15; D. (mouth) 10; (base) 9.5 cms.
China: Ming dynasty: early seventeenth century AD.
Cat. No. 78.

1974.2–26.37
Red lacquer four-tiered lobed box, carved with figures and prunus sprays. Interior and base black. H. 16.7; L. 15; W. 11.5 cms.
China: Ming dynasty: early seventeenth century AD.
Cat. No. 79.

1974.2–26.38
Red lacquer round box carved to a yellow-buff ground with branches of lichee on a metal core. D. 5.1 cms.
China: Ming dynasty: first half of the seventeenth century AD.
Cat. No. 82.

1974.2–26.39
Red lacquer dish carved to a dark buff ground with a design of paeonies. D. 14.5 cms.
China: Ming dynasty: sixteenth to seventeenth centuries AD. Attributed to Yunnan province.
Cat. No. 84.

1974.2–26.40
Dark red lacquer bowl, carved to a dark buff ground with birds and floral scrolls. Interior and base black. H. 6.3; D. 12.2 cms.
China: Ming dynasty: sixteenth to seventeenth centuries AD. Attributed to Yunnan province.
Cat. No. 85a.

1974.2–26.41
Red lacquer round box, carved to a yellow ground with paeonies. Interior and base black. H. 3; D. 6.4 cms.
?China: Ch'ing dynasty: probably seventeenth to eighteenth centuries AD.
Cat. No. 90.

1974.2–26.42
Black lacquer bowl-stand carved to the wood ground with chrysanthemums. D. 15.2 cms.
?Japan: eighteenth or nineteenth century AD.
Cat. No. 92.

1974.2–26.43
Red lacquer round box, carved with Chinese boys among lotuses. D. 21.2 cms.
?Japan: nineteenth century AD.
Cat. No. 95.

1974.2–26.44
Red lacquer dish carved to the wood ground with flying dragons, and below with a Guri style scroll. D. 16.8 cms.
?Japan: nineteenth century AD.
Cat. No. 96.

1974.2–26.45
Black and red lacquer cylindrical box with a Chinese immortal on waves. D. 18.3 cms.
Japan: ? eighteenth century AD.
Cat. No. 97.

1974.2–26.46
Red lacquer round box deeply carved with chrysanthemums. D. 10.7 cms.
Japan: late nineteenth century AD.
Cat. No. 98.

1974.2–26.47
Red lacquer five-case inro, carved with the story of Yüttsu. L. 7.2 cms.
Japan: eighteenth or nineteenth century AD.
Cat. No. 101.

1974.2–26.48
Red lacquer brush-holder and cover, deeply carved with birds and flowers. L.
(holder) 14.2; (cover) 6.3 cms.
? Japan: nineteenth century AD.
Cat. No. 102.

1974.2–26.49
Red, green and yellow lacquer flanged box, carved with vines, fruits and diaper
panels. Interior black and gold. H. 6.5; D. (flange) 15.5; (lid) 9.7 cms.
China: Ch'ing dynasty: eighteenth century AD.
Cat. No. 105.

1974.2–26.50
Red lacquer vase and cover carved with figures and various motifs. Interior black.
H. 24 cms.
China: Ch'ing dynasty: eighteenth century AD.
Cat. No. 106.

1974.2–26.51
Red lacquer cylindrical box carved with dragons and waves. Interior black. H. 7.1;
D. 18.6 cms.
China: Ch'ing dynasty: eighteenth century AD.
Cat. No. 107.

1974.2–26.52
Red lacquer cylindrical box carved with figures, trees and rocks. Interior black.
H. 1.5; D. 5.3 cms.
China: Ch'ing dynasty: eighteenth century AD.
Cat. No. 111.

1974.2–26.53
Red, green and buff lacquer box of irregular lobed shape, carved with figures and floral bands. H. 5.3; L. 12; D. 9.5 cms.
China: Ch'ing·dynasty: eighteenth to nineteenth centuries AD.
Cat. No. 113.

1974.2–26.54
Red lacquer cylindrical box carved with figures, vines and bats. Interior and base black. H. 9.3; D. 10 cms.
China: Ch'ing dynasty: seventeenth to eighteenth centuries AD.
Cat. No. 115.

1974.2–26.55
Red lacquer moulded fluted round box, stylized chrysanthemums forming crown of cover. Poem on base. H. 10; D. 24.4 cms.
China: Ch'ing dynasty: AD 1777.
Cat. No. 116.

1974.2–26.56
Black lacquer square tray with sloping sides. Mother-of-pearl inlay. L. 18.6; W. 18.6 cms.
China: Ming dynasty: sixteenth century AD.
Cat. No. 122.

1974.2–26.57
Black lacquer rectangular box inlaid with mother-of-pearl. H. 7.6; L. 33.8; W. 22.9 cms.
China: Ming dynasty: sixteenth century AD.
Cat. No. 124.

1974.2–26.58
Black lacquer octagonal tray with inset wickerwork panels and mother-of-pearl inlay. H. 7; D. 41.4 cms.
China: Ming dynasty: late sixteenth century AD.
Cat. No. 127.

1974. 2–26.59
Black lacquer three-tiered eight-lobed box with mother-of-pearl inlay. H. 21.8; D. 24.7 cms.
China: Ming dynasty: sixteenth century AD.
Cat. No. 129a.

1974.2–26.60
Black lacquer rectangular tray with inset wickerwork panels and inlaid mother-of-pearl. L. 36.4; D. 12 cms.
China: Ming dynasty: late sixteenth century AD.
Cat. No. 130.

1974.2–26.61
Lacquered table screen, the removable panel with raised lacquer and mother-of-pearl motifs on one side, and soapstone and mother-of-pearl ones on the other. H. 36; L. 29.5 cms.
China (possibly Ryukyu): Ming dynasty, sixteenth to seventeenth centuries AD.
Cat. No. 132.

1974.2–26.62
Brown lacquer rectangular box, with mother-of-pearl poem on lid, and inset wicker work panels below. H. 6.7; L. 17.5; W. 12.5 cms.
China: Ming dynasty: sixteenth to seventeenth centuries AD.
Cat. No. 133.

1974.2–26.63
Black lacquer cabinet with hinged cover and four drawers enclosed by doors; mother-of-pearl inlay; gold and silver; metal fittings. H. 30.4; L. 30.7; W. 23.5 cms.
China: Ming dynasty: seventeenth century AD.
Cat. No. 134.

1974.2–26.64 (1, 2)
Black lacquer pair of dishes, inlaid with butterflies and flowers in mother-of-pearl. D. 13.2 and 12.7 cms.
? Korea: eighteenth or nineteenth centuries AD.
Cat. No. 135.

1974.2–26.65
Black lacquer square tray, inlaid in mother-of-pearl and gold and silver leaf. L. 11; W. cms.
China: Ch'ing dynasty: seventeenth to eighteenth centuries AD.
Cat. No. 137.

1974.2–26.66
Black lacquer square tray, inlaid in mother-of-pearl and silver leaf. L. 10.7; W. 10.7 cms.
China: Ch'ing dynasty: eighteenth century AD.
Cat. No. 139.

1974.2–26.67
Black lacquer square tray with soapstone inlay and incised details in yellow, red and green lacquer. L. 10.9; W. 10.9 cms.
China: Ch'ing dynasty: eighteenth century AD.
Cat. No. 143.

1974.2–26.68
Red lacquer oval foliated tray, inlaid in mother-of-pearl. L. 22.7; W. 19.5 cms.
Ryukyu: seventeenth century AD.
Cat. No. 145.

1974.2–26.69
Black lacquer four-tier square box, inlaid in mother-of-pearl and gold and silver leaf with flowers. H. 7.4 cms.
Ryukyu (possibly Chinese): early eighteenth century AD.
Cat. No. 148.

1974.2–26.70
Black lacquer tray and stand, with red borders and mother-of-pearl inlay. H. of stand 8.4; L. tray 13.8; W. 13.8 cms.
Ryukyu: eighteenth to nineteenth centuries AD.
Cat. No. 150.

1974.2–26.71
Brown and red lacquer stand, the top plain, the sides inlaid in mother-of-pearl. H. 11; L. 27.5; top 24.8; W. 8.4 cms.
Ryukyu: ? late nineteenth century AD.
Cat. No. 152.

1974.2–26.72
Black lacquer rectangular box with sliding end, inlaid in mother-of-pearl. L. 23.2 cms.
Korea: nineteenth century AD.
Cat. No. 158.

1974. 2–26.73
Black lacquer cylindrical box, with incised designs filled in gold in the *ch'iang-chin* technique. Metal liner: handles and cover added in Japan. D. 24.9 cms.
Ryukyu: fifteenth century AD.
Cat. No. 161.

1974. 2–26.74
Red lacquer bowl-stand, with designs incised and filled in gold in the *ch'iang-chin* technique. H. 6.9; D. 17.5 cms.
Ryukyu: late fifteenth to early sixteenth century AD.
Cat. No. 163.

1974.2–26.75
Red lacquer circular dish with designs filled-in in light brown, grey, black and pale red. D. 16 cms.
China: Ming dynasty: Mark of Wan-li, AD 1595.
Cat. No. 169.

1974.2–26.76
Red lacquer circular dish, with designs filled-in in light brown, grey, black and pale red. D. 16 cms.
China: Ming dynasty: Mark of Wan-li (AD 1573–1619).
Cat. No. 170.

1974.2–26.77
Red lacquer octagonal tray, with designs filled-in in shades of red, brown, yellow and green, with gold outlines. D. 37.7; 41.1 cms across points.
China: Ch'ing dynasty: Mark of Ch'ien-lung (AD 1736–95).
Cat. No. 172.

1974.2–26.78
Red lacquer cylindrical box, painted in black, green, red and gold with children and birds. H. 7.7; D. 22.5 cms.
China: Ming dynasty: Mark of Chia-ching (AD 1522–66).
Cat. No. 176.

1974.2–26.79
Brown lacquer deep bowl of eight lobes, painted in red, green, yellow and gold. H. 6.4; D. 12.5 cms.
China: Ming dynasty: late sixteenth to early seventeenth centuries AD.
Cat. No. 177.

1974.2–26.80
Lacquer stem-cup, with designs in gold on a sprinkled gold ground. Silvered metal liner and base. H. 7.2; D. 8.2 cms.
China: Ming dynasty: early seventeenth century AD.
Cat. No. 178.

1974.2–26.81
Red lacquer three-tiered octagonal box, with design of birds painted in dark green, black, red and brown with gold outlines on a *nashiji* ground. Interior red. H. 28.2; D. 27.3 cms.
Ryukyu: late seventeenth century AD.
Cat. No. 179.

1974.2–26.82
Red lacquer eight-lobed dish painted in gold. The base black. D. 27 cms.
Ryukyu: seventeenth to eighteenth centuries AD.
Cat. No. 180.

1974.2–26.83
Red lacquer rectangular hinged box, with raised gilt designs on top, sides, and inside the lid. Metal fittings. H. 6.2; L. 21.4; W. 16.7 cms.
Ryukyu: seventeenth century AD.
Cat. No. 182.

1974.2–26.84
Red-brown lacquer ceremonial fan, with two slatted openings, decorated with painted gilt and inlaid mother-of-pearl designs. L. 45.3 cms.
Ryukyu: eighteenth century AD.
Cat. No. 183.

1974.2–26.85
Brown lacquer cup, incised and inlaid in red, yellow and blue lacquer. H. 8.3; D. 9 cms.
Burma: eighteenth to nineteenth centuries AD.
Cat. No. 188.

1974.2–26.86
Wooden mirror-case, with tray pivoting between upper and lower covers, lacquered in buff, red and black, incised and marbled. D. 18.1 cms.
Burma: eighteenth to nineteenth centuries AD.
Cat. No. 189.

1974.2–26.87
Black lacquer pedestal bowl, inlaid with mother-of-pearl, the interior red, base unlacquered. H. 12.8; D. 21.6 cms.
South-east Asia: eighteenth to nineteenth centuries AD.
Cat. No. 190.

A sabre of Sulayman the Magnificent

The swordsmith's art was highly esteemed in the Ottoman Empire. Its most notable achievement was the sabre (Turkish *kilij*) with its single-edged blade, curving gently and then straightening out for the last ten inches or so to the point where it was double-edged. Fine tempering and precise balance made it a superb weapon for thrust and slash.

The Museum already possesses an imperial sabre of about 1770 and another made by the swordsmith Ahmad Kashtah in 1604, and has now acquired an outstanding sabre blade of the sixteenth century—the period when Turkish arms were being carried to Eastern Europe and the Mediterranean. It is of finely damascened steel, 87 cms long; and decorated with gold inlaid inscriptions as well as raised designs on a gilded ground (**273**). On the side bearing the principal decoration, the lower end consists of one large and two smaller cartouches set in a design of palmette scrolls, of which the gilded matt ground consists of tiny circular punch marks (**274**). Each of the cartouches contains inscriptions. The large central one reads, "Alī is the only knight; Dhu'l-fiqār is the only sword'; the two smaller ones, 'Success [comes] only through God' and 'I put my trust in God'. To the left of this decoration, two verses are inscribed, the half-verses being separated by rosettes. These are in the *rajaz* metre and read:

> O Thou whose bounty is unceasing,
> Deal with us bountifully in whatever befalls us.
> Thou, the mighty one, spare us
> From thy destruction in the day of danger.

The other side of the blade is plain except for a panel of arabesque raised on a gilded matt ground (**275**). On the back edge of the blade there are two inscriptions within narrow panels which, from right to left, read: 'O Opener of the gates, open to us the best gate', and 'Qānūn [*sic*] Sultān Sulaymān in the year 926' (**276**). It is doubtful, however, whether these two inscriptions are contemporary with the sword's manufacture. The year 926 is equivalent to AD 1519–20: Sulayman succeeded to the throne in 1520. He certainly had not earned the sobriquet Qānūni, 'The Legislator', in the first year of his reign. Moreover, this inscription is executed in a technique quite different from that of the inscriptions on the side of the blade. In the latter, the gold has been carefully laid in a countersunk bed while on the back edge the gold has been burnished direct on a lightly hatched ground.

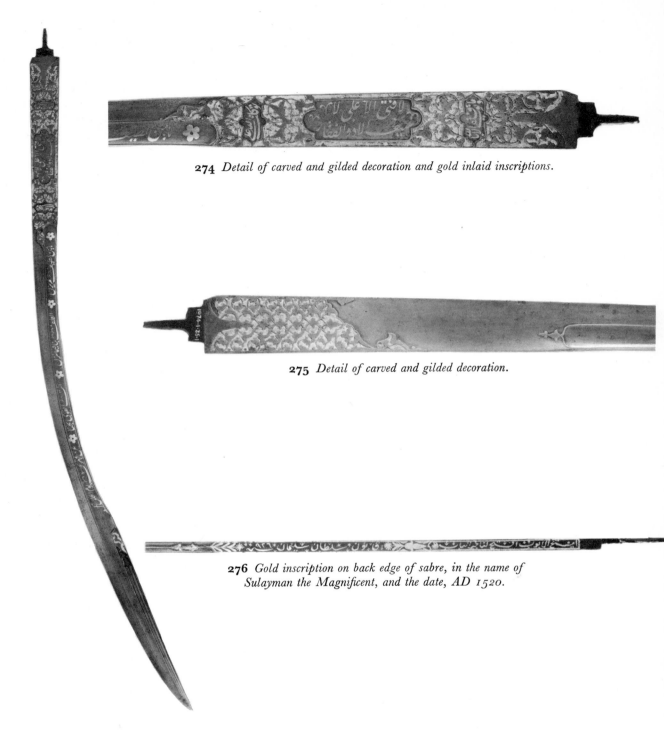

274 *Detail of carved and gilded decoration and gold inlaid inscriptions.*

275 *Detail of carved and gilded decoration.*

276 *Gold inscription on back edge of sabre, in the name of Sulayman the Magnificent, and the date, AD 1520.*

273 *Sabre blade of damascened steel with carved and gilded decoration and gold inlaid inscriptions. Turkey: sixteenth century AD. L. 87 cm.*
(Department of Oriental Antiquities 1974.1–25.1)

There are thirty swords bearing dedicatory inscriptions to Sulaymān in the Top-kapi Saray Museum. Of the seven which carry a swordsmith's signature the finest is a dagger made by Ahmad Tekelu in 933 H (AD 1526/7).[1] But there are a number of sabres which, by reason of their high quality, have been attributed to the sixteenth century, such as a sabre, signed by the master swordsmith Husain Khushqadam, and decorated with raised and gilded arabesque designs remarkably similar to those on ours.[2] Our sabre, therefore, may well have belonged to Sulayman the Magnificent and its dedicatory inscription based on records accessible to those who added it at some later date.

R. H. PINDER-WILSON
Deputy Keeper, Oriental Antiquities

1 F. Sarre and F. R. Martin, *Die Ausstellung von Meisterwerken Muhammedanischer Kunst in München 1910*, iii, Munich 1912, No. 248, Tafel 238–9.

2 U. Yücel, Turk Kiliç Ustalari, *Türk Etnografya Dergisi*, vii–viii, 1964–65, p. 18 and fig. 13.

A dancing Ganesa

The unmistakable god Ganesa with an elephant's head and broken tusk set on a corpulent and stunted human figure appears on this buff sandstone slab standing in a restrained dance posture, slightly flexing his right leg. His two upper arms carry the rosary and a bowl of sweetmeats on which his sharply curving trunk has come to forage while the lower two hold an axe and the severed part of his broken tusk (**277**). A snake, which serves as his sacred Brahmanical thread, running from his left shoulder and looping across to the right hip, rears its head in front of the left ear, shaken out of its usual position by the movement of the dance. The god wears pearled bracelets, anklets and a necklace, the two last together with a ring of bells. His head-dress consists of a pearled circlet outlining each temple and joined in the middle by a jewelled ornament. The god is naked except for a lower garment (*dhoti*) partly gathered up and falling in folds from the left thigh and between his legs. Behind the head with its nervous outspread ears is a plain circular halo.

277 *Dancing Ganesa in sandstone. Eastern India: south-eastern Uttar Pradesh. About AD 750. H. 99 cms. (Department of Oriental Antiquities 1974.2–25.1)*

The origins of Ganesa are obscure and no doubt primitive. His earlier cult as creator of obstacles implied a ritual of propitiation. Principally, however, he has become the remover of obstacles and is still widely worshipped to ensure success in the enterprises of secular life as well as in religious ceremonies. In a special sense he is a god of learning, being invoked at the opening of manuscripts. His name makes him commander of a class of demi-gods, the Ganas, who are associated with the great sectarian god Siva as his retinue. Ganesa is thus classed in the Saivite division of Hinduism, although at one period there was a movement which acknowledged him as supreme above the other gods. He is regarded as the son of Siva and Parvati, his consort, but various texts give different legends to account for the relationship and for his appearance.

In art and iconography standard images of Ganesa evolved by the time that the Gupta Dynasty (fourth to sixth centuries AD) had united most of Northern India and helped to create a classical type of artistic excellence. The disintegration of the Empire led to the rise of new regional schools which soon devised their own classical formulas. In their earlier stages they shared in the Gupta artistic legacy, particularly in respect of a naturalistic fullness in the treatment of volume. In fashioning a figure like Ganesa, the post-Gupta sculptor could combine that rendering of mass with the arrested movement of the dance which gave medieval Indian sculpture so much of its vitality. The present example is considered to represent an Eastern Indian offshoot of the Gupta style in transition to the more linear virtuosity of the later medieval schools.

WLADIMIR ZWALF
Assistant Keeper, Oriental Antiquities

PRINTS AND DRAWINGS

Some notable early prints

In recent years, despite the increasing scarcity of fine prints on the art market, it has still been possible from time to time to find interesting and sometimes important and occasionally unknown prints from the fifteenth and sixteenth centuries to add to the collection. Treating them more or less chronologically the earliest are two unknown dotted prints by the Master Bartholomeus. Such prints executed in the *manière criblée*, or dotted manner, significant examples of which now very rarely appear on the market, are a class of single-sheet prints produced mainly in the lower Rhineland in the second half of the fifteenth century which are technically allied to the woodcut in that they are printed from the relief parts of a metal plate.

The two dotted prints added recently to the Print Room's outstanding collection are of special interest in that they increase our knowledge of a master of such prints, who has been hitherto known solely by the unique impressions of four scenes from the Life of Christ in the Department.[1] The subjects of these are *Christ and the Woman of Samaria*[2] (Schreiber 2216), *The Raising of Lazarus*[3] (Schreiber 2218) bearing the signature 'Bartholmeus', *Christ's Entry into Jerusalem* (Schreiber 2221) and *Christ throwing the Moneychangers out of the Temple* (Schreiber 2228). Apart from Bernhardinus Milnet,[4] who signed an important print, the *Virgin and Child* (Schreiber 2482) also in the Department, Bartholomeus[5] is the only engraver of dotted prints, whose name is known to us. In addition to the clear stylistic links that his prints have with those by other engravers from the lower Rhineland and Cologne, we may note that the short inscription, *wyp gyp mir drinck* ('Woman give me to drink') on *Christ and the Woman of Samaria* is in a west Low German dialect. Apparently his name occurred then then only very rarely in South Germany and Schreiber tells us was common on the Rhine near the present Belgium and Dutch frontiers. It is quite likely as both Schreiber and Dodgson believed that this Master, who apart from the present set of prints is unknown, is probably identical with the 'Master of the Aachen Madonna', whose work is very closely allied stylistically. According to Schreiber it seems most probable that Bartholomeus was working about 1470. This dating is given a certain support in that the two prints newly acquired which also belong to the same series of scenes from the Life of Christ by Bartholomeus', are pasted on the inside front and back covers of a copy of Thomas à Kempis's *De imitatione Christi*, printed at Ulm by Johann Zainer in 1487.[6] The subject of the prints are the *Supper at Emmaus* (**278**) and the *Last Supper* (**279**) and are identical in size with the four already known. Despite the activities of the worm, they have been otherwise well preserved in the book. The impressions are clear and the colouring of yellow and green, and brown (somewhat faded) is much brighter than in the original four, which came from a manuscript of about 1500, and could have suffered when they were taken out. The similarities of style are self-evident, ranging from the facial types, the decorative patterns adopted on floors, and to the punches used for decoration, such as the fleur-de-lis, a six-rayed star with a black centre, and an eye-shaped ornament with a black centre. We find for instance, the fleur-de-lis has been used on the Samaritan Woman's dress in Schreiber 2216 and on the table-cloth in the *Last Supper*.

These prints have something further in common, for there is more than a suggestion that their compositions go back to the same or a closely related source. The

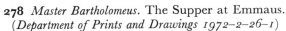

278 *Master Bartholomeus*. The Supper at Emmaus. (*Department of Prints and Drawings 1972–2–26–1*)

279 *Master Bartholomeus*. The Last Supper. (*Department of Prints and Drawings 1972–26–2*)

composition of *Christ's Entry into Jerusalem* (Schreiber 2221) was derived from a woodcut identical in its details with Schreiber 151 at Munich,[7] part of a Passion series, of which ten subjects are at Munich, dated by Schreiber about 1480. This series is in its turn apparently based on an earlier series of which there is a fragment (Schreiber 22a) at Vienna[8] of the Life of Christ, with six subjects arranged in two rows. The prints in the incomplete series at Munich, *Christ on the Mount of Olives* (Schreiber 192) and *Christ on the Cross* (Schreiber 430) are signed *Peter mäler ze Ulme*. The composition of the latter subject is identical with its representation on the sheet at Vienna. The same is true of the cut of *Christ before Pilate* (Schreiber 256) by Peter Maler and its rendering at Vienna. One of the subjects on the sheet, which has been torn in two, *Christ before Herod*, appears also in a fragment of a Block-book Passion, which Schreiber recorded at St Gallen, and in two sheets said to be in the British Museum (Weigel 261).[9] The present whereabouts of the fragment is not known however, and Weigel

261 is, in fact, at Weimar. All these relationships show how interdependent the craftsmen were who produced these early devotional prints. It is by no means always easy to be sure about the priority of some prints over others. For instance, a woodcut in Munich, *Christ and the Woman of Samaria* (Schreiber 141) described by Schreiber as a work of South German origin of about 1480, was said by Dodgson to be the model for the metalcut by Bartholomeus. D. Kuhrmann, however, has recently suggested that the Munich woodcut is probably a copy after the metalcut.[10] It is quite conceivable that the woodcut is itself a copy of an earlier print which has not apparently survived, and that both it and the metalcut derive from a common source.

The next print in date comes from the upper Rhineland, from the small Alsatian town of Guebwiller, half-way between Colmar and Mulhouse. It is a woodcut of an allegorical subject with explanatory verses printed below. This broadsheet is headed with the title *Nüw des [Jo]rs unsers lebens gesetzt durch Niclaus moler zu Gebwiler*.[11] The Museum has acquired two examples of this sheet, which in their present condition complement one another, in that the deficiencies of each is made good by the other. One has the text of the poem complete, but lacks a heading and the upper part of the woodcut (**281**). The other has the heading of the woodcut and the title, except for two letters, whose identity can, however, be easily guessed at, and has whole areas of the text of the poem missing (**280**). The woodcut is already known to us from a later impression without the text in Basel. It was catalogued by Bock [12] in his study of the woodcuts of the Basel master who has signed his work with the monogram D S. Bock decided that he could not accept the attribution of the present woodcut to this master, a decision with which I am unable to agree. Like the allegorical cut, the earliest woodcuts that have been attributed to him are also unsigned. These are those, ten in number, illustrating the amusing and lively *De fide concubinarum* of Paulus Olearius,[13] which cannot be precisely dated, but was printed at Basel between 1501, a date mentioned in the text, and 1505, when a re-print appeared at Augsburg. The liveliness of their satirical themes and the rendering of nature are just what we would expect of the designer of the cuts[14] for Petermann Etterlin's Swiss Chronicle of 1507.[15] Both sets are indeed generally accepted as by the Master D S and if one compares both his general approach to composition and the way he has tackled details in the Chronicle illustrations with the details of the broadsheet cut, which is incidentally also dated 1507 in the text, there can be little doubt that they were both designed by the same artist. One should notice, for instance, the very close similarities between the view of Lucerne [16] in the Chronicle and the landscape on the far side of the lake in the background of the allegory. Also the features of the young man in the broadsheet find many parallels both in the Chronicle, and elsewhere in the master's work. The rather wooden arrangement of the foreground protagonists is untypical for the

280 *Master* DS. *Allegorical woodcut illustrating verses by Niclaus Moler of Guebwiller based on the legend of St Barlaam and St Joasaph.* (*Department of Prints and Drawings 1973–4–14–13*)

281 *Master* DS. *Allegorical woodcut illustrating verses by Niclaus Moler of Guebwiller based on the legend of St Barlaam and St Joasaph.* (*Department of Prints and Drawings 1973–4–14–14*)

Master D s, but explicable if one remembers that this has been largely dictated by the Verses.

Fortunately we know a little of this man, Niclaus Moler, as he is referred to in the town records of Guebwiller, preserved there in the Archives Municipales.[17] He is listed in the 'Bannerordnung' of 1519 as a representative of the Smiths' Guild.[18] M. Ginsburger in his *Inventaire-Sommaire des Archives de Guebwiller*[19] identifies this passage in the document as a reference to an 'organization de sapeurs-pompiers' (firemen); however, it is much more likely that 'Bannerordnung' means what it most obviously suggests, that Moler was a standard-bearer for his Guild in that year. There are two further references in the tax assessments to Niclaus Moler, and several to a Lux Moler, who was no doubt a relative.[20] From the first of these we learn that Niclaus paid in tax in 1523 the relatively high sum of one pound and ten shillings,[21] and from the second, a note of Niclaus's widow's tax of ten shillings that he either died in 1526 or was dead by that year.[22]

Moler's verses are not very distinguished and in their content entirely unoriginal, for they are based on the legend of St Barlaam and St Joasaph,[23] which comes from a Buddhist legend and was transmitted by Byzantium to the West.[24] In Western Europe it became the source of a whole range of verses, prose accounts and dramatic pieces. The first prose version in German is by Bishop Otto II von Freising (1184–1220), which was soon followed, about 1220, by the verses of Rudolf von Ems.[25] In the Western version of the story, the son of the Indian King Abenner who, like Johnson's *Rasselas*, was preserved from a knowledge of the sorrows and evil of the outside world, is converted to Christianity and the life of a monk by the hermit St Barlaam. The first part of Moler's verses, 'Glichnüss der Welt' is a straightforward description of Barlaam's parable in which he explains to the young prince how man is so easily deluded by the vain glory of this world, 'Die Falsch eer [Ehr] der welt'. The second part is the key to its meaning, 'Uslegung der figur'. A man fleeing from a lion (in many versions it is from a unicorn) that symbolises death, has jumped up into a cleft of the branches of a tree that signifies the world. His feet are on a revolving stone ball, which is intended to indicate the waywardness of fortune. To his right is a threatening monster with four heads that signify the four elements. Gnawing at the roots of the tree are two mice, one white and the other black, representing day and night, that eat away time, and below emerging from the earth is a dragon with a gaping mouth, the Devil. The young man, however, ignores all these impending dangers and enjoys the drops of nectar that fall from the fruit of the tree and thus gives himself up to earthly sensual pleasures.

Moler rounds off his poem with an exhortation to the reader to have a special care for his morals in the time between Christmas and Shrove Tuesday. He also tells us that his broadsheet was published at Christmas 1507. In the midst of his pleasure (he is obviously referring to the feasting and celebrations connected with the twelve nights of Christmas), the reader should remember God's law and his Christian duty so that at the last he may obtain the crown of everlasting joy and felicity.

Representations of this allegory occur in Byzantine art as early as the eleventh century; that is, after the text had been translated from the Georgian into Greek. We find the subject is used as an illustration of Psalm 144, verse 4 (Vulgate: Psalm 143): 'man is like a thing of nought: his time passeth away like a shadow', in a Greek Psalter of 1066 (British Library, Add MS. 19352. fol. 182 *verso*).[26] Subsequently, the theme was taken up readily in the West, both by preachers, decorators of churches and manuscripts, examples of which can be found in the art of most West European countries. It is recorded that in the fifteenth century in South Germany there was a wall panel of this subject in Kloster Lorsch, near Schwabisch-Gmünd, which was probably based on Rudolf von Ems's text.

Two primitive woodcuts illustrating the same point in the legend that Moler describes occur in chapter 15 of the two earliest editions of it printed in Augsburg, *Die hystori Josephat und Barlaam* of G. Zainer of about 1475 and A. Sorg's of 1480, but neither of these is sufficiently close to count as a model for the broadsheet cut, although no doubt their text could well have been known to Moler. A woodcut of about 1460 which can be considered a forerunner only in that its message is the same as the broadsheet's is the *Young Man on the Tree of Life*[27] in Vienna (Schreiber 1867). The Devil tempts the young man with gold to which he helps himself, while at the same time attends to the warnings of both an Angel and God the Father. Could this be one of the earliest representations of someone 'having the best of both worlds'? The tree itself is being sawn through by two Devils. The sun and moon inappropriately placed near its roots are substituted for the mice of the Barlaam legend.

The next group of prints is by Urs Graf, and if he was not a pupil of the Master D s, he certainly was strongly influenced by him when he settled in Basel in 1509. There are the sixteen illustrations to a very rare little devotional book published in 1511 in a German and Latin edition of the Life of St Beatus,[28] the Apostle of Switzerland. The new acquisition[29] is a copy of the Latin edition which, although it lacks the title-page, includes each woodcut in the series. Other copies are in the Kunstmuseum, Basel (German edition, and a set of cuts from the Latin edition) and in the Zentralbibliothek, Zürich (Latin edition, incomplete). The series of cuts is also used on an undated broadsheet, preserved as two sheets in the Albertina, Vienna. According to tradition Beatus was baptised in England by the Apostle Barnabas, ordained in Rome by St Peter and then sent to Switzerland. There he is said to have lived and died in a cave at Beatenberg on the Lake Thun about 101. These woodcuts belong to the time when Urs Graf finally began to determine his mature style, and are of considerable charm and vigour. These characteristics are well illustrated by his woodcuts showing the Saint driving off a hovering dragon with his stick and of the Saint baptising converts (**282** and **283**). A very apposite comparison can be drawn between the series and his drawing in Berlin, signed and dated, most probably, 1513, the *Adoration of the Magi,* in which the bearded Kings have similar features to those of

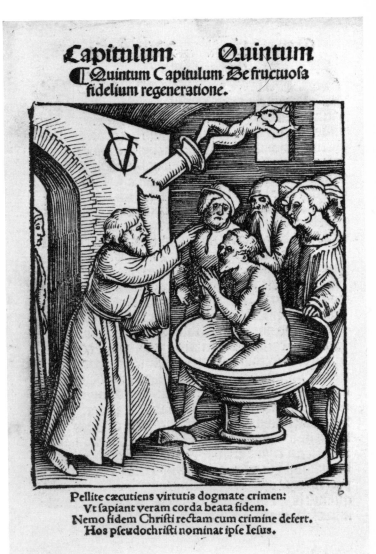

282 *Urs Graf. Woodcut from the* Vita Almi Confessoris et Anachorete Beati *(1511) showing St Beatus driving off a dragon. (Department of Prints and Drawings 1974-2-23-29)*

283 *Urs Graf. Woodcut from the* Vita Almi Confessoris et Anachorete Beati *(1511) showing St Beatus baptising converts. (Department of Prints and Drawings 1974-2-23-29)*

Imago beate virginis Marie

O benedicta dei genitrix: te crimine folam
Immunem natus contulit effe tuus.
Ipfe tuam formans animam fic virgo redemit:
Crimina φ primi nulla parentis habes.
Non fuit in toto concæptus fanctior orbe:
Si non de nato fint mea verba tuo.

284 *Urs Graf. Woodcut from the* Vita Almi Confessoris et Anachorete Beati *(1511) showing the Virgin and Child in Glory. (Department of Prints and Drawings 1974–2–23–29)*

285 *Hans Sebald Beham. Orpheus. (Department of Prints and Drawings 1971–6–19–5)*

the Saint. The Virgin in the drawing also resembles her image in the final cut of the series with the mark of the publisher, Adam Petri, below a Virgin and Child in glory, on a crescent moon (**284**). Tradition is combined with a strongly individual vocabulary, just as it is in another drawing dated 1513 of the *Virgin and Child with a Bird* now in Coburg, closely related in style to the whole series.

The final acquisition to be mentioned comes in a category encountered less often than formerly, a hitherto unknown print, in this case a woodcut of *Orpheus*[30] by Hans

Sebald Beham (**285**), an immediate follower of Dürer in Nuremberg, from where he had eventually to flee because of his revolutionary views. After comparison with similar woodcuts which are signed by Beham, such as his *Viol-Player*[31] of 1526 and the *Lovers seated before a Fence*[32] of 1522, and various other unsigned examples of about the same date, such as the *Seated Girl*[33] and its companion, the *Viol-Player*,[34] there can be little doubt that we are confronted here with an authentic work from the period 1520-5, which by chance has been passed over unnoticed. As, however, many of Beham's little woodcuts are rare, surviving only in ones and twos, it is not surprising, despite the thoroughness of cataloguers, that this small but distinguished print has escaped their net.

JOHN ROWLANDS
Deputy Keeper, Prints and Drawings

1 Campbell Dodgson, *Prints in the Dotted Manner and other Metal-cuts of the XV century in the Department of Prints and Drawings, British Museum*, 1937, Nos. 43-46.

2 References in the text to 'Schreiber' are an abbreviation for W. L. Schreiber, *Handbuch der Holz- und Metallschnitte des XV Jahrhunderts*, 8 vols., Leipzig 1926.

3 See A. M. Hind, *An Introduction to a History of Woodcut*, 1935, p. 189, repr. fig. 85.

4 For a discussion of this metal-cutter see C. Dodgson, *Burlington Magazine*, xxv (1914), p. 169 f.; A. M. Hind in *op. cit.*, pp. 183-4 clears up various errors about other supposed impressions of the British Museum *Virgin and Child*.

5 A. M. Hind, *op. cit.*, p. 190.

6 Hain 9091; *Catalogue of Books printed in the XVth century now in the British Museum*, Part II, Germany, Eltvil-Trier, p. 530. This octavo volume bound in contemporary blind-stamped pigskin over wooden boards, lacks the title-page, and two blank leaves. According to an inscription in an old hand the book belonged at an early date to the Convent of Aspern near Vienna. Another inscription states that it was still their property in 1653.

7 P. Heitz, *Einblattdrucke des fünfzehnten Jahrhunderts, No. 31* (W. L. Schreiber, München, Graphische Sammlung, Part 2), 1912, repr. plate 114.

8 See F. M. Haberditzl, *Die Einblattdrucke des XV Jahrhunderts in der Hofbibliothek zu Wien, I* (die Holzschnitte), 1920, No. 32, repr. plate X.

9 See T. O. Weigel and A. C. A. Zestermann, *Die Anfänge der Druckerkunst in Bild und Schrift an deren frühesten Erzeugnissen in der Weigelschen Sammlung erläutert*, 2 vols., Leipzig 1866.

10 *Die Frühzeit des Holzschnitts* (Exhibition Catalogue, Staatliche Graphische Sammlung), Munich 1970, No. 93 (as unique: South German, *c.* 1480).

11 Very recently I have been shown in a private collection in Germany another example of the broadsheet, in which the missing letters in the title are as indicated within the square brackets.

12 E. Bock, *Die Holzschnitte des Meisters D.S.*, Berlin 1924.

13 E. Bock, *op. cit.*, Nos. 1-10; Campbell Dodgson, *Prussian Jahrbuch*, xxviii (1907), p. 33, Nos. 18-27.

14 E. Bock, *op. cit.*, Nos. 14-17.

15 *Kronica von der loblichen Eydtgnoschaft . . .*, Michael Furter, Basel.

16 E. Bock, *op. cit.*, No. 15.

17 Miss C. Andersson of Stanford University, California, has very kindly volunteered to examine the records at Guebwiller on my behalf. I am very grateful for her most helpful assistance.

18 See Guebwiller, Archives municipales: liasse B.B.7.

19 Published 1928, see p. 6.

20 See Guebwiller, Archives municipales: liasse B.B.7, folios 15 and 88 ff. in the section beginning folio 82 entitled 'Ratzbuch der statt gebwyler angefangen Anno 1500 und fünf yar . . .' where he is listed as one of the 'Amptlutt' [Amtleute], officials of the town.

21 Guebwiller, Archives municipales: 'Gewerffbuech Anno MXXiij' c.c.47.

22 Guebwiller, Archives municipales: 'Gewerffbuech Anno MXXvj' c.c.47.

23 See Louis Réau, *Iconographie de l'Art chretien*, Tome III (Iconographie des Saints), Paris 1958, pp. 177–8.

24 J. Mavrogordato describes the Story of Barlaam and Joasaph as the only instance in Byzantine literature of the novel, 'written in a fluent and rhetorical style' (see *Byzantium: an Introduction to East Roman Civilization*, edited by N. H. Baynes and H. St L. B. Moss, 1948, pp. 238–9).

25 Mrs Gerda Calmann very kindly brought to my attention the very fine verse translation made from an oriental source by Friedrich Rückert (1788–1866) in which the tale is told and explained very much in the manner of Moler's version (see *Gesammelte Gedichte von Friedrich Rückert*, Bd. I, Erlangen, 1834, pp. 67–9).

26 See S. Der Nersessian, *L'Illustration des Psautiers grecs du Moyen Age*, II, Paris 1970. London, Add. 19,352, pp. 57, 69.

27 F. M. Haberditzl, *op. cit.*, i, p. 34, No. 168, repr. plate CVIII.

28 *Das Lebē[n] des heiligen bychtigers und einsidlers sant Battē[n] des ersten Apostel des oberlands Helvecia geheissen*, and *Almi Cō [n] fessoris et Anachorete Beati . . .*, both Basel, Adam Petri, 1511.

29 Register No. 1974–2–23–29 (1–17).

30 Register No. 1971–6–19–5. 11.7 × 7.6 cm.

31 F. W. H. Hollstein, *German Engravings, Etchings and Woodcuts . . .*, Vol. III, Amsterdam, n.d., p. 247, P. 1232.

32 Hollstein, *op. cit.*, p. 244, P.1229.

33 Hollstein, *op. cit.*, p. 248. P.1234.

34 Hollstein, *op. cit.*, p. 247, P.1233.

Drawings by Sebastiano del Piombo and Agnolo Bronzino

In 1974 the Department of Prints and Drawings acquired two sixteenth-century Italian drawings of exceptional beauty and significance. One (**286**) is a study of the Virgin and Child by Sebastiano Luciani, better known either from his birthplace, Venice, as Sebastiano Veneziano, or from the sinecure office of Superintendent of the Sealing ('Piombo') of the Papal Briefs to which he was appointed in 1531, as Sebastiano del Piombo. The drawing, first recognized as the work of Sebastiano by Mr Philip Pouncey, and sold as lot 2 in Messrs Sothebys' sale of 27 June 1974, is in the artist's favourite medium of black chalk heightened with white bodycolour on blue paper. Chalk is a fragile medium, easily damaged by rubbing, but this sheet is in an exceptionally good state of preservation: the paper has faded to a greyish-green, but the crispness and sharpness of the drawing itself is unimpaired, preserving every nuance of the draughtsman's touch. Sebastiano's drawings are rare—only about forty are known which can be unquestionably attributed to him—and this new acquisition is a precious addition to the four already in the collection.

286 *Sebastiano del Piombo :* The Virgin and Child. *Black chalk heightened with white bodycolour on blue paper.* 25.5 × 78.7 cms. *(Department of Prints and Drawings 1974–9–14–1)*

Sebastiano began his career in Venice as a pupil successively of Giovanni Bellini and of Giorgione, but in 1511 he moved to Rome, then a centre of intense artistic activity dominated by the rival and incompatible personalities of Michelangelo and Raphael. He soon attached himself to Michelangelo, who not only procured commissions for him but gave him practical help with them in the form of drawings: sometimes, as with the S Pietro in Montorio *Flagellation*, a design for a complete composition; sometimes, as with the National Gallery *Raising of Lazarus*, a study for a group of figures. Until recently our whole conception of Sebastiano del Piombo as a draughtsman has been distorted by the fact of this collaboration, for ever since the late nineteenth century, critics have shown a persistent tendency to discard the traditional and—as Johannes Wilde demonstrated some twenty years ago—correct attribution to Michelangelo of drawings connected with these joint works, and to reattribute them to Sebastiano.

No such ambiguity attaches to the newly discovered drawing, for it agrees exactly in handling and style with the well-defined group of those certainly attributable to Sebastiano on the strength of their connection with works in which Michelangelo can have had no share. It perfectly illustrates the hybrid, Veneto-Roman, nature of his formation: the technique of black chalk heightened with white on *carta azzurra* is one that he brought with him from Venice and to which he remained faithful throughout his long career in Rome. Venetian, too, is the exquisitely rendered play of silvery light across the forms. The forms themselves, however, are Roman, for the pose of the Child (though not his placing in relation to the Virgin) is directly copied from Raphael's *Madonna di Foligno* (now in the Vatican Gallery). Raphael's full-length seated Virgin holds the Child on her left side. His right hand clasps her mantle, His right foot rests on her left thigh, and His left foot stands on the clouds which support the whole group of figures. Sebastiano's Virgin is seen half length. The horizontal line which supports the Child's right foot, together with the perspective and placing of His other leg, show that she is behind a low parapet in front of which is a flat ledge filling the whole foreground. She holds the Child on her right side, His Raphaelesque pose skilfully adapted so that He is stepping down from the parapet on to the ledge, with His right hand resting on the Virgin's left shoulder.

Its derivation from the *Madonna di Foligno* gives the drawing an added interest in the context of the Museum's collection, in which there is a study by Raphael for his group of the Virgin and Child in the, for him, quite exceptional medium of black chalk on blue paper—a medium so unusual that the drawing was at one time seriously believed to be by Barocci. It has already been suggested that the *sfumato* effect of broadly handled black chalk on *carta azzurra* argues knowledge of Venetian practice, and that the unfamiliar appearance of the drawing may reflect the moment in

Raphael's development when he was in contact with Sebastiano. The *Madonna di Foligno* dates from 1511–12, exactly at the time of Sebastiano's arrival in Rome. The first work that he undertook there, in the Sala di Galatea of the Farnesina, was commissioned by Raphael's patron Agostino Chigi, so it is more than likely that at that time the two artists were in contact. But it does not necessarily follow that Sebastiano's drawing of the Virgin and Child dates from the same time. Its style and technique are in fact characteristic of his full maturity, after 1530. (It may be compared, for example, with the study in the British Museum for the group of standing women in the late fresco of the *Visitation* formerly in S Maria della Pace.) As the indication of the ledge and parapet shows, this is a design for a complete composition. No painting of it is known, but the Virgin's features were clearly drawn from the same model as those of the Virgin in the *Madonna del Velo* (Naples), a painting datable after 1530, the composition of which is likewise based on a prototype by Raphael—the lost *Madonna di Loreto*. The foreground is similarly occupied by a flat ledge behind which the Virgin is standing, but the Child is lying on this while she, with both hands, removes the veil that was covering Him.

The Museum's new drawing, if not an alternative solution for the Naples picture, must have been a study for another painting of exactly the same type.

The other drawing (**287**) was also acquired in the London sale-room. Sent to Christies with an old attribution to Giulio Romano, it was there identified by Mr Annesley and Mr Russell as the work of the Florentine painter Agnolo Bronzino (1503–72), and was bought for the Museum at the sale on 26 March 1974 (lot 18). In his *Drawings of the Florentine Painters*, Berenson dismissed Bronzino in a single paragraph; but more recent research (notably by Professor Craig Smyth) has led to the emergence of many more drawings than were known to Berenson, and has produced a much better balanced and more favourable estimate of his quality as a draughtsman. Only two other drawings by him are in the Museum collection: a design in pen and wash heightened with white for the decorative border of a tapestry, and a three-quarter length portrait drawing of a man, in black chalk (probably a study for a painting). The new drawing, also in black chalk, is a significant supplement to this meagre representation in being a figure composition, and of an unusually elaborate and complete kind. The previous history of the Sebastiano drawing is unrecorded, but the Bronzino bears the collector's marks of Thomas Banks (Lugt 2423), his son-in-law Baron Henri de Triqueti (Lugt 1304), and Count Rey de Villette (Lugt 2200^A). For Banks (1735–1805), one of the foremost English neo-classical sculptors, this drawing must have had a particular appeal, for in conception it is entirely sculptural. The effect it makes is not of a group of flesh-and-blood figures but of a high relief in polished marble; and though the figures depart entirely

287 *Agnolo Bronzino: unidentified subject. Black chalk. 26.9 × 41.2.*
(Department of Prints and Drawings 1974–4–6–36)

from the classical canons of proportion and attitude, there is a marmoreal frigidity about the group that a sculptor of Banks's period would have found particularly sympathetic.

The style of the drawing is closely dependent on Bronzino's master and life-long model, Jacopo Pontormo (1494–1556); so much so, indeed, that the possibility of its being by the older artist had seriously to be considered. The child held by the woman kneeling in the left foreground, if completely visible, would be seen to have the extraordinarily elongated and distorted proportions that are characteristic of him. But Bronzino's personality is unmistakably apparent in the head of the bearded man in the right background.

The subject as yet remains mysterious. The compilers of the sale-catalogue suggested, on the grounds that no men of fighting age were represented, that it might be an episode from *Exodus*. It has further been suggested that the drawing may be in some way connected with the series of frescoes of scenes from the Old Testament which

Bronzino completed after Pontormo's death in the choir of S Lorenzo in Florence, and which were all destroyed in the eighteenth century. This explanation would account for the very strong Pontormesque flavour of the drawing; and certainly its style seems compatible with a dating in the 1550s.   J. A. GERE

Keeper, Prints and Drawings

A drawing of the Assumption of the Virgin attributed to the circle of Sebastiano Ricci

In 1974 the Museum acquired by private purchase an eighteenth-century Venetian drawing of the *Assumption of the Virgin* which on stylistic grounds it was possible to attribute to the circle of Sebastiano Ricci (**288**). The drawing is typical of early Venetian rococo draftsmanship in its free painterly handling; the plastic values of seventeenth-century drawing have been abandoned in favour of an effect of scintillating light created by broken line. Although the source for this open rococo style of drawing may ultimately be found in the work of the peripatetic Luca Giordano, it was developed and fully practised by Sebastiano Ricci and Antonio Pellegrini in the early eighteenth century in Venice. Executed in black chalk on cream paper, the outlines have been strengthened by brownish-red watercolour applied with the tip of the brush. Such a duplication of line, repeating the meandering sometimes zig-zagging black chalk underdrawing is a graphic technique employed by Ricci, and supports the view that the drawing was made with his example in mind.

In composition, too, the drawing recalls a model by Ricci: the painting of the *Assumption of the Virgin* in the Karlskirche, Vienna (Pallucchini, *La Pittura veneziana del Settecento*, 1960, pl. 26), commissioned by the Imperial Court and made by the artist at the very end of his life in 1733/4. The drawing does not agree in every detail with the painting: in the former the Virgin is erect as she rises from the tomb and she is accompanied only by three putti, the Apostles kneel below; in the latter the Virgin, surrounded by groups of angels and putti, is seated on clouds while below some of the Apostles flanking the tomb are standing. But a common feature of the two is the tall candelabrum which appears on the ground in front of the tomb, an object which is rarely so conspicuously displayed, if at all, in scenes of the Assumption and which gives particular character to the Karlskirche painting. A further point of resemblance is the exaggerated treatment of the attenuated upward reaching arms of the Apostles.

It is probable that the drawing was made in connection with an altarpiece whose destination is suggested by a faint inscription in chalk on the right-hand side which

288 *Circle of Sebastiano Ricci*, The Assumption of the Virgin, *black chalk on cream paper, the outline strengthened with brownish-red watercolour.* 32 × 21.5 cms. (*Department of Prints and Drawings 1974–12–7–1*)

reads: *Maria a san tomà*. A likely interpretation of 'san tomà' of the inscription is that it refers to the church of S Tommaso in Venice which is abbreviated by convention to S Tomà; 'Maria' would seem to identify the subject of the drawing, the Assumption of the Virgin. The purpose for which the drawing was made would easily be accounted for were a painting of this subject to exist in S Tomà, but unfortunately this is not the case. According to early guides to Venice none of the altars in the church were adorned with a painting of the Assumption, but it cannot be ruled out that such a painting may have been planned for the church which was extensively altered in the middle of the eighteenth century and was decorated in the rococo manner by Jacopo Guarana in 1755. At this time some of the older altarpieces were replaced.

Finally, in considering the authorship of the British Museum drawing four other drawings of the Assumption, two by Gaspare Diziani (Venice, Correr 5627 and 5645; Pignatti, *Eighteenth-century Venetian Drawings from the Correr Museum*, Exh. cat., London 1965, no. 20), one by Giuseppe Diziani (Tricesimo, Udine, Coll. Miotti; Bettagno, *Disegni veneti del Settecento della Fondazione Giorgio Cini e delle collezioni venete*, Exh. cat., Venice 1963, no. 23) and one by Nicola Grassi (Scholz Collection; Muraro, *Venetian Drawings from the Collection Janos Scholz*, Exh. cat., Venice 1957, no. 89) should be mentioned here as they each show an attempt to vary the composition of Ricci's prototype, the Karlskirche painting, and it is possible that a further relationship between the drawings may exist. One of the two drawings by Gaspare Diziani has been dated *c.* 1733, the time when Ricci was at work, on his painting for the Karlskirche. Such a date would seem too early for the British Museum drawing.

NICHOLAS TURNER
Assistant Keeper, Prints and Drawings

An unrecorded drawing by Dante Gabriel Rossetti

No British artist is more fully documented than Rossetti. Seven years after his death, his brother published an invaluable year-by-year account of his activity;[1] ten years later, a list of works, as complete as was then possible, 396 in number, was appended to H. C. Marillier's monograph;[2] in 1971 appeared what will remain the definitive *catalogue raisonné* by Virginia Surtees, comprising 766 items together with several hundred related studies and replicas.[3] But no *catalogue raisonné*, however thorough, can hope to achieve finality, and since 1971 a number of unknown and unrecorded works have come to light.

One of these, acquired by the Department of Prints and Drawings after its appearance in a provincial auction-sale, is a rough sketch in pen and brown ink and wash inscribed in the artist's hand 'Hamlet & Ophelia' (**289**).[4] This is a particularly interesting addition to the Museum's small but very choice Pre-Raphaelite collection, since it joins Rossetti's highly finished pen-and-ink drawing, dated 1858, of the same episode in the play.[5] Rossetti, essentially a 'literary' artist, is at his most successful when illustrating some highly charged moment of spiritual or emotional tension between a man and a woman. Having decided to take a subject from *Hamlet*, it was thus almost inevitable that he should have chosen the episode in Act III, scene i in

289 *Dante Gabriel Rossetti*; Hamlet and Ophelia, *pen and brown ink and wash*. 25.8 × 10 cms. (*Department of Prints and Drawings 1974–4–6–11*)

which Hamlet feigns madness in order to test Ophelia's constancy. The 1858 drawing treats the subject more elaborately: the *dramatis personae* are likewise restricted to two, but the little oratory in which they are is over-furnished with complicated bric-à-brac, including panels carved with subjects symbolizing, in Rossetti's own words, 'rash introspection';[6] while the 'intricate stairs and passages' in the background suggest the shadowy labyrinth of intrigue and cross-purposes in which Hamlet finds himself. Rossetti later admitted that 'perhaps after all a simpler treatment might have been better',[7] and it cannot be denied that beautiful though the 1858 drawing is in its fanciful complexity, the exclusive concentration in the other on the two personages powerfully intensifies the dramatic effect. The new drawing, which from its style must date from the mid-1850s, may represent the 'simpler treatment'. He had had this subject in mind some years before 1858: in a letter of August 1854 he says he is doing a design of Hamlet and Ophelia 'deeply symbolic and far sighted',[8] and the style of the sketch in Birmingham,[9] though this corresponds in all essentials with the 1858 drawing, suggests a dating towards the beginning of the decade.

A label formerly on the back of the frame records that the drawing belonged to Henry Holiday (1839–1927), now remembered chiefly as a designer of stained glass for the firm of Morris & Co. and, as a painter, for only one work—the once widely popular and much reproduced picture of *Beatrice denying her Salutation to Dante* (Walker Art Gallery, Liverpool), a painstakingly academic rendering, painted *c.* 1880, of a subject which Rossetti had made particularly his own. Holiday was on terms of friendship with Rossetti in about 1860, but how and when the drawing of *Hamlet and Ophelia* came into his possession is not known. A faint pencil inscription in the lower right-hand corner reads 'D. G. Rossetti to . . .'. The name of the recipient is tantalizingly illegible, but it seems to be 'S. Solomon'. Simeon Solomon (1840–1905) was one of the Pre-Raphaelite circle in the 1860s, and a friend of Rossetti and of Holiday.

J. A. GERE
Keeper, Prints and Drawings

1 William Michael Rossetti, *Dante Gabriel Rossetti as Designer and Writer*, London, 1889.

2 H. C. Marillier, *Dante Gabriel Rossetti: an Illustrated Memorial of his Art and Life*, London, 1899.

3 Virginia Surtees, *The Paintings and Drawings of Dante Gabriel Rossetti (1828–1882): a Catalogue Raisonné*, Oxford 1971.

4 1974–4–6–11. Sold Bath, Messrs Jolly, 4 March 1974, lot 175, bt. 'Agnew'.

5 1910–12–10–8. Pen and ink. Surtees, no. 108.

6 See Surtees, no. 108.

7 Letter of 18 February 1870, to George Eliot (see Surtees, no. 108).

8 *Letters of Dante Gabriel Rossetti*, ed. O. Doughty and J. R. Wahl, Oxford 1965 etc., i, p. 214.

9 Birmingham City Art Gallery 460'04. Pencil on pale grey paper. Surtees, no. 108A.

10 Henry Holiday, *Reminiscences of My Life*, London 1914, pp. 75–6.

A study for the Portrait of Serena Lederer
Gustav Klimt

The acquisition of this drawing in 1974 represented the first attempt by the Department of Prints and Drawings to embrace the work of the leading progenitor and first President of the Vienna Secession. Gustav Klimt's (1862–1918) reputation for posterity has largely depended upon his role as an exponent of those pictorial innovations which characterized Viennese *Jugendstil*. *Music 11*, Klimt's mural for the music salon of Nikolaus Dumba, attests to his repudiation by 1898 of conventional illusionism, in the use of flat, ornamental design, juxtaposed, however, with the human figure, for which he reserved a three dimensional treatment. This tension between naturalism and stylization reached a climax in the minutely articulated mosaic patterns of Klimt's murals for Josef Hoffmann's dining room in the Maison Stoclet, Brussels (1905–11). His portraiture, not surprisingly, evinces a more conservative approach; only in 1902, in the portrait of his mistress, Emilie Flöge (Historisches Museum der Stadt Wien), did Klimt essay an overt espousal of the decorative devices already employed in his allegorical compositions.

From the mid 1890's Klimt concentrated exclusively upon female sitters, largely drawn from the upper echelons of Viennese society, whose portrayal appeared as part of a thematic triumvirate celebrated in the Klimt room of the First Vienna Art Exhibition of 1908. The important point of departure for Klimt's mature portrait style was 1898, and the picture of Serena Lederer (Collection of Erich Lederer, Geneva) belongs to a group of portraits executed before 1902, in which the sitter is placed within a decorative void. The artist combined fidelity to external appearance with a free, painterly rendering of dress and great delicacy in the interpretation of attitude and facial expression, which imparts a luminous ethereality to the finished work, reminiscent of Whistler's handling of similar subjects. Within the context of Viennese portraiture, Klimt must be seen in conjunction with the host of lesser artists who populated the pages of *Ver Sacrum*, the organ of the Vienna Secession; Koloman Moser, Josef Engelhart, Franz von Stuck and Théo van Rysselberghe, to name but a few. Serena Lederer was in fact given such a context by Moser, when he incorporated the painting into a display of contemporary portraiture at a Secession exhibition in 1901, subsequently reproduced in *Ver Sacrum*.

The British Museum drawing was originally part of the estate left by Klimt at his death and belongs to a group of studies for the same portrait, now distributed between the Albertina and the Historisches Museum der Stadt Wien. It appears to represent the final stage prior to the squared sketch in the Albertina; other drawings

290 *Gustav Klimt, Study for the* Portrait of Serena Lederer, *conte crayon.*
(*Department of Prints and Drawings 1974–7–20–34*)

depict the sitter frontally and then with her arms bent behind her back. Economy of line distinguishes Klimt's draughtsmanship from that of his Viennese contemporaries, who practised a more academic and highly finished manner; Toulouse-Lautrec provides a closer parallel and his influence upon Klimt became explicit during the latter part of Klimt's career.

The portrait of Serena Lederer has further significance in relation to Klimt's patronage, as it marked the beginning of a long and profitable friendship between the artist and the industrialist, August Lederer, who amassed the most important private collection of Klimt's work in Vienna. In 1914 and 1915 Klimt executed two more family portraits, a highly decorative treatment of the Baroness Bachofen-Echt, Serena Lederer's daughter (Collection of Erich Lederer), and a more restrained study of her mother, Charlotte Pulitzer (destroyed in 1945). Above all, August Lederer installed the reviled ceiling painting *Philosophy*, in a room specially designed by Hoffmann, together with a number of Klimt's other controversial public works.

The drawing of Serena Lederer therefore serves as eloquent testimony both to Klimt's linear virtuosity and to a vital phase of artistic patronage.

FRANCES CAREY
Assistant Keeper, Prints and Drawings

WESTERN ASIATIC ANTIQUITIES

A Sumerian foundation deposit from the Temple of Nanshe at Siraran

With the aid of the National Art-Collections Fund an unusual Sumerian foundation deposit has been acquired by the Museum. It comprises a limestone tablet (9.8 × 7.4 cms) and a copper peg surmounted by a plinth on which stands a bull-calf surrounded by reeds (H. 19.4 cms, W. 12.0 cms). The same inscription appears on both the peg and the tablet, and records the rebuilding by Gudea, a ruler of Lagash, of the Temple of the goddess Nanshe in Siraran in *c.* 2100 BC: 'For Nanshe, the mighty queen, the mistress of the embankment, his mistress—Gudea, the ruler of Lagash, made the (ritual) appurtenances resplendent. In Siraran, her beloved city, he built for her (and) restored on its (original) site her E-Siraran, a mountain soaring above temples'. The city of Siraran is now represented by the modern mound of Zerghul,

291 *Copper bull-calf from the Sumerian foundation deposit at Siraran. (Department of Western Asiatic Antiquities 135993)*

some 30 kilometres to the south-east of Tello, so it is undoubtedly from there that the foundation deposit comes. Before reaching the London art market, it had been in a Continental private collection for many years. The temple of Nanshe at Siraran has a long history in the Sumerian period: it was first built by King Ur-Nanshe (*c.* 2500 BC) and later rebuilt by both Uru-ka-gina (*c.* 2350) and Gudea. The British Museum already possesses a gate-socket from the Temple of Nanshe at Siraran, so the addition of one of the foundation deposits is especially welcome.

It will be fully published in a forthcoming issue of the journal *Syria*.

EDMOND SOLLBERGER
Keeper, Western Asiatic Antiquities

PLATES

I. Comic actor seated on an altar
(Magenta Ware, Cat. no. 10; GR 1873.10–20.2)

II. The Malcolm celestial globe
(OA 1871, 3–1,1)

III. William Blake: illustration to Young's *Night Thoughts*, page 7
(PD 1929–7–13–141)

IV. A painted linen shroud from Egypt
(EA 68509)

PLATE I

PLATE II

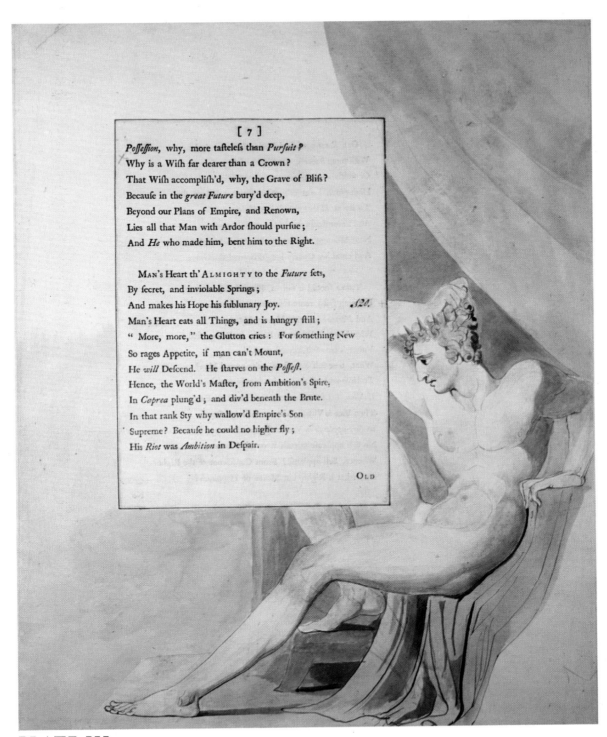

[7]

Possession, why, more tasteless than *Pursuit* ?

Why is a Wish far dearer than a Crown ?

That Wish accomplish'd, why, the Grave of Bliss ?

Because in the *great Future* bury'd deep,

Beyond our Plans of Empire, and Renown,

Lies all that Man with Ardor should pursue ;

And *He* who made him, bent him to the Right.

MAN's Heart th' ALMIGHTY to the *Future* sets,

By secret, and inviolable Springs ;

And makes his Hope his sublunary Joy.   *520.*

Man's Heart eats all Things, and is hungry still ;

" More, more," the Glutton cries : For something New

So rages Appetite, if man can't Mount,

He *will* Descend.   He starves on the *Possess*.

Hence, the World's Master, from Ambition's Spire,

In *Caprea* plung'd ; and div'd beneath the Brute.

In that rank Sty why wallow'd Empire's Son

Supreme ? Because he could no higher fly ;

His *Riot* was *Ambition* in Despair.

OLD

PLATE III

289

PLATE IV

Index